Peter May

Peter May

A Biography

Alan Hill

ANDRE DEUTSCH

First published in 1996 by
André Deutsch Limited
106 Great Russell Street
London WC1B 3LJ

A CIP record for this title is available
from the British Library

ISBN 0 233 98970 6

Printed and bound in Great Britain by
St Edmundsbury Press, Bury St. Edmunds, Suffolk

To Don
a true friend
who shared my cricket pleasures

Foreword
by Sir Colin Cowdrey

Peter May was a fine all-round games player and a cricketer in the highest class. History will record that he was one of England's greatest batsmen.

Our lives were thrown together when we shared a cabin on SS *Orsova*, the luxury liner which took the MCC team to Australia in September 1954, a voyage of twenty-three days. It was a memorable tour where, under Len Hutton's captaincy, we won the Ashes. Peter and I became very close friends and batted a lot together. Over the next seven years we had more partnerships at Test-match level than, perhaps, any other England pair.

Alan Hill has researched his subject with enormous care and details the story of Peter May, as the batsman, the captain and the person, in a splendid way. His book is a delightful read and will be much enjoyed by those who really love the game.

Colin Cowdrey

Contents

Illustrations

Line illustrations

'Majestic'. Cartoon by Roy Ullyett, from *The Greatest of My Time* by Trevor Bailey *(page 113)*.

Scorecard of the first Test match at Edgbaston, 1957, against the West Indies *(page 139)*.

Photographs

Acknowledgements and thanks for the use of the photographs are due to the following: Mrs Virginia May; Kathleen and Richard Robinson; The Headmaster, Charterhouse School; Brian Souter; G. H. G. Doggart; British Newspaper Library; A. J. McIntyre; Surrey County Cricket Club; Kent County Cricket Club; Justin Edrich; Peter Nathan; Michael Pearce.

Author's Introduction

This is the celebration of a life of a dedicated man whose early death in December 1994 was lamented by all who knew him. Peter May, sadly, was not able to rejoice in another celebration at his beloved Oval. He was looking forward to his installation as Surrey president during the club's 150th anniversary in 1995. Peter's name is recorded on the President's Board in the Oval pavilion – *honoris causa*.

In happier circumstances, his presidency would have been a pleasurable reminder of an anniversary occasion in May 1947. This event, delayed by the Second World War, coincided with his first appearance, as a Charterhouse schoolboy, for a Surrey eleven in a match to raise funds for the club's centenary appeal.

Peter May blossomed as a great cricketer in splendid surroundings and on the true pitches at Charterhouse and Fenner's at Cambridge. They enabled him to grow in assurance as the outstanding batsman of his generation. The benefits of these formative years were shown by his unrivalled expertise on all wickets in England and throughout the world.

Peter always acknowledged these endowments as a cricketer. He would undoubtedly have welcomed the moves to provide improved facilities, especially for children, to enable them to take part in sport and fulfil their potential. He was a vice-president for nine years of the London Playing Fields Society, which has launched a public appeal. The Peter May Memorial Appeal, under the patronage of Field Marshal The Lord Bramall and the chairmanship of Lord Prior, has a target of £7.5 million.

The immediate aim, says Peter Nathan, the chairman of the Playing Fields Society and a Charterhouse contemporary of Peter May, is to use the funds to update facilities in an area of significant social need. The Wadham Lodge Sports Centre at Walthamstow is to be established as a centre for performance and excellence in cricket. It will be renamed the Peter May Sports Centre. The other grounds to benefit from the Appeal will be Morden Park; Fairlop Oak at Hainault; and Prince George's at Raynes Park.

In its own way, my biography of a humble and modest champion seeks to present another memorial. It is designed to evoke a brilliant chapter of achievement and to call for a renewal of standards in the game, so resolutely upheld by Peter, for another generation. A host of celebrities and others of lesser renown, all of whom cherished Peter, have provided a variety of ingredients for my record. I must especially thank Peter's widow, Virginia, and her family for both authorising the book and giving their support in my endeavours. Sir Colin Cowdrey, who has kindly supplied the foreword, recalls a friendship which never wavered and was blessed with trust on and off the field.

I must gratefully acknowledge the courteous assistance of the British Newspaper Library staff at Colindale, Jeff Hancock, the Surrey CCC librarian, and Mrs Ann Wheeler, the Charterhouse School Librarian, for placing their archives at my disposal. My thanks are also due to the late Derek Lodge for his comprehensive statistical work. This was valuably complemented, at short notice, by David Kendix.

The emergence of Peter as a cricketing prodigy at Charterhouse has been portrayed in vivid colours by Lord Prior, Sir Oliver Popplewell, Peter Nathan, Philip Snow (a long-standing friend of George Geary, Peter's influential school coach) and John Perry, who shared a school bench for five years at the Godalming school and delights in his association with a 'man of simple tastes'. Happy reminiscences of Peter – and his parents – during his boyhood at Reading were the splendid yield of talks with his cousins, Kathleen and Richard Robinson. They both place stress on his single-minded attitude to sport and his kindly nature.

Alan Shirreff, Peter's Combined Services captain, Don Kenyon and the late Roley Jenkins recall the astonishing maturity – and ability to take control of a situation – during his National Service days. They have helped me to recapture his mastery against the odds in the unexpected victory over Worcestershire in 1949. Walter Hadlee, the New Zealand captain in that year, remembers how highly he and his fellow tourists rated Peter. Even at that early stage, he impressed them as an England player of the future.

My recital of the Cambridge years has been enhanced by the memories of his university peers, Hubert Doggart, John Dewes, Dennis Silk, Raman Subba Row and the Rt. Rev. David Sheppard, Bishop of Liverpool. John (J. J.) Warr, another of this assembly, has added his praise as well as allowing me glimpses of an intensely shy man who was at his happiest and best within his family, or among a close group of friends. Warr, along with others, debunks the image of Peter as an aloof man. Divested of his ceremony as a public figure, Peter had an engaging and lively sense of humour.

Peter's stature as the lynchpin of the Surrey batting during the great years in the 1950s is attested to by many of his fellow players, colleagues as well as opponents, who figure prominently in the text. Bob Appleyard, a formidable rival in Yorkshire, remembers that Peter drew upon, for his sustenance as his cricketer, not only the views of those within the game, but other knowledgeable observers outside cricket circles.

The testimonies of his England contemporaries during Peter's record-breaking reign of forty-one consecutive Tests bear witness to his zeal and sympathetic command. 'Peter had immense pride and maintained a code of conduct as an example to be followed by others,' comments Peter Richardson. 'He believed that everybody was trying until proved otherwise.'

Geoffrey Howard, the MCC manager on the tour of Australia in 1954–55, has looked back on a memorable series which marked the emergence of a young guard headed by Peter May. Peter's astonishing progress has also been charted by many rivals from overseas. Alan Davidson, Neil Harvey, Arthur Morris and Ray Lindwall were fervent in their praise of him during reminiscent talks at Arundel in 1995. Davidson in particular recalled Peter's resilience, as a young player, and how he came through the ordeal of a first encounter with Lindwall when the Australians visited the Oval in 1953.

Willie Watson, the former Yorkshire and England batsman now resident in South Africa, was a fellow Test debutant in 1951. This was the year in which Peter, while still an undergraduate, travelled to Headingley to score a century which did not pale in eloquence beside his England partner and mentor, Leonard Hutton. Watson recalls the composure of the twenty-one-year-old Peter, whose batting was acclaimed by the Yorkshire partisans. Peter's gifts are also acknowledged by his South African contemporaries. Jackie McGlew remembers a fierce competitor, who was 'born to win'; and Trevor Goddard recalls how Peter revealed his stature as a true sportsman, uncomplaining in adversity and amid lapses in form on the tour of South Africa in 1956–57.

The disappointments of this series were swiftly erased by the remarkable batting marathon against the West Indies at Edgbaston in the following summer. Peter and Colin Cowdrey were associated in a recovery against the odds to haul England back from the brink of defeat. Together they buried the spinning bogey of Sonny Ramadhin, who had mesmerised the England batsmen in 1950 and promised to do so again. Ramadhin, in conversation at Lord's during his benefit year in 1995, ruefully recalled the implacable defence confronting him at Edgbaston. It did not prevent him – and his cheerful bowling companion, Alf Valentine – from extolling the majesty of May. 'Peter batted with the exuberance of a West Indian,' they both said.

Peter May, the 'unusually retiring man', in the words of Sir Colin Cowdrey, shunned the limelight as a celebrity cricketer. Empire-building was not his style, but he was never to be underestimated as a competitor. Richie Benaud, another in the combative mould, unreservedly awards the palm to his old rival as the greatest cricketer to be produced by England since the war. 'Peter was not only a great orthodox player, but a wonderful improviser. He would have been brilliant in the one-day game.'

ALAN HILL
Lindfield, Sussex
May 1996

Chapter 1
Entry of a Cricketing Wonder

Beneath the shade of the great and glorious tree on Charterhouse Green, a hushed group of onlookers let the minutes tick by. They were watching an innings, his first school century, which announced the arrival of Peter May as the outstanding batsman of his generation.

One of the knot of admiring spectators, standing under the canopy of branches, was a fellow pupil, Peter Nathan. He recalls that school matches then began at 11.30, with lunch at 1.30. 'Those like me who were not playing had to be back in their house five minutes before the interval. But I was not going to move until I'd seen the whole of the morning's play.' Nathan remembers the 'exquisite timing' displayed in the innings against Harrow. 'Peter already had many of the strokes for which he became famous; his only weakness at that time was hitting the ball hopefully in the air down to long leg.'

A cricketing wonder was glimpsed on this June day in 1944. It was a sporting episode which had an extraordinary impact on the school. The slim, immaculately clad fourteen-year-old, his brows furrowed in concentration, was already the combative master. His bat was the caressing sword which blunted the keen pace of a future Olympic sprinter, Alistair McCorquodale. Peter May and Tony Rimell rejoiced in their pursuit of runs on the sun-baked Green. They shared a partnership of 100 runs for the fourth wicket. 'Though trying hard,' commented *The Carthusian*, 'the Harrovians could not stop the fluency with which these young batsmen scored. It was a delightful exhibition of batting. Once or twice every over the ball sped swiftly across Green to the boundary, vainly chased by some luckless Harrovian.'

The school report at the end of the season glowed in the discovery of a precocious talent. 'May, at the age of fourteen, seemed to be irrepressible. Once he had gained his place in the side, he never looked back, and time after time more than justified his inclusion at such a tender age.'

1

The eulogy might also have dwelt upon his unswerving character. From his early boyhood in Reading, Peter May bristled with determination. His cousin, Richard Robinson, now a retired West Country farmer, was a boon companion in those years. They both attended the Marlborough House Preparatory School in the town. Richard, because of family circumstances, was a guest of Peter's parents. He was, in fact, more of a surrogate son, accorded the same affection and discipline as Peter and his younger brother, John.

Pictures in a family album show Richard as a mischievous scamp with tousled hair and stockings steadily disappearing into his shoes. Alongside him, Peter gleams with tidiness, only deviating from the well-brushed look when, begrimed and happy, he is caught up in the excitement of a school cross-country race. 'Peter was perfection really, but I was different,' says Richard, shrugging his shoulders at the memory. 'I didn't care if I lost, or played badly at sport, so long as I'd enjoyed myself. Peter was even then more analytical. If he had been bowled out, he would want to know why.'

The quiet, reflective Peter had been born into a strict and well-regulated household. The influence of his parents, both of staunch Methodist persuasion, was to lay the foundations for an ordered life. He was born on the eve of a new decade, on 31 December 1929, the first son of cousins, Thomas Howard May and Eileen May. Eileen's father was the Rev. Howard May. He was the younger brother of Thomas May, the joint grandfather of the May and Robinson children. The initials of later distinction – P. B. H. – combined the latter two names with those of Peter's grandmother whose maiden name was Barker, and his father, who was always known as Howard. Peter's birth came six weeks too late for his mother and father to collect a prize. Grandfather Thomas had offered £10 to the parents producing his first grandson. This handsome gift went instead to the Robinsons – and to Richard, who won the race to the cradle.

The challenging grandfather was renowned for his civic pride. Thomas May was a town councillor and served as a Methodist preacher on the Reading Wesley Circuit for fifty-three years until his death, at the age of seventy-two, in 1936. He displayed vigour and zeal as an astute business-man. In 1880, he had joined Alfred Callas in his ironmongery business in Reading. In 1900, he was appointed a partner and managing director of the newly designated private limited company. After his death, the business, trading under the title of wholesale ironmongers and builders' merchants, passed into the custody of his sons, Howard, who specialised in electrical contracting, and Arthur. They remained as joint directors of the firm until it was sold on their retirement in the early 1960s.

The grooming of a great cricketer unfolded under the guidance of encouraging parents. At the Mays' semi-detached home in Wescott Road on the outskirts of Reading, the atmosphere was happy and hospitable. Sport ranked high on the domestic agenda. Eileen May was an accomplished tennis player. The engaging lilt in her voice carried the notes of her earlier musical training. She was the driving force behind all the family activities. Eileen and others drawn into practices were the cricket allies. They fielded and bowled to Peter and his brother, John, born in November 1932, on a dual-purpose tennis court, which occupied the whole of the garden behind the house. Smashes and volleys off the racket were often stilled amid the clamour for cricket. The nets were lowered to permit the execution of other strokes on the hard, true surface.

Sir Colin Cowdrey remembers his visits to the May home at the start of his friendship with Peter. The impression lingers of a routine of precise timekeeping. 'We would have a game of snooker or billiards after supper followed by a milk drink at bedtime. Breakfast was at 7.30 sharp. We had to arrive downstairs, shaved and smartly dressed. Father went off to his store at five to eight.' This was a regime which, Cowdrey believes, carried the legacy of a meticulous and well-organised mind when Peter ascended to the cricket stage.

Billiards was a game in which, as Peter Nathan observed during his weekends at Reading, the other Peter could have blossomed as a top-class exponent. Richard Robinson recalls that a full-sized table was installed in an attic room. Silence was golden in this sporting sanctum when wet days kept them indoors. The boys, instructed by their father, calculated the angles at billiards and snooker in studied contests. One special treat of Peter's childhood was an outing with his father to London to watch the Australian record-breaking champion, Walter Lindrum. Howard May and his friend, the Marlborough House headmaster, were snooker addicts. It was perhaps fortunate that they were such good friends when Peter and Richard were caught throwing stones near the school The two boys escaped with a stern reprimand.

The large hall at Wescott Road was also commandeered by Peter and Richard for cricket and football on inclement afternoons. The games were of an exuberant nature, endangering and occasionally demolishing the light fitting illuminating the hall. It was then 'lights out' in more than one sense, as the boys were firmly shepherded to bed. Howard May also instituted a policy of self-defence and recruited a local boxing instructor to supervise weekly boxing sessions. This physical training did enable Peter to turn the tables on an aggressor at Charterhouse. Peter was a wiry boy, but not especially strong until he grew to manhood. One story places him again in the boxing ring at school. He was matched with an opponent, thickset and confident of his superiority. Peter overcame his qualms to unleash a fierce blow and send the heavier boy sprawling on the canvas.

Acting as a counterpoise to the sporting vigour was the emphasis on education in the May family. Peter's other cousin and Richard's sister, Kathleen, describes an evident fascination with learning and a devotion to literature. She remembers a sitting-room lined with bookcases at Wescott Road. They housed volumes of Shakespeare; Lawrence's *Seven Pillars of Wisdom*; and the favoured works of Kipling, all standing proudly in handsome bindings. Howard May scoured the review columns and regularly ordered books that appealed to him.

Consistent with this background was an imperative to propel Peter and John – and Richard too, who later went to Repton School – towards higher education. Kathleen Robinson recalls one shrewd and instructive letter received by her parents from grandfather Thomas. The message arrived after her father had been promoted to a new post. 'My advice is, be careful with the extra money,' he wrote. 'Don't live right up to your income, but put a little by for the sweet boy and girl *which you have to educate* and care for.'

It is generally believed within the family that Eileen May was especially keen that her sons should go to Charterhouse. The decision was inspired by the recommendation of a relative, a scholastic authority and former master at the Surrey school. Before this was implemented there was an intermission at Leighton Park School in Reading. Peter, then aged nine, was directed there after Marlborough House closed on the outbreak of war in September 1939.

Bob Relf, one of three cricketing brothers who played for Sussex, was the first of Peter May's cricket mentors at Leighton Park. It was a happy coincidence, in view of Peter's later association with the Gilligan family, that Relf should be his guide. Relf had first played for Sussex in 1905. He was still a member of the county team when Arthur Gilligan took over the captaincy in 1922. Relf also shared, with his young pupil, the same birthplace; as did Peter's future England and Surrey colleagues, Alec and Eric Bedser and Ken Barrington and Tom Dollery, of Warwickshire.

Poaching first-class counties were once wryly rebuked by the Berkshire CCC secretary for relying heavily on this cricket nursery for their success.

Bob Relf was a veteran campaigner, with memories of batting with the august C. B. Fry in Edwardian days at Hove. Aggression had been the keynote of his batting, combined with a 'wonderful nerve when things were going badly'. The phrase rings true of the man, and the same tribute would later be paid to the lanky boy striding dutifully beside him. A. J. Gaston, the Sussex historian, said of Relf: 'He is one of the finest acquisitions our county has obtained of the professional element. I like his style immensely.' Relf, along with his brothers, had an integrity which again could as easily have been attributed to Peter May. All who met him, observed one writer, were struck by his extraordinary conscientiousness and intense anxiety to do everything right.

Relf was in his seventies by the time Peter attracted his notice at Leighton Park. The uninhibited and punishing style of the boy cricketer greatly appealed to him. Although Peter was much younger than most of the school team, he strongly advocated that his pupil should be selected for the first eleven. Such a step had no precedent, said the masters, and Relf's request was turned down. He did not, however, let matters rest there. Waiting for Peter when he moved to Charterhouse in 1942 was another vigilant tutor, George Geary, the old Leicestershire and England all-rounder. Relf, as Geary's predecessor at Charterhouse, had alerted his fellow professional to the promise of Peter. The time was not far distant when an astonishing young sportsman would be crowned as the undisputed ruler of his schoolboy kingdom.

Chapter 2
Splendours at Charterhouse

'It was as if an Olympian had deigned to play skittles with mortals.'

Frederic Raphael

The sharp spires of Charterhouse School loom tall and breathtaking at the crest of the steep slope that rises above the Surrey town of Godalming. It was founded in 1611 by a Tudor entrepreneur, Thomas Sutton, for forty scholars and eighty brethren. Anthony Quick, in his history of the school, recalls the original premises in London, lying beneath 'the harsh serrated edges of the Barbican towers in buildings reminiscent of an Oxford or Cambridge college'.

By the summer of 1872 the school governors had exchanged the cramped quarters and the fog and fumes in the slums of Clerkenwell for the clean air of the Surrey hills. The surroundings at Godalming were 68½ acres on the Deanery Farm Estate, purchased at a cost of £9,450. In their haste to conclude the deal, the governing body found that their expenditure on the new buildings exceeded by £30,000 the £90,000 they had received from the Merchant Taylors' School for their London site. The miscalculation, however careless and unrewarding, did not detract from the desirability of the new home. Here was a magnificent setting where the light was strong and free from smoke and, as generations of future cricketers would affirm, with first-rate conditions for batting.

Quick sets a scene of imposing grandeur. 'As the traveller came over the brow of the hill, the main front of the school rose up in all its glory. On the left Saunderites, on the right the chapel, both capped with towers, and the Founders' Court, with the principal tower, set at the centre of the site behind the court and facing the travellers.'

The housemasters at Charterhouse in earlier times were often likened to the barons of feudal days. They ran their houses as private businesses; one especially affluent undertaking was ranked and known as the Ritz.

6

Generally, however, modest economics dictated the fare available to pupils. A minimum diet was provided for the boarding fees. Anything else, such as a cooked dish for tea, was added to the bill. Tea at Charterhouse is still referred to as the 'homebill'. The spartan years of the Second World War, including the imposition of rationed food, is etched in the memories of Old Carthusians of that period. Invite one of them out to dinner, it is said, and note the consumption of bread rolls with their tucker.

The roll-call of distinguished Old Carthusians over more than a century includes from the worlds of literature, journalism and music such luminaries as William Thackeray, Robert Graves, Osbert Lancaster, Henry Longhurst and Ralph Vaughan Williams. Robert Baden-Powell, the founder of the scouting movement, was educated there, as was interestingly, in the light of Peter May's background, John Wesley, the evangelist and founder of Methodism. Charterhouse is also linked to drama, with a splendid theatre dedicated to the memory of another former pupil, the playwright Ben Travers, doyen of the Aldwych farces. Travers, who lived into his nineties, returned to lay the foundation stone of the theatre at Charterhouse in 1980.

Peter May, along with other Charterhouse pupils of his time, was privileged to have as a vibrant guardian, head and housemaster, Sir Robert Birley. Birley was a scholar and historian of vast intellectual energy. He had made his name as an assistant master at Eton before moving to Charterhouse in 1935. The intimations of a future war were already apparent to him at the time. Shortly after his appointment, he wrote to his predecessor, Frank Fletcher. 'You guided the school through the last war. I shall have to guide it through the next.'

The Charterhouse headmaster was given the irreverent soubriquet of 'Bags' Birley, because of the protruding flesh beneath his inquiring eyes. 'A large figure, he looked an academic with his high forehead, his stoop, his untidy suits and a certain lack of physical co-ordination,' wrote Anthony Quick. Sir Robert, one of the great figures of public schools, cared deeply for people. He was always prudent in his approach, seeking to cajole rather than command. His innate shyness was a quality he shared with many of his young charges. The barriers were lowered when he spun into animated discussion. 'A boy would be dullard indeed if Birley did not communicate some of his excitement in his research into topics that fired him,' observed Quick.

Lord Prior, another of Birley's protégés at Charterhouse, reflects on a 'very remarkable man, an enthusiast for life and bursting with ideas'. He recalls the interest shown by his old headmaster in Peter May. 'He handled Peter very well because he recognised that here was a phenomenal boy. I think he was a bigger influence behind the scenes than perhaps even Peter realised.'

Peter May entered Saunderites House at Charterhouse in the autumn term of 1942. He was registered in the Upper IV, immediately below the Scholars' form. It was a sign that he possessed credentials other than sport. John Perry, another former Carthusian and lifelong friend, shared a bench form with Peter in five years at the school. Perry, now a Torquay hotelier, resided in Verites House, situated along with Saunderites (the principal house) and Gownboys in the central block.

Perry vividly recalls Peter's first appearance, as a 12-year-old, in the nets. It was the custom at the beginning of the cricket quarter at Charterhouse for new boys to be vetted as possible candidates. Perry walked out one day with other Verites pupils to await their inspections. 'Suddenly, in a blur of action, we saw this boy come back off his right foot and hammer the ball into the offside net.' The procession of boys stopped as if called to attention on the drill square. A chorus of excited gossip ensued: 'Who, for goodness sake, is this fellow? He is marvellous,' they all said. Perry adds: 'It was clearly obvious from that moment that Peter was a tremendous young prospect.'

It did not dissuade Robert Birley in his decision not to allow an immediate promotion to the first eleven. 'Peter was quite mature in physical terms as a boy,' recalls Jim Prior. 'In sporting terms he was two or three years ahead of anyone else. But it was considered a mistake to push him too quickly.' Many years later Sir Robert did confess that he had erred in caution, but his counsel was a caring and responsible action. First eleven cricket, even for someone as talented as Peter, would have been too severe a trial.

May was instead placed in the Under-16's team for one probationary year. He was delivered into the disciplined ministry of the implacable Robert Arrowsmith. The Charterhouse classics master was a martinet to be feared. He was a stickler for cricket etiquette and would forcefully express his views. Jim Prior remembers Arrowsmith, later a Kent cricket historian of renown, as a 'walking encyclopaedia' on the game. Arrowsmith did have the saving grace of immense enthusiasm. The often irascible man had to combat the jarring pains of arthritic hips. School-teaching sessions in the summer included a period of work before breakfast. Arrowsmith always wore a tweed cap, which he threw towards his chair when he entered the classroom. 'If it landed on the chair, we knew we were all right,' says Prior. 'If it missed, then you could guarantee we were in for a rough time.'

Eileen and Howard May visited Godalming during their son's proving season in the Under-16 eleven in 1943. Mrs May watched Peter's buoyant batting on 'The Wilderness'. John Perry remembers: 'Peter got a lot of runs that day. I can see her now, sitting on a little mound beside the ground. She was a very proud mother.'

Peter May and John Perry were jointly engaged in modern language studies at Charterhouse. Their tutors included Harry Marsh, later headmaster at Cranleigh, who taught French, and 'Herr Doktor' Gerstenberg, as German instructor. The highly Germanic presence of this teacher was a source of mirth in the classroom which somewhat diminished his authority.

There came a time when the two friends were installed as class monitors. They did not make a commendable start in their new roles; in fact, it may have been Peter's sporting prowess that saved them coming under the lash of the cane. A golden rule at Charterhouse involved a concession known as 'raising a cut'. It gave pupils the opportunity to abandon a lesson if a teacher failed to appear after ten minutes of the advertised time of a class. The English master on this occasion was W. C. Sellar, one of the authors of *1066 and All That*. John Perry relates that Sellar was a lugubrious man at the best of times. 'Peter and I kidded ourselves that he was late. In point of fact, it was nine minutes and 55 seconds. We scarpered one way and in walked Sellar through another door.' The master had beaten his time limit by just two seconds, but he was not setting a good example in punctuality. His anger at the abrupt leavetaking was, though, awesome in its ferocity. The misdemeanour was reported to the headmaster. The subsequent call to Birley's study was an uneasy interlude. The trembling boys escaped with a searing reprimand. They were chastened and subdued for many days afterwards.

Peter, than aged fourteen, was promoted to the Charterhouse first eleven in 1944. He was asked by his captain 'if he would like to take no.4'. He politely acknowledged his place in the batting order and replied: 'That will be fine by me.' The age gap between the two boys, one almost a child and the other nearly an adult, conjures up a piquant cameo. Parity in relations was not then possible; but the 'likeable and lovable' Peter soon established a meeting of cricket minds.

Addressing social demands was, though, a more difficult task. At home in Reading, Peter had been given a simple upbringing, which led to a certain unworldliness alongside his more sophisticated elders at Charter-house. Anyone with special talents, either as a scholar or sportsman, could find himself in an embarrassing situation. For instance, the term 'hash (slang for 'work') pro' was used to denigrate rather than congratulate a bookish pupil. Peter, the paragon of modesty, was not a subject for disdain. He disarmed those who affected to sneer at accomplishments.

Peter was always self-effacing and he found the acclamation he received at school and afterwards a source of acute embarrassment. His intense shyness was another cross he had to bear. It says much for his resolve that he overcame this disability. Peter very quickly revealed an inner strength. 'He was never subjected to bullying at school because he was so respected and liked as an exceptional sportsman,' says Jim Prior.

Peter's deference to his captain as a first eleven debutant was magnified when he was ushered into the presence of the Charterhouse coach. 'George Geary was a mountain of a man, a towering international sportsman,' remembers John Perry. 'He was more than just a cricket professional and always extremely generous.' Another memory concerns a visit made by Geary to Perry's hotel in Shrewsbury in later years. 'George always wore a grey trilby hat, large and of 1930s vintage. He came into our restaurant, wearing the hat and an MCC blazer from his 1928–29 tour of Australia. It was a stunning entrance – the conversation of the diners stopped as George made his way to our table.'

Peter May always remembered how Geary's broad shoulders matched the breadth of his grin. He was also struck by the hands which produced wonders from a cricket ball. 'They were the largest hands I had seen, in fact, until I was introduced to the Bedser twins.' 'George,' added Peter, 'was an adviser and guide rather than a coach. He picked out natural ability, and encouraged it. He did not stifle and smother it with a maze of technicalities to baffle the impressionable young mind. He never said too much, but whatever he did say demanded an attentive ear.'

Geary never sought to quench the sense of adventure among his pupils; if the strokes were not too hazardous, his reasoning was, why shackle a possible source of runs? He was, however, adamant on an adherence to the basics of batting. 'Keep your head still,' he instructed. 'Stand still as long as you can. When you move your feet, move quickly, but the longer you stand still, the later you'll play the shot.' The advice was supplemented by the veteran's unerringly pitched deliveries for each and every stroke. Peter always acknowledged his good fortune in possessing a top-class bowler as a coach. At an early age, he rapidly gained in assurance and was schooled in the priorities of balance and footwork as a batsman.

In one coaching session, after Peter had taken full toll of a sequence of full tosses, George entered the attack. He knew a greater challenge was needed to test the mettle of the boy. At once he teased and beat Peter with his slower ball. Geary then sent down two lightly flighted medium-pace deliveries. Peter played each of them firmly from the middle of the bat. Geary's next ball was the slow leg-cutter which had deceived Peter before. It was countered this time by a stern, defensive stroke. 'He sorted it out quickly,' said Geary. 'You get some boys who are useful cricketers, but they never seem to sort it out. But he was different. I could see that he had a real cricket brain.'

George Geary, the eldest of sixteen children of a Leicestershire boot-maker, was himself self-taught as a cricketer. He reputedly cycled each day from his home village of Barwell, fifteen miles from Leicester. There he rolled the county wicket and bowled all day before returning home, again by cycle, to roll the Barwell ground before dark.

He first played for Leicestershire in 1912. Ewart Astill, another county stalwart, also gave long and distinguished service. The careers of Geary and Astill, both England all-rounders, were inextricably linked. They were two of the four survivors from the pre-First World War era, still playing in 1938 when Geary retired. Geary played in fourteen Tests against South Africa and Australia, at home and overseas, and also toured India and the West Indies. He last represented England, at the age of forty-one and under the captaincy of Bob Wyatt, against Australia in 1934.

Geary's contemporaries attested to his unwavering accuracy through marathon bowling spells. The chronicles record his feats in the triumphant series in Australia in 1928–29. In the final Test in the sweltering heat at Melbourne, Geary established a then Test-innings record. He bowled 81 overs (486 balls) and conceded only 105 runs for his five wickets. The economy of his high, easy action – the dovetailing of his medium-pace and acutely breaking leg-cutters and stock off-spin – produced a career aggregate of 2,063 wickets. His spinning ploys gave him 12 wickets, including his best Test figures of 7-70 on the mat at Johannesburg, in the 1927–28 series in South Africa.

The Leicestershire man was also a valiant batsman, improving with age, so it was said, as he scored three of his eight centuries in his final season. On his debut against Australia at Headingley in 1926, he was associated with the Yorkshireman, George Macaulay, in a match-saving ninth-wicket

11

stand of 108 runs. His all-round status was sealed by his ability as a slip fieldsman. The enormous hands grasped over 450 catches, two of which, to dismiss Woodfull and Macartney, off the bowling of Larwood, were placed in the near-miraculous category. These were to prove conclusive in the overthrow of Australia in the Oval Test in 1926.

One of his most remarkable bowling performances was the capture of 10 wickets for 18 runs in one innings against Glamorgan at Pontypridd in 1929. Geary would hardly have expected that it would be superseded three years later by Hedley Verity's 10 for 10 at Leeds. He was even less overjoyed by his wife's reaction when he returned home from his triumph in Wales. George was rightly well pleased with himself as he sank into his armchair. He waited patiently for an overture. It was not forthcoming and silence reigned. At last, George said: 'Done well today, missis, all ten wickets for 18.' Mrs Geary offered no comment on his achievement. Instead, she pointed to the kitchen hearth. 'I've left you the stove to black-lead,' she said.

Geary, as the cricket coach holding court in the tiny attic room at the top of the Crown pavilion at Charterhouse, was a delightful raconteur. He enthralled his young listeners, Peter May among them, with extravagant tales. His most enduring impressions were of touring India between the wars. Above all his cricket feats, he best remembered the days of tiger-hunting, dining off gold-plate, and residing in suites in Maharajahs' palaces. 'George made the east sound just as mysterious and colourful as did Kipling in his books,' recalled Peter. 'You would think that India possessed the richest maharajahs, the most precious diamonds, and the biggest elephants and fiercest tigers ever known.'

Sir Oliver Popplewell, QC, another wartime Carthusian and former MCC president, remembers Geary as 'friendly and sensible and good with boys'. He relates one instance of the Charterhouse coach's roguish sense of humour. It was the custom at Charterhouse to entertain visiting teams to pre-match dinners. One Wellingtonian, having celebrated rather freely and prematurely, was discovered the next morning in the long-jump pit. He was quite clearly unfit to play in the match and journeyed home. Four years after this episode, he returned to Charterhouse for another match. Geary, performing his usual duties as umpire, gave the young man guard when he came in to bat. He looked inquiringly down the wicket and said: 'Feeling much better now, sir?'

In 1947, his last school year, Peter May strode into the spotlight as Charterhouse captain. The school suffered only one defeat, by Winchester, in a triumphant season. In that year, said Frederic Raphael, it was difficult to imagine what could be missing from May's game; he turned cricket into a kind of one-man show. 'When he played in the house matches, scoring as many runs as were needed to bowl out the opposition, it was as if an Olympian had deigned to play skittles with mortals.'

John May was also a merited member of the Charterhouse team that summer, having been presented with his first eleven colours by his brother. He had joined Peter in Saunderites House in 1945. He possessed many of the physical attributes of the elder May, but lacked the determination which might have placed him in the first-class game. Minor Counties cricket with Berkshire was a meagre advance following the outstanding promise he had shown at school. His inattention once brought a stern rebuke from George Geary. John could not overcome the habit of pulling across the ball. It frustrated the Charterhouse coach. Geary stressed that this would prove John's downfall if he persisted with the errant stroke. Some years later John returned to Charterhouse with a visiting eleven. He had not eliminated the fault and was out in both innings swinging across the line. 'Do you agree with what I used to tell you?' asked Geary. 'Yes, I know, you're right,' replied John, with an apologetic smile.

The lapses were not so severe as to prevent John from following Peter as the Charterhouse cricket captain. In 1950 he headed the school batting averages with 502 runs at an average of 41.83. He was also a member of the school Fives team for four years and captain in his last year. The younger May is also remembered as one of the best soccer half-backs the school had produced since the war, and his prowess was acknowledged by appointment as captain in 1950. Peter Smithson, one football colleague of those years, recalls a fearless performer and the pleasures of playing with him. John May was held in esteem as a quick bowler at Charterhouse; his house tutor unhesitatingly described him as a 'West Indian bowler before his time'. John's reputation engendered fright in one opponent facing him for the first time in a house match. Smithson related: 'As he came thundering up to the wicket to bowl the first ball, the small boy at the other end stepped away from the wicket. He explained to the umpire that he had had a fly in his eye. As John ran up to deliver the next ball, the same thing happened again.' This performance was repeated for the next four balls until the umpire decided to intervene and end the batsman's distress. 'Over' was called without a ball being bowled!

John, like Peter, was cherished for his integrity in sport and in his later profession as a chartered accountant. He was, again in common with his brother, very supportive of his partners and colleagues and mindful of his clients' needs. Peter Smithson remembers that John did, however, have one curious 'blind spot' – an obsession with ancient motor cars. 'John always seemed to be the proud possessor of the oldest car and once acquired he would never get rid of it. They were for ever breaking down or failing to start.' John's wife, Liz, became aware of this eccentric pursuit at a very early stage in their marriage. His favourite old Sunbeam Talbot actually broke down in the middle of Dartmoor on the journey to their honeymoon hotel.

After John May died, at the age of fifty-five in 1988, those who had enjoyed his company – on the cricket field, the golf course or at the bridge table – recalled a modest and engaging man who, as Peter Smithson said, 'was great fun to be with'.

From their schooldays Peter Nathan recalls a remarkable instance of Peter May's fortitude which, in this case, concerned his brother. John May was playing in a match against Harrow on the day in 1946 when their mother died. Nathan was strictly instructed by Peter to maintain a silence on the bereavement until the end of the game in the afternoon. He did reluctantly accept the edict, which specifically included John. It was a gesture of brotherly protectiveness. Nathan today reflects that, in controlling his own distress, Peter gave evidence of his sense of duty and character.

The stature of Peter May at Charterhouse is expressively noted in one story told by Jim Prior. He describes the humbling experience of examining Peter's bat. 'The bats you generally pick up in the club pavilion or at school have lots of red marks all down their edges, with very few in the middle. Peter's bat was not at all like that. His just had a sort of dent in the middle where every ball had struck and it was only when one looked at his bat that one realised what a very great cricketer he was. His bat was always straight, reminding me again of my old master who used to tell us boys to look at the sweaters of the old pros. The right elbows and the area around the right ribs would be worn into holes, caused by the constant friction between the elbow and the ribs as shots were always played keeping the right elbow tucked in.'

In his four years in the Charterhouse eleven, May scored 1,794 runs and averaged 54.36. That he was unquestionably the best schoolboy batsman in the country was evidenced by his aggregate of 651 runs in 13 innings at an average of 81.38 in 1947. The progress of the 'star boy cricketer' had not escaped the notice of Harry Lewis, the Berkshire secretary. In the previous season Peter was invited to play for Berkshire against Bucking-hamshire. Bill Stokes was May's first senior cricket captain. He recalls that this 'delightful young man' scored around 20 before he was trapped lbw by Victor Lund. 'Peter batted immaculately,' says Stokes. 'He was very upright, with a straight bat: one could see instantly that he would go far. It was sad for Berkshire but Surrey claimed him under the school qualification. First-class cricket awaited him, and rightly so.'

Peter's remarkable run tally in 1947 included undefeated centuries against Harrow and Eton. E. M. ('Lyn') Wellings, the former London *Evening News* cricket correspondent, thought that May, even at seventeen, might have had a measure of success in county cricket.

Peter had first played at Lord's two years earlier for the Public Schools against a Lord's XI. He was dismissed for nought and one. But there was no shame in being dismissed by Trevor Bailey and Freddie Brown.

In 1946, Charterhouse defeated Winchester, their great rivals, for the first time since 1936. Tony Rimell, setting a fine example in the field and leading the eleven for the second year in succession, also secured victories over Harrow, Wellington, Cranleigh and Westminster. Only rain in the match against Eton frustrated the ambition to win all the school matches in one season. Charterhouse, during Rimell's reign, was regarded as the best of the southern schools. Rimell was later reunited with May and Popplewell at Cambridge. He won his blue in two years at university and later represented Hampshire.

As an all-rounder, commented *The Carthusian*, Rimell had probably been unequalled at Charterhouse. 'Whether fielding, bowling his teasingly flighted off-breaks, or batting, he was always interesting to watch. His running between the wickets, especially when partnered by May, was a joy to behold.' Oliver Popplewell, brimming with infectious confidence, also held sway as a wicket-keeper and prolific run-scorer. His all-round abilities were a major factor in the victories over Wellington and Winchester.

Peter May, rapidly maturing as a batsman, was complimented on adding the late-cut to his repertoire. 'It is a delightful stroke which, combined with his graceful leg-glide and fluent off-drive, enables him to dominate any field which is set for him.' *The Carthusian* tellingly added that so many of his innings were left unfinished because of the weakness of opponents, who failed to make many runs off the bowling of Rimell and Whitby.

Bob Whitby, volatile and rebellious, had arrived, as a fifteen-year-old at Charterhouse, straight from India. He did not easily make the transition

15

from his opulent lifestyle in Calcutta. He was, though, an outstanding all-rounder, an aggressive opening batsman, a fiercely competitive bowler, and superb close fieldsman. He was close to winning a blue at Cambridge. Later he became Prince Charles' housemaster at Gordonstoun. Whitby played with May for the Public Schools against the Combined Services at Lord's in 1946. 'His fast bowling was superb and, at times, unplayable,' enthused *The Carthusian*. Whitby took seven wickets for 38 runs, including six clean bowled, against Harrow. This was only marginally inferior to his eight wickets for 16 runs in the victory by four wickets over Winchester. He took 40 wickets at an average of 10.48 runs in a memorable season.

John Perry, described by *The Cricketer* as a 'fastish bowler of unrhythmic action', remembers the exhortation of Wilfred (W. W.) Timms. Timms, formerly with Northamptonshire, was the master-in-charge of cricket at Charterhouse. 'You must always bowl your in-duckers against Winchester. They're not very comfortable against them,' said Timms. Perry missed the victory over the Wykehamists because of injury, but he was in the side when Field Marshal Montgomery, who had a son at Winchester, attended the fixture at Godalming in June 1945.

'We were all very serious as Monty and Birley walked around Green,' recalls Perry. 'Peter was batting, trying to save the day. Suddenly, he was out to a magnificent catch. Monty looked up and said: "There's always a turning-point in these battles".' He had no doubt been appraised of the dangers posed by Peter's batting.

Exceptionally heavy rain on the morning of the match had delayed the start until after lunch. Winchester, on a wicket drying rapidly in the wind and sun, were dismissed for 102. Perry, in one over, took three wickets in four balls. Charterhouse, in their turn, were also confounded by the perils of the wicket. They lost five wickets for 37 runs and the Carthusian hopes then rested with May, doggedly resisting the Winchester attack on a spiteful pitch. A superb catch at short extra-cover led to his downfall. It was a conclusive dismissal. Peter was top scorer with 25 (out of a total of 68). Winchester, favoured by winning the toss, were victors by 34 runs.

A resentment still lingers among May's Charterhouse contemporaries at the criticism of his fielding. Peter was never a natural athlete. By his own admission, he was not a greyhound in the field. But he was unfairly omitted from one schools' representative match in 1946. The reason given for his non-selection was inadequate fielding. It was based flimsily on minor blemishes. They included a dropped catch in the deep and in the lee of the pavilion, and two misfields during the earlier match between the

Southern Schools and the Rest at Lord's. Peter Nathan considers this was a misguided verdict. 'Peter's fielding on this and other occasions was immaculate.' The intention of the perfectionists among the selectors was in the nature of a challenge. 'There was an element of trying to punish him; a call to do better next time without weighing up all of Peter's attributes as a batsman,' says Nathan.

John Perry also rallies to his friend's defence. 'Peter was a first-class extra-cover and, when he captained the school, equally fine at mid-off or mid-on.' Another writer in *The Cricketer* reinforced the memory of the 'hard and accurate throw, which, combined with a little cunning, ensnares the wickets of incautious batsmen'. Perry regards the prowess as a consequence of the emphasis placed by Bob Arrowsmith on fielding practice at school. 'This was one of the rigours of any Charterhouse cricketer's life.'

In 1947, again at Lord's, May was intently watched by another influential judge, Archie Fowler, the MCC chief coach. Peter scored 148 (out of 270) for the Southern Schools against the Rest and 146 (out of 239) for the Public Schools against the Combined Services. Wellings enthused about the latter innings in *Wisden*. 'His class as a batsman and ideal temperament was obvious from the start of his big innings against the Combined Services. The first short ball bowled at him he hooked with complete assurance and impressive force to the Tavern boundary. It was an innings of the highest class, played at a time when the other batsmen were failing badly. He had a wide range of strokes, and he was always looking for opportunities to use them.'

Peter Nathan batted with May in the match against Eton in 1947. He recalls that Peter, quite early in his innings, survived after hitting an enormous skier to mid-on. The catch was dropped, but before that happened Peter refused his partner's call for a run. 'Peter then asked me to scamper to the other end. I was run out. The great thing, though, was that Peter was not dismissed because he went on to get this monumental score for a one-day game.' Peter reached his 100 in less than two hours and was unbeaten on 183.

In the helter-skelter run chase, Peter was also dropped at the wicket and was then involved in another run-out. His brother, John, was the victim this time. The declaration halt was called at 277 for 8 and then, perhaps with a hint of apology for running him out, Peter entrusted Nathan with the ball. The cushion of a large total was also a consideration in this act of generosity, but Nathan, purveying his slow leg-breaks, did not let his captain down. He took five wickets for 29 runs, as Eton were dismissed for 108.

Nathan, in his assessment of May's skills as a boy, stresses the magnet of Charterhouse's reputation as a cricket school in those years. 'There was a great demand among club sides, including such as the Free Foresters, to visit us. They often included former or current county players, whose opposition endowed Peter's performances with increased significance.' Among these visitors in 1944 was a future England colleague, Sergeant Godfrey Evans. Evans, representing the Royal Army Service Corps, gave notice of his excellence as a wicket-keeper. But he scored only four runs. Peter, on patrol in the long field, took the catch off a steepling big hit at fine-leg. Evans eagerly accepted his chance to even the score. He took the catch to dismiss Peter when Charterhouse batted.

Other more sombre headlines took precedence over the emergence of the brilliant boy cricketer at Charterhouse. A terrible conflict weighed heavily on people's minds. The bombardment of London by German aircraft at this time led to the strengthening of rooms in each house to act as shelters. In July 1940 it was not clear whether the school would reassemble in September. In this crisis, one of the hastily prepared defensive lines against an anticipated German invasion ran along the Wey valley within a few hundred yards of the school.

The threat of invasion had receded by the time Peter took up residence at Charterhouse. The assault from the skies did, however, continue unabated. Air-raid precautions at the school were supervised by Edward Lovell; the Home Guard was run by Tommy Thompson; and a junior training corps was marshalled by Frank Ives. Peter, in his last year at school, rose to the rank of sergeant in the Corps. Digging for victory was a catchphrase of the war years. Potatoes and vegetables were grown and Jim Prior, befitting his future tenure as Minister of Agriculture, kept pigs as a valuable supplement to the rations.

The last chapter in the aerial bombardment of Britain unleashed the flying bomb, the V1 or, as it was nicknamed, the 'doodlebug'. The eerie missiles were launched in the closing weeks of the cricket quarter of 1944. 'They came in low and were unnerving, as no-one could tell when they would cut out and where they would land,' wrote Anthony Quick. Charterhouse survived unscathed, but one pupil, emerging from a shelter after one had passed over the school, remarked to a master: 'Wizard doodle, sir!'

Although Charterhouse escaped without mishap, scarcely a week passed without Robert Birley lamenting the loss of former pupils in the school chapel. 'We had to listen to the news of those who had been killed in action. It was most distressing,' remembers John Perry. One of those who died was Tony Lovett, a superb cricket captain, who had demonstrated a potential to match Peter May as a leader. Lovett had left Charterhouse at eighteen. He died in a flying accident within twelve months of his departure. Altogether 340 Carthusians lost their lives in the war.

The end of the war in Europe brought a salutary sermon from Robert Birley. On a Sunday evening after VE Day he reflected that the rise of Nazism had been the result of a spiritual emptiness in Germany. Carthusians, he said, who had so many opportunities to develop a full life, should consider it a duty to help others not so fortunate. 'Never let this country be a house with empty classrooms,' he declared.

During his last year at Charterhouse Peter May was captain of soccer, hockey and fives, as well as cricket. He could not be considered the quickest on the football field; pace and panache were noticeably absent in his game. The compensation was his industry as a 'fetcher and carrier' at inside-forward; and he did stun defences with the opportunism of his shooting. As a sporting all-rounder, Peter also excelled with his intuitive passing at hockey; and, with his brother John, he was thrice the winner of the Kinnaird Cup, the amateur championship for Eton Fives.

Peter never held pretensions as a bowler, but his 'slow, floating off-spin' did win house matches at Charterhouse. In his report, as head monitor, he betrays more than a hint of joy at the victory by Saunderites over Robinites by 99 runs in the house match final in July 1947. 'On Wednesday the unexpected happened. P. B. H. May went on to bowl, and, with his first ball, completely beat the Robinite captain ... this was the beginning of the end. The Saunderites' hopes rose – but not too high for we had a habit of losing these matches when once we had got on top. However, with the May brothers bowling for the rest of the match, the remaining eight wickets fell for merely 42 runs. These two bowlers seemed to be inspired and took all the wickets between them.' The last Robinite wicket fell at 74, and, continued Peter, 'we could hardly believe our eyes'. The Saunderites' triumph was achieved after a lapse of twenty years. Peter exultantly ended his match report with the words, appropriately capitalised and underlined: 'WE HAD WON THE CUP'.

In his last year, Peter was also engaged in a farewell thespian tribute to the revered Robert Birley. A performance of Gilbert and Sullivan's *Trial by Jury* was staged in Brooke Hall. 'There was an incalculable amount of work put into this production,' reported Peter. 'The producer deserves especial mention for his great patience and originality in adding various small actions to this light opera.' Peter himself was cast in the role of the 'learned judge'. This was a portrayal which has gained retrospectively a fulsome and, perhaps, indulgent critique. Peter Nathan, one of the invited guests at the production, insists: 'I witnessed and heard Peter singing quite brilliantly and professionally as the judge.'

There were other voices who cherished Peter's integrity and talents on the cricket stage. Eddie Paynter, the Lancashire and England batsman, came down to Charterhouse to umpire in a match against an MCC eleven. He watched May strike an elegant century and was deeply impressed by the certainty of the innings.

It is, however, the authoritative view of George Geary to which we must return. Philip Snow, the brother of Lord (C. P.) Snow, the novelist and physicist, had first met the Charterhouse coach in the early 1930s. At that time Geary ran the winter indoor nets in the dining-room at the then Leicestershire headquarters at Aylestone Road. Snow, as Bursar at Rugby School, persuaded Geary to come out of retirement and coach again at Rugby in 1960. Geary was then aged sixty-six, and he was to continue to maintain his vigil behind the nets for another decade.

Snow recalls that George's 'sparkling, rich brown eyes' did not dim in watchfulness with the passing years. Geary needed no persuasion to delve into his abundant store of reminiscences. He once told Snow: 'May is the best young 'un I ever saw in the nets, or out in the middle, before and beyond his time. And I've seen a good many lads all over the world in my time since the First War.'

Geary always modestly disclaimed the slightest influence in May's cricket apprenticeship at Charterhouse. 'Peter was so full of natural gifts as a batsman that he would have discovered himself in any case.' May, as his devoted pupil, scorned the reticence of his old coach. 'George might tell you that he could teach me nothing about the game that I did not know. Treat that with a large pinch of salt,' he said. Perpetuating today the memory of a wise counsellor at Charterhouse is a memorial seat beside the cricket Green. Geary would also have been proud to know that an annual award, bearing his name, of bat and pads is given to the most promising Under-16 cricketer of the year.

Another perceptive group of Surrey stalwarts looked on as Peter May, in his last year at school, played at neighbouring Broadwater in May 1947. May's prolific run-making that summer had earned him a county trial. He was a member of an Errol Holmes's Surrey XI opposed to a Farncombe and District team. The match was staged in aid of the Surrey centenary appeal, delayed by two years because of the war.

Brian Castor, newly returned from a Japanese prisoner-of-war camp, was to become one of the key architects in rebuilding Surrey cricket after the war. He was to prove a commanding and influential secretary of the club in the post-war era. Castor had been apprised of May's promise, but he had never seen the boy play. At Broadwater, he watched Peter garner runs of impressive quality. He instantly knew that he had sighted a player who would become an inspirational figure. His pavilion companions were Errol Holmes, the former England and Surrey captain, and Stan Squires, a redoubtable campaigner who played for the county from 1928 to 1949.

An exchange of glances among this inspectorate compelled a question waiting to be answered. 'Douglas Jardine at his best,' was the unanimous cry. Peter May, beneath his mask of boyish shyness, would soon measure up to this comparison. His gifts, like those of his distinguished predecessor, were to be ruthlessly honed for his own conquests.

Chapter 3
Making Waves Ashore

'Peter was such a self-effacing fellow. It was difficult to believe that he had an iron will to win against the odds.'

Alan Shirreff

Auspicious beginnings carry perils for the stars in their courses. A question that will always remain unanswered is whether Peter May would have faltered had he been plunged into the tour of Australia in 1950–51. As he said, his own lucky star continued to shine in another stirring voyage. Fair winds blew to speed the cricketing sailor through the shallows of Services cricket. The paternal care of George Geary at Charterhouse was reinforced when he found other guiding hands during his National Service in the Royal Navy in the late 1940s.

Observant men from overseas were compelled to admire the promise of a diligent apprentice in 1949. The witnesses were the touring New Zealanders. Walter Hadlee, their captain, missed the match against the Combined Services at Gillingham through injury. May's scores were negligible in quantity, but his innings did arouse the keen interest of the tourists. Hadlee recalls that Mervyn Wallace, his vice-captain, and the rest of the team unreservedly extolled the potential of the young serviceman.

At the end of the tour, A. J. ('Jack') Holmes, the chairman of the England selectors and a former captain of Sussex, was the New Zealanders' guest at a lunch in Paris. Holmes invited his hosts to express a view on candidates under consideration for the following year's tour of Australia. Mervyn Wallace responded by describing May as the best young player they had seen on the tour of England.

May, then aged nineteen, had also been noticed by another onlooker, who wrote in the *Playfair Cricket Annual*: 'He was the outstanding performer, both in concentration and stroke-range. He is uncommonly well-equipped for his years, and his technique against spin, as the New

Zealanders were quick to spot, is remarkably mature. His on-side play is particularly strong although he is inclined at the moment to overdo the cross-bat push off his legs.'

Peter did not gain selection for Australia in 1950–51. Three of his future Cambridge University colleagues – David Sheppard, John Dewes and John Warr – were included in an experimental party under the leadership of Freddie Brown. The trio of raw recruits were subjected to a bruising baptism in Test cricket. Alec Bedser, with due grievance, has lamented the accent on unproven youth in Australia and the decision to leave more experienced campaigners kicking their heels at home.

Bedser and Len Hutton stood alone in their majesty in the lost series. Bedser took 30 wickets at an average of 16.06 runs each; and Hutton, lordly in his command, scored 533 runs at an average of 88.83. The aggregate included an unbeaten 156 in the fourth Test at Adelaide. The unexpected failure of Denis Compton, handicapped by a knee problem, was another element in England's defeat. In the circumstances, the inspiring lead of Bedser and Hutton ought to have at least ensured parity with Australia. Even so, the series for England was not completely shrouded in gloom. They lost two Tests at Brisbane and Melbourne by only 70 and 28 runs respectively and finally ended a sequence of seven successive Test defeats with a victory by eight wickets in the last match at Melbourne.

The omission of Peter May was for him perhaps a blessing in disguise, an acknowledgement that his talents should be carefully nursed before he was thrust on to this major stage. Alec Bedser does, however, believe that May, among all the emerging batsmen of the time, alone merited a place on the Australian tour. John Warr considers that Peter would assuredly have gone to Australia had he been on view on the more prominent platform at Cambridge, a year earlier, in the summer of 1949. Walter Hadlee recalls a later meeting with May during the 1954–55 tour of Australia and New Zealand. The question of his earlier non-selection provided one talking point. 'Peter felt that he had not been quite ready for international cricket at that time,' says Hadlee.

Sir Oliver Popplewell has emphasised May's good fortune in playing challenging Services cricket against other aspiring county players out of the glare of the spotlight. The National Service interlude enabled Peter to gain in maturity and negotiate less taxing hurdles before going to university. Before entering the Navy in 1948, Peter had been accepted for Pembroke College, Cambridge. His initial service training was carried out at HMS *Royal Arthur* at Corsham, near Chippenham. He was destined to meet for the first time and play against many of his future first-class partners and rivals during this period. At Corsham, in one match, he was opposed to Arthur Milton, the Gloucestershire and later England opening batsman. Milton was 'still in khaki' and on Army leave. He was a member of a local wandering side called 'The Willows', which played against village teams in the area. 'They were a wonderful bunch of lads, just back from the war and happy to be home,' he recalls. 'This young boy played against us. He gave us a real towelling and hit the ball everywhere.'

From Corsham, May was posted to Yorkshire and HMS *Ceres* at Wetherby for instruction in the supply and secretarial branch. During this summer he turned down an invitation to represent Harrogate in the Yorkshire League. He preserved his loyalty to *Ceres* and was content to play in the less exalted Harrogate and District League. There was also the enriching experience of talks with Maurice Leyland, the Yorkshire county coach and a renowned Dalesman.

It is difficult to credit Peter with seafaring ambitions; and as 'Writer P. B. H. May', he was not in danger of succumbing to seasickness. His duties, when he returned south to Chatham and the office of the Commander-in-Chief, Nore, were clerical with strong and alluring crick-eting interludes. The question of a commission, even if he had held the necessary qualifications, did not arise since commissions were not then open to National Servicemen. John Warr has amusingly reflected that, as a Petty Officer, he outranked both May and Oliver Popplewell, another Royal Navy Writer. Warr's superior status was gained through his service accomplishment, with no particular aim in mind except to pass the time, in taking an electronics course.

May's role as 'Writer' baffled many people, especially when it was abbreviated on cricket scorecards to 'Wtr'. He remembered that this once led to a heated debate during a match at Lord's. 'My name on the card was surrounded by a most high-level wardroom – the name seeming like a small dinghy among a fleet of battleships!' The members were perplexed by his designation. Finally one of them arrived at a solution. 'Waiter,' he announced in some glee. 'Of course, chap's the mess waiter.' It was a moment of merriment; Peter overheard the remark and chuckled at the idea that he was at Lord's to carry out the drinks.

George Wenham was associated with Malden Wanderers, a premier Surrey club side, and also as scorer for the London Club Cricket Conference (C. C. C.) in the postwar years. He recalls his first meeting with May in July 1948 during a two-day match between the Navy and the C. C. C., played at the gunnery school at Whale Island, Portsmouth. The Conference captain was A. C. L. Bennett, whose work with the BBC prevented him from playing regular county cricket, although he did occasionally lead Northamptonshire in the late 1940s. It was said that he should have captained Surrey in the first year after the war, except that the letter of appointment was sent to the wrong Bennett.

It was a glorious summer's day at Portsmouth. The sun shimmered on the waters of the harbour. One of the marquees on the ground, recalled Wenham, accommodated the officers and seemed to contain nearly every retired admiral or commodore from Portsmouth to Petersfield. The Marine Band played during cricket before lunch on this festive occasion. Deploying his strokes thumpingly in unison with the music was a young Writer, who had travelled down from his Yorkshire base. Wenham, as the Conference scorer, watched Peter May score a very impressive half-century in the Navy's first innings.

In 1949, a return match between the Conference and the Navy was played at Hastings. Allan Rae, the West Indian opening batsman, was in the Conference ranks. The Navy team included John Manners and Michael Ainsworth, both respectively century-makers for Hampshire and Worcestershire in county careers curtailed by their service duties.

Keith Walker, the Malden Wanderers leg-spinner and a Surrey trialist, took 200 club wickets in that season. At Hastings he outwitted May. Wenham recalls that Walker, a friend at Rutlish School at Merton, bowled medium-paced leg and top spin, coupled with a quick seamed ball. His style resembled that of the Australian fast-medium bowler of later years, Max Walker; in delivery the ball appeared to emerge over the top of his head. It was his quick leg-break which dismissed May cheaply in the Navy's first innings.

Walker went on to complete a notable double in the Navy's second innings. The feat of dismissing May twice in one match was one to be cherished, but before this happened Peter had to re-establish his pride. He provided evidence of his youthful authority, as the Navy battled to save an innings defeat. This time he was intent on a century. He had reached around 80 when, as Walker recalled: 'I bowled a top-spinner to him first ball and he played it perfectly. I did the same with the second and third balls and each of them met with the same response. When I bowled the fourth ball I again tried the top-spinner. Peter now judged it to be the leg-break and he was out lbw.'

Wenham, in a postscript to this achievement, considers that the standard of club cricketers in the 1940s was of such quality that many of them would have featured in championship or one-day county matches today. Playing against them and others of higher stature in representative games as a serviceman was of inestimable value. It was an essential spur for May in his progress towards true growth as a cricketer.

May was third in the national averages in 1949. He scored 693 runs in 12 innings at an average of 63.18 runs each. Leading the first-class field were Joe Hardstaff and Len Hutton. Peter regarded his own high place in the list as freakish. It did not, he said, bear comparison with the number of innings, between 40 and 56, played by his illustrious seniors. It was possibly a misleading rating, but May did thrive fruitfully in his forays with the Combined Services and the Royal Navy.

At Worcester, in late August, he was almost brazen in his adventure. The county attack included three England bowlers. At one stage Worcestershire appeared assured of victory inside two days. The visitors were only 34 runs ahead, with three wickets left, in their second innings. The events of a remarkable match are described by Alan Shirreff, the Services captain. 'We had been destroyed by Dick Howorth, Reg Perks and Roley Jenkins. Jenkins took three wickets in four balls in this innings and ten in the match. Worcestershire claimed the extra half-hour, hoping to finish the match off. But Peter May, with the help of Bob Wilson, defied them.'

May marshalled the Services tail to such advantage that the eighth and ninth partnerships (with Wilson and Ford) more than doubled the score. He scored 175 (out of a total of 337) to add to his 97 in the first innings. *Wisden* enthused about an innings of 'great authority' by the former Charterhouse schoolboy. 'May batted for four-and-a-half hours. He tempered aggression with watchful defence, and the majority of his nineteen fours were the result of beautifully timed drives.'

Alan Shirreff, recalling this early instance of May's mastery, says: 'Peter, of course, stood technically head and shoulders above the rest of us. But he was such a modest, self-effacing fellow that it was difficult to appreciate that, deep down, he had an iron will to achieve success, and win against the odds.' At Worcester, Peter took charge of a deteriorating situation. Don Kenyon and Roley Jenkins were among his rueful opponents at New Road. 'We could not stem the flow of runs,' says Kenyon. 'It didn't matter who bowled at him; he hit the ball very hard.'

In a conversation shortly before his death in 1995, Jenkins confessed that he had an opportunity to halt May's commanding innings. He was acknowledged as one of the best and safest cover-points in the country. 'I dropped Peter when he had only scored around 30. I used to "catch pigeons". The ball, as it sped off his bat, was going reasonably comfortably to my right hand. But it took a swerve to the left, and I couldn't grasp it in time.'

Dick Howorth took a more reserved stance in his early assessment of May. 'I don't know how good he is going to be. He can't yet hit the ball on the off-side.' It was a tempered verdict by the England left-hander. Peter was, perhaps, then indulgent in his preference for the on-side. It was always one of the glories of his game and curiously pronounced during his salad days. Frank Tyson remembers how even in later years Peter would exult in his 'old right hand, his guide and master'. Raman Subba Row, in his morning greeting at The Oval, would ask: 'How's your right arm?'

Tom Graveney offers another glimpse of May in command at Bristol. 'Peter looked a class player and he was then only a beginner.' May hit 80 before being dismissed by Graveney's brother, Ken, in the first innings of the match against Gloucestershire. He followed this with an unbeaten 90 in the second innings. George Emmett and Andy Wilson both scored centuries for Gloucestershire, but the Services were close to another victory in a tense finish.

There were, of course, inevitable hiccups to harden Peter's resolve in this summer. Signalman Tyson, in the match between the Army and the Royal Navy at Lord's, scattered the stumps before May had had a chance to sight the ball. It was Tyson's only wicket in the match, and the Navy were untroubled in winning by nine wickets.

In another match against the Public Schools at Lord's, Peter twice failed to the general disappointment of his growing band of admirers. In the second innings he was teased into giving a return catch, brilliantly accepted by a sixteen-year-old boy from Tonbridge School, Colin Cowdrey. Cowdrey, the gifted all-rounder, took seven wickets with his leg-breaks in the match. Robin Marlar, the Harrovian off-spinner, though meeting with minor success, was considered the most promising of the Schools' bowlers on view at Lord's. 'He may prove to be the best of the lot,' commented a writer in *The Cricketer*. 'On a suitable wicket he can spin the ball like a Goddard and also make it go away at a quicker pace, a very awkward combination.'

Another talented sixteen-year-old, Michael Stewart, the Alleyn's School captain, also presented his credentials in the match. Stewart hit 63, as the Schools gallantly strove to reach their victory target of 159 runs in two hours. They failed by 19 runs, with two wickets left and their pride intact. It was a close call, for as *The Cricketer* reported: 'The Combined Services appeared to have almost over-strained the quality of mercy by their selection of a side which excluded their better tried veterans and left the honour of the Forces in the hands of a youthful band of warriors of junior rank.'

Peter May was given an instructive master class by the Kent and England leg-spinner, Doug Wright, at Gillingham. Wright took eight wickets, including five wickets for three runs in three overs, in the Services' first innings. Peter was dismissed for nought. It was a decisive spell by Wright and effectively sealed the outcome of the match. Kent's innings victory was ensured by a century by Les Ames augmented by a last-wicket stand of 74 between Brian Edrich and Fred Ridgway. May and A. H. Parnaby, who had played for Durham and the Minor Counties, were the avenging Services batsmen in the follow-on. They resolutely took toll of their first-innings sorcerer. Wright did capture another five wickets, but this time he faltered in length against a determined assault. Peter's contribution was a brisk half-century, as he and Parnaby added 111 runs.

May mildly described his duel with Wright in the bitter east wind at Gillingham as 'an interesting experience'. 'When he was pitching it and making the ball bounce unusually high at a far greater pace than the normal leg-spinner, Doug could be devastating. He was not far off doing me first ball in the second innings. It pitched middle-and-leg and I was pretty sure that it was the googly, so I took a swing at it. I'd guessed right. It went for four.'

The batting revels of Peter May gained him wider recognition in 1949, the last of his National Service summers. There was another example of his burgeoning talents in a jaunty solo for the Royal Navy against the Royal Air Force at Lord's. Once again, he shouldered the responsibility of restoring his team's fortunes. The Navy had lost seven wickets for 91 runs before he thankfully found a partner with staying powers. He thereupon unfurled his strokes to hustle to an unanticipated declaration. The extent of his authority is revealed by the fact that his unbeaten 162 came out of a total of 283. The next highest score of 58 was made by his stoutly resistant ally, Hodges, who defended nobly in Peter's company. The match, in the end, was dominated by the batsmen on both sides. But it was May who ignited the torch in his pursuit of runs in adversity. His 58 runs in the second Navy innings gave him a match aggregate of 220 without dismissal.

Peter May typically overstated the case when he said that he had gorged on trifling morsels during his service days. His feasting bat then, and later, was charged with a hunger for runs. The bounty of his aggression was increased when he entered a splendid new company at Cambridge.

Chapter 4
The Best of his Generation

'Peter was not an empire builder, looking for honours for himself. But he was a great competitor, never to be under-estimated.'

Dennis Silk

Peter May, unlike the vainest of actors, did not believe his own notices. The accumulated praise was as resistible as an agony column. He stumbled uneasily in the spotlight. 'With his usual modesty,' observes his friend, Peter Nathan, 'he would not wish to appear in any match in which he was easily the best'.

'The talisman of Peter's thinking was not to tell the world, but let others find it out,' says another lifelong admirer, John Perry. A doting cricket public did exercise this option to voice a concerted hymn of praise. At Cambridge, May became a member of an illustrious batting quartet, one of the finest in university history. His boyish, courtly charm snared him as a pin-up idol and the subject of respectful adoration. The force of his appeal was tellingly described by his History tutor, David Joslin. Joslin recalled a routine procedure, which was the starting point of most of his supervisions with May.

'There was invariably a pile of autograph books, which belonged to the children of Fellows and various chums of these children,' said Joslin. The presentation of the books was such a common occurrence that Peter automatically went through a signing ritual. The tutor handed over the books and Peter, in turn, gave him his essay. Relating this anecdote, a correspondent in the *Pembroke College Gazette* comments: 'Whether this exchange of paper was fair only posterity can judge.'

The intimations of glory at Charterhouse were just ripples waiting to swell into a thunderous flood. May's school centuries were simply hors d'oeuvres for a vast banquet of runs. He was, for one brief summer, the junior, overshadowed, and cast in a subordinate role at Cambridge.

His arrival at Pembroke College in 1949–50 coincided with the dominance of Hubert Doggart, John Dewes and David Sheppard. All three were to take other routes in life which mostly excluded cricket. Doggart and Dewes went into the scholastic professions. Sheppard progressed to high office in the ministry, culminating in the honour of being appointed the Bishop of Liverpool in 1975.

Hubert Doggart, the Cambridge and future Sussex captain, was a brilliant all-round sportsman. He was one of three generations to achieve distinction at Cambridge; his father, Graham, and son, Simon, also won their blues at the university. Doggart made what must be regarded as a sensational debut in 1948. He started his career as a Cambridge batsman with 215 not out against Lancashire. It is the highest innings in modern times played by an English batsman in his first game in first-class cricket. John Dewes, the formidable left-hander, from Aldenham School, was Doggart's partner in a then English record second wicket stand, unbroken, of 429 against Essex in the following year. Dewes, another superb schoolboy cricketer, had, at nineteen, first represented England in the 'Victory' Test against the Australian Services at Lord's in July 1945, and he made his Test debut proper against Australia at The Oval in 1948.

David Sheppard, the youngest of the trio and from Sherborne School, made his debut for Sussex against Leicestershire at Hastings in 1947. Two years later he won his county cap after scoring 204 against Glamorgan at Eastbourne. Sheppard was to establish a Cambridge record of 1,281 runs, including seven centuries, in his captaincy year in 1952.

Peter May would subsequently supersede his Cambridge seniors and become, in their reckoning, the best of his generation. Oliver Popplewell, a late-order university batsman of this time, remembers the awesome command of Cambridge's opening quartet. He says that it was something of an event if he got to the wicket at all. So prolific were the undergraduate stars that the opposing counties did not dare field other than their best elevens.

May and Sheppard were awarded their blues after an extraordinary match against the West Indian tourists at Fenner's in the early summer of 1950. Cambridge, having topped 500 on the first day, finally declared at 594 for four. The mammoth total was achieved against an attack which included all but Pierre and Gomez of the regular bowlers. Sheppard (227) and Dewes (187) were associated in a magnificent opening stand of 343.

'At no time,' reported Michael Melford in the *Daily Telegraph*, 'was this cricket one would expect from undergraduates against Test match bowlers.

Dewes and Sheppard played with great mastery throughout the day, with scarcely a false stroke and with runs coming in an uninterrupted flow.' The Fenner's pitch was one of the truest ever prepared by a groundsman, Cyril Coote. Melford remembered an ominous moment in the second over of the match when Dewes hit Prior Jones like a bullet along the ground through the covers without moving his feet at all.

Sonny Ramadhin and Alf Valentine, soon to be the scourges of English Test batsmen, were annihilated by lightning strokes. By tea, the opening partnership was approaching 300. May went to the wicket at a quarter to seven with the score at 487 for 2. The earlier fall of Dewes had let in Doggart, who had sat with his pads on for nearly six hours. He made merry with a fluent 71 to add to the displeasure of the forlorn bowlers. Sheppard and Doggart put on 144 in an hour and a half. At the last, it left May and Stevenson with walk-on parts in the batting extravaganza. It was really pure gluttony to score yet more runs.

The larceny of the batting robbers continued in conditions preposterously weighed against bowlers. The West Indians, with equal fervour, produced a crushing counter, amassing 730 for three. Everton Weekes was unbeaten on 304 and Frank Worrell hit 160. They put on 350 in three and a half hours.

David Sheppard recalled how, on this bitterly cold May day, they did drop some easy catches to allow the tourists to stamp their authority. Worrell, especially, profited from his escape. 'The real lesson we received was from Weekes: cutting and hooking anything short with tremendous power, very quick to skip up the wicket to drive the slow bowlers, and driving in all directions off the back foot, which I had never really seen done before, he massacred our bowlers.'

Hubert Doggart remembers that when Weekes was in the 290s he was overheard muttering to himself as he prodded the hard, unyielding Fenner's pitch on a length. 'Play carefully,' was his whispered exclamation, 'Weekes, man, you're in the nineties.'

The *Daily Telegraph*, in its postscript to a remarkable episode, reported that it was not so much a cricket match, more a readjustment of the record books. It added rather sourly: 'The crowd, delighted though they were by such majestic hitting, were left to wonder whether or not this could be regarded as a satisfactory game of cricket.'

The batting plunder at Fenner's was followed less than two weeks later by the fiasco of the Test Trial at Park Avenue, Bradford. The hitherto flourishing undergraduates, not yet wise in the affairs of cricket, were cruelly dispatched on an impossible pitch. More experienced campaigners, including the Australians in 1948 and the West Indians earlier on in 1950, had also had cause for concern on the notorious Bradford wicket. May, Doggart and Sheppard and Donald Carr (Oxford) represented the Rest. Dewes, happily for him in the England team, was excused the travail of his university colleagues. It was without a doubt a cricketing travesty, expressing more the spectacle of *Grand Guignol* entertainment. The wicket had not been covered for twenty-four hours before the match. Heavy rain had produced a spiteful pitch, totally unsuitable for a fair examination.

Jim Laker, a Yorkshireman who played for Surrey, was here on his home ground, and took eight wickets for two runs. May, dismissed for nought, and Doggart were among those confronted by his spin. Sheppard, opening the innings, did not number among his victims. Trevor Bailey trapped him lbw before the ensuing rout. By a quarter past one, the Rest, put in to bat by Norman Yardley, were all out for 27. The match ended in victory for England by an innings before lunch on the second day. Sheppard said Laker's figures would have been nine for two if Godfrey Evans had not stumped Fred Trueman off the bowling of Alec Bedser. It was a characteristic example of Evans's agility. In a whirl of action, he clung on to the lifting ball outside the leg stump and scattered the bails before Trueman could ground his flailing bat.

Len Hutton, admittedly against more modest forces, demonstrated that runs could be scored. It was, though, his uncommon genius which allowed him to conquer the evils of the pitch. His 85 showed that he was without peer as the master on bad wickets. It was a lesson to be digested by the hapless students.

Hubert Doggart was Peter May's chaperone at Bradford. He had arranged with his tutor at King's College to look after Peter, who was engaged in his first year examinations at Cambridge. 'I had to take him out in the evening, guard him like some champion dog at Crufts – all so he could play in that ill-fated Test trial. I had to promise that I would watch him en route and, once we had arrived in Yorkshire, prevent any communication of the exam papers.'

Peter May, along with his unhappy partners, had other preoccupations to divert his mind. He thought the match, played so early in the season and on such a pitch at Bradford, was the 'very height of futility'. 'The conditions were too extreme and the experience too brief,' he said. However, if one disregards the merits of the exercise, there can be no doubt that Laker would have bowled out the best of rivals. John Arlott was quick to praise the feat, which, he said, was achieved on a 'one in 300 sticky wicket, with the ball leaping about like a salmon. It was perfect for his off-spin. Laker habitually spins the ball far more than most of his type. On this occasion, he "dug" it in more than usual, using little flight, and giving the batsmen no chance to get to the pitch of the ball.'

The verdict, whatever the opposition or circumstances, is that only a great exponent of spin could have come within touching distance of Laker's performance. Of the two runs Laker conceded, one was the product of an impish full toss to Eric Bedser. It was delivered to allow him a run to get off the mark, an act of rare charity by Laker. Since the fielder was Eric's brother, Alec, it is probably fair to suspect that there was an element of collusion between bowler, batsman and fieldsman.

The chastened undergraduates, returning home after the calamity at Bradford, doubtless remembered the privilege of a good, predictable wicket at tranquil Fenner's. Peter May readily acknowledged the advantageous conditions. 'It was wonderfully true and heartbreaking for bowlers. But it did force them to bowl to a length.' For batsmen, he said, it did have one drawback: the ball did not lift and thus banished the hook shot. This would explain his infrequent use of the stroke in first-class cricket. He thought it was of dubious merit and, in any event, he had other more productive shots at his command. Raman Subba Row, another Cambridge contemporary, also remembered the perfection of the Fenner's wicket. 'It encouraged and bred front-foot players. If you played forward, it was quite difficult to get out.' Subba Row endorses the general verdict that it was the best possible teaching ground for both batsmen and bowlers.

The wickets at Fenner's were nurtured by a man steeped in cricket traditions. Cyril Coote, the doyen of groundsmen, was also a sharp but astute critic. He was a guide and counsellor to a whole cavalcade of aspiring undergraduates for over four decades. Coote, handicapped by a soccer injury which left him lame, still shone in Minor Counties cricket. As a left-handed opening batsman, he scored nearly 3,000 runs for Cambridgeshire between 1932 and 1939. Coote captained the county in the two seasons preceding the Second World War and again from 1946 to 1949. His farewell innings against Berkshire observed the unities of preparation. John Warr recalls the dedication, measured on this occasion to Coote's own desires. 'He prepared the wicket, won the toss and decided to bat. He then went in first and scored 200.'

Peter May shared with David Sheppard the distinction of scoring a double-century in his first year at university. He scored 227 not out against

Hampshire at Fenner's. He was associated with Dewes and Mike Stevenson in two partnerships of over 200, the second an exhilarating display lasting only five minutes over two hours. The innings of May and Sheppard were among thirteen three-figure scores registered that summer to establish a university record. It was, otherwise, a moderate season for May. He scored 637 runs in 17 innings. Dewes and Sheppard each hit over 1,000 runs to win deserved hurrahs. E. M. Wellings, writing in *Wisden*, did perceptively maintain the conviction that May was likely to make the greater advance. The England selectors thought differently. Doggart, Dewes and Sheppard, the latter two also gaining selection for the tour of Australia in the following winter, played in Tests against the West Indies.

In the meantime, during the university vacation, May took his first steps on the Surrey ladder. He recalled: 'It is a measure of how well I was treated by everyone at The Oval from the start that, if all the batsmen were fit and in form, the two senior professionals, Laurie Fishlock and Jack Parker, would take it in turns to stand down for me. This was just one of their kindnesses in my early years with Surrey.'

Peter May might well have been preceded as a Surrey player two years earlier by Colin Cowdrey, who was qualified to play for the county. Geoffrey Howard, then assistant secretary at The Oval, recalls that an approach was made to Cowdrey because of his phenomenal record at Tonbridge School. The offer was turned down; and Howard was then instructed by the Surrey committee to direct another inquiry to May, who was then serving in the Navy. Peter was more than willing to accept the invitation. He scored 34 for the Surrey second eleven against Norfolk at Lakenham in 1948. Geoffrey Whittaker, who also played in the match, laconically remarked: 'He's not bad for an amateur.'

May remembered that his entrance into the Surrey first eleven in July 1950 carried extra responsibilities. There was an air of expectancy, justified by their position in the table, that Surrey could hoist the championship pennant at The Oval for the first time since 1914. As a newcomer, his nerves could well have jangled in this situation. Against Gloucestershire at Bristol he scored only two runs in the match, losing his wicket in the first innings to the wily veteran, Tom Goddard. He was then thrust into a confrontation with Yorkshire at The Oval. It was his first meeting with Bob Appleyard, who was starting out on a magnificent career sadly curtailed by illness. May and Appleyard were to become fiercely combative rivals, their duels enhanced by a mutual respect.

The honours in this first encounter went to Appleyard and Yorkshire.

Surrey were bowled out for 127 and 97, and lost by seven wickets. Peter was dismissed for nought and one, bowled by Appleyard in the first innings, and lbw to Wardle in the second. Appleyard, in the second of his two appearances for Yorkshire in that season, finished with four wickets for 47 runs. He recalls: 'I realised that I wasn't good enough merely as a fast-medium bowler. I could bowl an off-spinner. At The Oval, after about five overs, I ran up and bowled a slow spinner. The batsman (Fletcher) had a tremendous swipe at it. It pitched and turned and knocked his middle stump out. The dismissal was amazing to me and even more so to my own side. No one had seen me bowl off-spinners.' Despite his haul of wickets, including the swift dismissal of May, Appleyard was given a wigging by his captain, Norman Yardley. 'Make your bloody mind up,' he told the recruit. 'How can I set a field when you're bowling like that?'

Surrey regained their poise to win their next seven matches, beginning at Worcester. May was dropped twice early in his innings. He then, perhaps recalling his exploit as a National Serviceman against these opponents, proceeded to hit his first championship century. The Worcestershire spinners, Jenkins and Howorth, were once again harassed in defeat. 'It was none too soon,' said Peter. 'Indulgent though they were, Surrey were not going to go on playing me indefinitely while I was not even reaching double figures.'

May was the steadfast sentinel in the crucial match against Lancashire at The Oval. It provided ample confirmation of his coolness in a crisis. Surrey were sixteen points behind Lancashire, their only challengers. They did have one precious game in hand, but it was imperative to deny their Red Rose rivals the bonus of first-innings points. This was Lancashire's last match of the season and those four points would have given them the title outright. Surrey's opponents included Brian Statham and Roy Tattersall, both of whom were to be swept into national prominence in the following winter, when they were belatedly flown out to reinforce the MCC party in Australia and New Zealand.

At The Oval, after the early loss of Washbrook and Place, Lancashire sacrificed enterprise for caution. The dourness of their batting rebuked their championship ambitions. Jack Parker took five wickets for 30 runs, as Lancashire were dismissed for 221. May, now installed as no. 3 in the Surrey order, was reassuringly composed in a troubled reply. His discipline was sorely needed. Surrey lost three wickets, those of Fishlock, Fletcher and Constable, for 39 runs. Dark clouds glowered to mock the batsmen. Statham and a young Australian from Manchester University, Tom

Dickinson, bowled with spirit and venom. Peter calmed the heartbeats of the partisans and took charge of the game. Parker, with a half-century to place alongside his bowling success, and Arthur McIntyre, unbeaten on 44, were his allies. The two batsmen between them helped May add 164 runs and so ensure the decisive advantage. By the time May was out, eight runs short of a deserved century, the battle had been won.

Peter was quietly pleased. 'I batted for nearly five hours, and although I did not make 100 I took satisfaction from being able to play an innings of this sort against good bowling, and when it mattered,' he recalled. Surrey went on to beat Leicestershire by ten wickets to share the championship. May's own contributions at a testing time were acknowledged by the award of his county cap.

His progress on this and other stern fields was so remarkable that everyone expected him to do well in the varsity matches at Lord's. He was supremely equipped for the big occasion. His heroics as a batsman consigned to laughter any suspicion of temperamental fallibility. 'We'll be there at the finish', was a motto he shared with Godfrey Evans. Yet a strange quirk of cricketing fate decreed uneasy struggles in his three games against Oxford between 1950 and 1952. In five innings his total was only 119 runs, with a highest score of 39 in 1950. The lapses were in marked contrast to his otherwise unblemished standards in those years. In his Cambridge career he averaged over 60.

The inter-varsity matches, with maturing celebrities in their throng, were exacting and keenly contested events. In 1951 the match attracted nearly 11,000 paying spectators. Its importance on the sporting calendar matched Henley and Wimbledon. 'It is the central theme of university cricket,' Peter May said in one interview at the time. 'Our main thought right from the beginning of the season is to find the best team for that one match. For sheer rivalry I know nothing else like it in first-class cricket. I can only compare it with the grimmest house match at school.'

The concluding words were those of a boy as yet unschooled in the rigours of Test cricket. But the essence of his message was clear; there was a tension surrounding the matches. Peter's more mature view was that he and others dwelt too heavily on the importance of these showpiece occasions. They allowed them to upset their judgement. 'Certainly,' he said, 'most of the batsmen, myself included, did not play the bowling on its merits as we did against the counties – often against some of the best bowlers in the country.'

Cambridge arrived at Lord's in 1950 as a team of high-scoring renown.

Sheppard and Dewes had twice accumulated over 340 for the first wicket, but the Light Blues did not live up to their imposing credentials. Sheppard, with 93, alone prospered in the first innings. Dewes and Doggart were deluded by pace and spin; May, involved in a dreadful muddle, was run out for seven; and Cambridge were all out for 200. Clive Van Ryneveld, a future South African captain, and Ramish ('Buck') Divecha, who toured England with India in 1952, were the principal contributors to their downfall. The power of the Cambridge batting was surprisingly contained. But equally, as Billy Griffith, writing in *The Cricketer*, foretold, their bowling lacked the penetration to dispose of the much improved Oxford batting. He thought from the outset that a draw was a sensible prophecy.

The one exception to Griffith's reservations on the bowling was the hostility of John Warr, who bravely defied the handicap of a pulled muscle to play in the match. In his four years at Cambridge Warr took 169 wickets. David Sheppard remembers: 'John was never genuinely fast, but he was lively and a tremendous trier. He could make the ball swing away from the bat and he kept the batsmen guessing with a good change of pace.' Warr took four wickets for 44 runs and Oxford were bowled out for 169.

Peter May made amends for his first innings confusion, as he and Mike Stevenson prevented a batting catastrophe. Cambridge were 88 for four, only 119 ahead, at lunch. The fifth-wicket pair added 81 and Doggart's declaration at four o'clock was of the token variety. 'He was never in the happy position of having both runs in the book, and the time for his doubtful bowling to do its work,' concluded Billy Griffith.

Depending on your allegiance, worse was to follow in the varsity match of 1951. Oxford, against the odds, pulled off a remarkable win by 21 runs, with 17 minutes to spare. Cambridge's stock was high after three victories on tour. Within their ranks were four players – Sheppard, May, Warr and Marlar – who represented the Gentlemen against the Players eight days later. Sheppard and May offered only brief glimpses of their true form. Superlative fielding was the key to the Oxford success. Conversely, so *Wisden* reported, it was the runs which Cambridge slackly conceded in the field which tipped the scales in the Dark Blues' favour.

This was a match in thrall to spin. Divecha, bowling his offbreaks to a tight leg-side cordon, took nine wickets, including seven for 62 runs in a marathon spell of 43 overs in Cambridge's second innings. The Indian bowler made a considerable impression on the umpire, Dai Davies. Davies was one of the great characters of cricket. Wilf Wooller, the Glamorgan captain, once said that Davies had the talent to become a magnificent preacher. Old Dai had an incomparable gift of repartee. At Lord's, he bisected the syllables to confer new citizenship on the bowler of the hour. 'Di-vecha,' he said. 'How nice it is to see a Welshman playing today.'

David Sheppard was unexpectedly preferred to Peter May as the Cambridge captain for 1952. Today he expresses his astonishment at his promotion ahead of May. John Warr reveals that the appointment of his successor was decided by just one vote. 'Peter was a better cricketer than David. But he had not performed at all well in the varsity matches. Peter was not seen as a charismatic figure. Undergraduates tend to be swayed by considerations of success or failure on what they believe is the big day, and the choice fell on the future Bishop of Liverpool.'

Peter May again failed against Oxford in 1952, but there were mitigating circumstances. By a curious mischance, the eclipse of May in successive years at Lord's was attributable to the athleticism, on the first occasion as substitute fieldsman, of a 'little fair-haired boy', the Australian, Alan Dowding. Dowding won cricket and soccer blues at Oxford and captained the team in 1953.

In 1952, as Dennis Silk recalled, 'Peter slightly mishit the ball to deep mid-wicket and Dowding, running full tilt from square-leg, took a quite amazing catch.' At first he seemed to have misjudged the flight of the ball, but he eventually held it head high in front of the Tavern. Dowding was much esteemed in Australia as a fieldsman and clearly deserved his reputation. Apart from this 'noble catch', as *The Times* described it, his fast running, clean picking-up and accurate returns were other tokens of his industry. To add to Cambridge's mishaps, he also ran out Popplewell and Wait.

Once again, Cambridge had taken the field as strong favourites to break their barren spell. Both Sheppard's and May's averages were in the 70s; and Cuan McCarthy, the South African Test bowler, and Robin Marlar had taken well over 100 wickets between them. The omens appeared good when Oxford, despite a stylish half-century by Colin Cowdrey, were dismissed for 272. Robin Marlar was the dominant bowler; his seven wickets were the product of clever variations in pace and judicious spin.

Cambridge, in their reply, looked to have established an unassailable position and a platform for victory. Sheppard scored a century, the first by a Light Blue in a university match since the war. It was his seventh 100 of the season. He and Subba Row put on 119 for the fifth wicket. Oxford required 136 to save an innings defeat but, as *Wisden* reported, 'they showed a welcome revival of spirit'. Even so, the Dark Blues, buffeted by the fierce onslaught of McCarthy and Warr, were apparently engaged in a lost cause. They lost six wickets for 86 before Dowding and Alan Coxon came together in a determined rearguard action, Dowding resisted for two-and-a-half hours for a valiant 52. Sheppard claimed the extra half-hour in the hope of sealing his captaincy with a fulfilling and cherished success. In the end he had to concede that Oxford, unflinching in extremity, deserved to share the honours in an unforeseen draw.

Peter May, disappointed but nevertheless unbowed by his university match lapses, was casting his eyes towards new horizons. He was not, as Dennis Silk declares, an empire builder, despotically intent on claiming his own territory. His style was to forgo honours simply for himself. The struggles in varsity cricket were left behind in triumphs on other fields in 1951. David Sheppard noted a strengthening of May's defence and an even greater determination to unleash his flowing range of strokes. His driving was one of the glories of a wonderful year.

The news that he was batting at Fenner's emptied the lecture theatres. They ran down to watch him play,' recalls Dennis Silk. Other curious followers would neglect their daily tasks to laud the shy undergraduate when, in 1951, he travelled north for a prestigious date at Headingley.

Chapter 5
Gathering Momentum at Headingley

'His batting, over nearly five hours of a tense and grilling day, had a steadfast calmness and concentration of purpose remarkable in a young man of twenty-one.'

E. W. Swanton

Two events coincided with pleasing symmetry over two fulfilling weeks in July 1951. They linked for the first time two players, one the established master, and the other an exciting pupil. At Kennington Oval, on the first morning, thousands scrambled for admission. They questionably included a group of Surrey schoolboys, who had eluded a queue inspection by a local headmaster. He thought that their combined act of absenteeism had stepped beyond the bounds of acceptance.

The truants were, perhaps, forgiven their indiscretion, as another lesson engaged their attention at The Oval. On a ground celebrated in his name, and upon which he had broken the Test record in 1938, Leonard Hutton reached the milestone of 100 centuries. It was accomplished with a soothing and classically executed cover-drive, which is still fixed in the memory as a dream of style.

Hutton's innings was soon to be twinned with another which lost nothing in eloquence. Peter May, the twenty-one-year-old Cambridge undergraduate, was assured of celebrity status when he partnered the newly crowned Yorkshire centurion at Headingley. May's century on his Test debut against South Africa proclaimed him as the most promising batting prospect in post-war cricket. His 138, bridged by a weekend interval at a secret retreat in the Yorkshire countryside, was watchfully compiled in an innings lasting twenty minutes over six hours. His success brought fresh laurels to Cambridge cricket. The last English batsman to score a hundred in his first Test was another Cantab, Billy Griffith. He was preceded by Paul Gibb at Johannesburg in 1938–39. May's century was also the first by an undergraduate since Stanley Jackson, another man of Fenner's, achieved the feat in his second Test against Australia in 1893.

May's route to Headingley was only checked by yet another setback in the varsity match. The resilient young man, in a phenomenal summer, did not linger long in the shadows. Less than two weeks later he returned to Lord's to kindle the expectations of the watching selectors. He was a member of the Gentlemen's eleven captained by Nigel Howard, against the Players. Sheppard, Warr and Marlar were the other Cambridge representatives, all seeking renewal after the reverse against Oxford. The Players won by 21 runs to replicate exactly the victory by the Dark Blues. May, coming in at 53 for 2, flourished handsomely in defeat. He hit a sparkling 119 and his rivals, as he carried out his bat, included the formidable bowling quartet of Alec Bedser, Brian Statham, Roy Tattersall and Malcolm Hilton.

Denis Compton, captaining the Players, had been at his resplendent best with 150 in their first innings. May, partnered by the exuberant Doug Insole, provided the counter with his own refreshing assault. 'There were none at Lord's for this match who were not prepared to accord him full marks both for good sense and quality,' commented Billy Griffith in *The Cricketer*. 'He drove beautifully and, to our great delight, often *over* the heads of the inner ring of fielders. He reflected his class by the certainty of his strokes which produced many runs wide of mid-on.'

The pattern was set at Lord's for a remarkable scoring sequence: one peak period of less than a month produced a yield of 871 runs. May completed his 1,000 runs on 27 June; yet with the aid of two centuries, including one before lunch, in the match against Essex at Southend, he doubled his aggregate by 10 August. His second 1,000 runs was reached early in his second innings against Essex. He went on to score a century to add to five others in this sequence. In his eight innings following the varsity match he scored five centuries, and was only twice dismissed for less than 100.

The departure of Dewes and Doggart, coupled with the absence of Sheppard, resuming his studies after the tour of Australia, meant that May was now the bulwark of the Cambridge batting. He hit hundreds against Sussex, Warwickshire and Middlesex, the latter his third in four innings at Fenner's. He then augmented his challenge with an unbeaten 178, his highest score of the university season, against Hampshire at Bournemouth.

May's selection for the fourth Test at Leeds, ahead of Tom Graveney and Reg Simpson, was greeted with especial glee in Cambridge. The

41

'College Servant' in the *Cambridge Evening News* expressed his joy in verse. 'Peter May, the critics say,/Merits his place by England play./We'll hope and pray young Peter may/prove his worth on Test Match day.'

The devotions of the writer were not misplaced; but May, without lapsing into immodesty, knew that he had forced the selectors to 'pick him'. Even so, there was a surge of pride when he switched on the wireless after Sunday tea at his home at Reading. It was exciting to hear his name announced and the family rejoiced with him. On the following day he went back to the county match at Lord's to enjoy the fillip of a century for Surrey against Middlesex. The 'Masterly May' headlines on the evening newspaper placards – and Surrey's subsequent victory – were the best possible prelude to his first Test match.

England's selectors, possibly more enterprising than those in office today, made five changes after the third Test against South Africa was won by nine wickets at Old Trafford. Tom Graveney, having made his debut at Manchester, gave way to Compton who returned after an injury. Statham and Laker were omitted; and, most surprising of all, Godfrey Evans was also excluded from the team. The bonus for Yorkshire followers was the merited selection, as Evans's replacement, of Don Brennan. Brennan, the thirty-three-year-old Bradford amateur, and his Surrey counterpart, Arthur McIntyre, were highly regarded technicians behind the wicket. The buoyancy of Evans, the infectious cheerleader and player for the big occasion, deprived them of more opportunities at Test level.

Frank Lowson, another Yorkshireman and the third of the Test debutants at Leeds, did for a time arouse hopes of a distinguished future as an opening batsman, but leg problems, including surgery for varicose veins, denied the Bradford man the rewards of his dedication. Lowson's batting style was strongly reminiscent of his Yorkshire partner, Leonard Hutton. Indeed, he had so closely followed his example that he seemed like a clone of the master. There were times when his cover-drive was so much a copy of Hutton's that people had to look twice to make certain who had hit it. It reflected, like a picture in a mirror, more than a little of the elegance daily paraded for his tuition.

E. W. ('Jim') Swanton was approving of the much-changed England team at Headingley. 'Five changes is more than a winning side has suffered for a long time, but the pruning is not as drastic as it might at first glance appear. Resting Evans was always probable and he will not be out of the side for long. His method is such that when he is out of form his brilliance deteriorates into the erratically spectacular.' Swanton linked Graveney with

Peter May as two of England's batting discoveries. 'May,' he wrote, 'is without doubt one of the best young batsmen we have seen since the war.'

The South Africans came to Leeds 1-2 in arrears, having won the first match at Nottingham by 71 runs. It was their first Test victory for sixteen years and their second in England. Roy Tattersall, with twelve wickets in the match, masterminded the equalising victory at Lord's. Alec Bedser, in his turn, matched Tattersall with an aggregate of twelve wickets in the England success at Old Trafford. He set, not for the first time, a standard that was unsurpassed in both teams. His seven first-innings wickets gave the enduring Surrey bowler a total of 150 wickets in 36 Tests.

There were treacherous conditions after rain in the final stages of a match at Old Trafford. Hutton and Ikin had to withstand a barrage of short-pitched deliveries from Cuan McCarthy before coaxing the winning runs. McCarthy, flaxen-haired and fiery, displayed an antagonism in keeping with his prowess as a boxer. He was not always accurate but he was capable of inducing terror in batsmen. Given pace in the pitch, he could be a nasty proposition. David Sheppard recalled one virulent encounter between Cambridge and a modest MCC team at Lord's in which the hapless opponent was Harry Sharp, the Middlesex batsman. 'Cuan bowled him as fast an over as I have ever seen, including one bumper at which Harry waved his bat just as our wicket-keeper, Gerry Alexander, was catching it over his head twenty yards back.' John Warr looked on with some amusement. 'Harry,' he said, 'that would have gone in the Mile End Road if you'd hit it.'

McCarthy was also involved in a more ugly episode against Sussex at Hove in 1952. He struck the veteran, Jim Langridge, on the head with a ball which rose frighteningly off a length. Langridge, then aged forty-five, was knocked unconscious and taken to hospital. A local butcher in the crowd said the sight of Langridge's twitching limbs as he lay on the ground reminded him of slaughtered bullocks in their death throes. Langridge did survive the nightmare experience, but Robin Marlar, another Sussex man, said: 'Jim Langridge was killed by that blow on the temple, but it took him fifteen years to die. He became a very old man by the following season.'

Aggression, thoughtless and fraught with tragic consequence on this occasion, has been the endowment of all great fast bowlers. For McCarthy, soon to incur no-ball problems which effectively ended his first-class career, it was not a statement of his character. He was acknowledged as an engaging and pleasant man in most circumstances. The boisterous young giant later exchanged cricket for a life as a farmer in Dorset.

His express bowling did, though, not go unnoticed by Peter May, since both men were now not only at Cambridge but at Pembroke College. David Sheppard remembered a question posed by Peter when they batted together against the South Africans in 1951. 'Is he as fast as Lindwall?' asked Peter, with a wry grin and perhaps contemplating other challenges of extreme pace in the years ahead.

Sheppard had cause to recall the intermittent menace of McCarthy. He and Hubert Doggart had taken part in a second-wicket century stand for Sussex against the South Africans at Hove. In nine overs, on a drying pitch, McCarthy achieved a hat-trick and dismissed the last eight batsmen for 14 runs. There was further evidence of his dominance at Cambridge in 1952. In that summer he easily headed the university bowling averages with 44 wickets at 17.20 runs each.

Louis Duffus, the South African commentator, chronicled the misadventures of the South Africans in 1951 and how injuries and illness had affected them to an alarming degree. The key bowler, Athol Rowan, one of the finest off-spinners of that time, carried the burden of a persistent and painful knee injury. Michael Melle, the fast bowler, had to undergo an operation that prevented him from playing for several weeks. The great exception amid the epidemic was the veteran medium-pace bowler, Geoff Chubb. Chubb, known as the 'Iron Lung' of South African cricket, was chosen at the age of forty for his first tour. It was to prove a rewarding swansong for a man whose career had started twenty years earlier. He amazed everyone with his undiminished stamina and accuracy, bowling the most overs, more than 800, of a kind that tax the energy. Chubb took the most wickets (21 in five Tests) and 76 in all first-class matches on the tour.

Duffus described the disparity in the performances of the South Africans on the tour as resembling the personality change of Robert Louis Stevenson's classic character. The Jekyll team were, he said, judged by South African aspirations, eminently successful. 'They won the first Test match, made a record score, and earned a favourable draw in the fourth and were by no means outclassed in the other games of the series. The Hydes were woefully unpredictable, inconsistent, and unexpectedly incapable of mastering opposition that was often only moderate in strength.'

The biggest single setback the South Africans faced was the blow that broke the thumb of Dudley Nourse in the fifth match of the season at Bristol. 'Had he not been Nourse and captain of the team he would not have played again,' said Duffus. 'His innings of 208 at Nottingham in the first Test, played with this handicap and in agony through over nine hours, was in my experience unsurpassed for sheer courage.' The injury did gradually heal but its legacy was a slump in form. 'The middle stud in the shirt front of South African cricket dropped out and revealed a nakedness in aggressive batting that influenced the whole tour,' concluded Duffus.

A changing of the guard was now imminent alongside the similar realignment and infusion of youth in England. The rivalry between the two countries was to grow in intensity throughout the decade. In 1951, the unseasoned Springboks were exposed as raw recruits; but such players as Roy McLean, John Waite, Jackie McGlew and Hugh Tayfield (who was flown to England to understudy Athol Rowan) were to become a resurgent force under the ardent command of Jack Cheetham.

By Peter May's side on the train journey to Leeds was Alec Bedser, who has since remarked on the composure of his young companion. Bedser, though, was well aware of the pressures awaiting him in an alien setting and before a sharply critical Yorkshire crowd. He knew that young southerners, and particularly amateurs from Cambridge or Oxford, had to show convincing proof of their abilities before the reception thawed into warmth. Peter's reputation at Fenner's was not exactly scorned, but it did need to be evaluated in sterner circumstances. One observer of this scene, R. C. Robertson-Glasgow, commented: 'Above all other spectators, those of Yorkshire tend to believe only what they see.'

Alec Bedser was quietly encouraging, making the necessary introductions, and coaxing and gentling his charge into the social preliminaries at Leeds. One of the more far-reaching of the introductions made was to Harold (A. H. H.) Gilligan, the former Sussex and England captain, and the ICC representative for South Africa. Gilligan was in attendance as one of the supervising officials at the Test. His escort at a cocktail party at the Queen's Hotel was his daughter, Virginia. She remembers this first meeting with her future husband. 'Peter was very shy as I was.' Virginia, well versed in the rudiments of cricket as a Roedean all-rounder, always happily accompanied her father on his liaison duties. At the family home at Shamley Green in Surrey, she had mingled as a girl with a host of visiting celebrities. 'They were all wonderful heroes in my days of watching cricket. It was a tremendous thrill to meet and talk with them.' Alas, it cannot be claimed, in the best traditions of the novel, that her meeting with Peter at Leeds was the forerunner of a whirlwind romance. One suspects that it would, too, have been out of character for both of them. Virginia reflects: 'Peter was much too occupied with his cricket. It was his life. I didn't come into the picture until much later.'

The seething crowds on Test match days in midsummer at Headingley converge in an atmosphere of high contentment. There is a rustle of anticipation, tangible in the gossip and banter, and the ground is transformed into a beleaguered fortress. On the opening day of the Test against South Africa all the gates were closed before lunch, with an estimated 35,000 crammed inside the famous arena. Queues had begun to form at 6 a.m., three-and-a-half hours before the opening time. Four men had got up at four and motored from Whitby to take their places among the waiting people by seven o'clock. The crowds encircled the ground and flowed into the side-streets; one queue stretched for a distance of nearly two miles back from the Kirkstall Lane turnstiles and down Cardigan Road.

Five hundred people were locked out, some of them forlornly loitering and prepared to seek admission at any price. 'We don't mind what it costs us,' was the plaintive chorus. The tale of fervour, particularly striking in the immediate postwar years, continued throughout the match. The total attendance figures reached 116,000, with receipts of £26,000, and they were then the highest of any Test between the two countries.

Headingley once again did not betray its tradition as a featherbed. It was a heartbreaking wicket for bowlers and probably incited them close to mutiny when Don Bradman was in his pomp. The great man scored two triple centuries at Leeds in the 1930s. Yorkshire acknowledged his eminence by making him a life member of the club.

There was more tall scoring at Leeds in 1951. Both England and South Africa exceeded 500 on yet another amiable wicket for batsmen. There were lamentations in other quarters at the snailpace rate of 47 runs an hour throughout the match, but it did not quench the enthusiasm of the packed ranks of spectators revelling in the warm sunshine.

Freddie Brown, the England captain, lost the toss for the eleventh time in fourteen Tests to shackle his attack with an insuperable burden. The position worsened when Bailey strained his back and withdrew for treatment. His new-ball partner, Bedser, made an early breakthrough to dismiss Waite and thus equal Maurice Tate's tally of 155 wickets. It was an important scalp but the merest slip in an orgy of scoring, which consigned the match to an inevitable draw. Eric Rowan, before he was superbly caught by Bedser in the gully off Brown, batted for over nine hours. His 236 surpassed the double century of Nourse at Nottingham and established an individual record score by a South African. Clive Van Ryneveld assisted him in the addition of 198 runs, another record, for the second wicket. Roy McLean, more brightly, caught the gleam of the sun with his audacious strokeplay; and Percy Mansell, in his first Test, faltered nervously to fall within 10 runs of a century.

South Africa finally totalled 538 and, between them, Bedser, Brown, Tattersall and Hilton bowled 217 overs in the innings. Tattersall, in fact, was singularly parsimonious in conceding only 83 runs in 60 overs. Theirs was a marathon stint beyond reproach; and, as Wilfred Rhodes succinctly remarked: 'The wicket was the boss.'

Billy Griffith, writing in *The Cricketer*, patriotically noted a surge in batting standards, more in keeping with a Test match, when England began their reply. For the Yorkshire crowd there was the stirring spectacle of Hutton and Lowson going out to bat. Twenty-one years had elapsed since a Yorkshire pair had last opened for England. Paul Gibb had been Hutton's ally in the 'timeless Test' at Durban in March 1939.

In the early evening vigil on the Friday there was a concerted intake of breath around the ground. Hutton, on six, was missed at slip in the third over by Mansell off McCarthy. It was a costly error and South Africa were penalised for their caution. Unaccountably, with an enormous cushion of runs, Chubb was permitted only one slip and a gully. After his escape, Hutton remembered where he was and what was expected of him. Brilliant sunshine dappled his frail shoulders on another day of artistry on the Saturday.

'Yorkshire,' wrote Jim Swanton in the *Daily Telegraph*, 'rejoiced in the skill of their newest Test player, Lowson, but hardly more than all others present who could recognise the marks of pedigree. His strokes had about them a rhythm which was strongly suggestive of Hutton. The judgement of length was such that he was always in position with time to spare, and the whole leisurely motion seemed to make it so easy for him to steer the ball through the in-field.'

Lowson, brilliantly caught by Mansell at backward short-leg off Athol Rowan, scored 58. His was an auspicious debut, but he must have been disappointed to fall just one run short of a century opening partnership. The attention was now focused on Peter May, dipping his head apparently nonchalantly, as he strode out for his first Test innings. He knew that here was a perfect opportunity to impress in tailor-made batting conditions. But it was an ordeal for a fledgling cricketer and there were other distractions.

'Headingley had no sightscreen and, as I went out to join Len Hutton, I was aware of the intenseness of the light,' recalled Peter. 'It was a hot day, and the sun, dancing on the white shirts and frocks of the basking crowd, produced a dazzling glare behind the bowler's arm.'

There was one ball left of Athol Rowan's over. Peter completely lost sight of it in the mottled background of the crowd at the Kirkstall Lane end. 'When in doubt – push out', was the message flashed by his brain. In the split-second which divides safety from disaster, it was imperative that he gauged the right line of the delivery. 'A moment later – it seemed, at the time, like an eternity – I felt the ball on the bat,' he recalled. 'Although Rowan's natural turn enabled it to snick the inside edge, I had the bat well forward to smother the spin.' The ball evaded the clutching hands in Rowan's leg trap and scuttled away, accelerating rapidly down the hill. Peter had begun his Test career with a boundary conjured in near desperation. He later remembered his subconscious reaction to this first ball and blessed his good fortune in being able to play a crucial innings. 'I used to say three things to myself going out to bat: "Grit your teeth, do your best, but enjoy it".' He certainly obeyed the first two of his personal directives, but enjoyment was suspended in the trauma of the anxious opening at Headingley.

Bill Bowes, an illustrious member of the Yorkshire bowling pantheon and later a wise observer in the press box, provided a musical analogy in describing the promise of Peter May. 'Just as a pianist can be recognised from the opening chords, so could a cricketer be seen in Peter before he played a shot.' The sporting hands of May produced a concerto in a major key at Leeds. The echoes of his and Hutton's driving resounded throughout the day. It is not fanciful to say that he did not pale by comparison with his senior partner. Roy Tattersall, one of the watching England team, thought that May's performance was of such quality that he did not appear to be the aspiring pupil.

As a personal witness of the scene, my attention was boyishly directed towards Len Hutton, my Yorkshire hero; but the thread of memory weaves in accord with the views of May's command. He was tall and willowy, his hair neatly trimmed, and he looked vulnerably gauche enough to invite a bond of sympathy, not that it was needed. The upright presence; the picture-book stance; the comforting, unflurried approach, all instantly conveyed his authority. Among the other pleasures of this first acquaintance was to watch him in the field and note the clean pick-up of the ball when running full tilt and his unerring throw straight over the bails.

Jim Swanton reinforces the impressions of the punishing stroke-play of Hutton and May. He described the flourish of Hutton's bat, as the Yorkshireman thrice struck boundaries through the covers. The acceleration came after Hutton had been uncharacteristically becalmed, scoring one run in twenty minutes and taking three hours to reach his half-century. It was, at last, batting to relish, and Mann, the South African bowler, was compelled to adjust his field. Hutton had warmed to his task. 'Thereafter,' noted Swanton, 'Mann bowled to Hutton with an inner ring of five on the off-side, as well as two extra-covers policing the boundary.'

The strategy, as a defensive exercise, was absurdly futile. It was an object lesson, surely not lost on Peter May, to watch Hutton still pierce the field with a regularity that froze the South Africans into statuesque immobility. Hutton duly reached his appointment with his century, his 102nd; and his partnership with May, glowing in rapport, was worth 129 runs.

From my seat in the upper circle – Monday at half-price – at Leeds' Theatre Royal, I had watched the Court Players in Alan Melville's *Castle in the Air*. The title of the play in the week of Peter May's triumph at Headingley now seems entirely appropriate. Peter, in the days leading up to the Test, must have pondered on his own daydream. It was always within his grasp, but only a special kind of person could have fulfilled it in reality.

Douglas Jardine, celebrated and reviled as the England captain in the bodyline tour of 1932–33, was among the spectators at Leeds. He looked on with approval, as May displayed the governance which had first attracted attention when he was a Charterhouse schoolboy. Jardine also noted a tenacity and the lack of indulgence which was in accord with his own relentless style. Jim Swanton awarded his own palm of honour to May. 'His batting, over nearly five hours of a tense and grilling day, had a steadfast calmness and concentration of purpose remarkable in a young man of twenty-one. His false strokes could be counted on the fingers of one hand.'

Swanton enthused about the 'swift succession of telling hits' and the drives to all points of the arc between extra-cover and mid-wicket. 'The basis of his play was the forward defensive push with which he safely negotiated Rowan's off-breaks for over after over.'

Billy Griffith dwelt upon May's composure and the evidence of technical ability far beyond one of his years and experience. 'I have seldom seen the dead-bat defensive stroke better played. He, too, drove with elegance on the off-side, and there was the hallmark of the highest class in the way he forced the ball wide of mid-on.' May's campaign against the probing spin of Rowan and Mann owed more than a little to his scrutiny of the technique of his elders, Hutton and Denis Compton.

The apprenticeship of May and others of his generation was also to profit from an understanding of the 'V' plan in batting. The example of Hutton was diligently followed. It showed them how gradually to widen the arc of their strokes. The lesson, absorbed from their master, was to start an innings by playing only just wide of mid-on or mid-off. Then, from a position of strength and ease, it was permitted to fan out the shots square of the wicket.

May made light of the nervous nineties on his great day at Leeds. Two glorious straight drives carried him to a coveted goal. The century was greeted with tumultuous applause by the Yorkshire partisans. Bill Bowes said that he had not seen the crowd rise so spontaneously to anyone since Hugh Bartlett, the Sussex batting cavalier, ferociously put Yorkshire to the sword in 1938. On that occasion, Bartlett had defied belief in hitting Hedley Verity for six sixes in two overs. He scored 94 in 75 minutes before being caught by Maurice Leyland on the long-off boundary.

Peter May, in less extravagant fashion, had quickened the pulse of the multitude. He said how he was especially touched that the reception should be accorded not to an old friend, but to a young stranger in their midst. He felt accepted. 'I shall remember the ovation for the rest of my life. I'd never heard anything like it before and it does things to you.'

While thrilled by the acclaim, Peter had also to run the gauntlet of press attention as the new cricketing hero. In an episode worthy of the corridors of espionage, he had to thank his school and university friend, Oliver Popplewell, for his release. Popplewell provided the shelter of a 'safe house' – and Sunday lunch at the home of his future wife at Ripon.

There was also the belated acknowledgement of his talents by Gubby Allen. It was Allen's custom to visit Cambridge every year to play for the Free Foresters against the university. In the previous year he had seen May get out rather irresponsibly to a careless stroke. Allen, always forthright in his comments, told Peter: 'That was the most unconscious shot I have ever seen.' Peter did not think he was as bad as all that but, inwardly fuming, he accepted the criticism. The telegram received from Allen at Leeds was a signal that Peter was now accounted more responsible. It read: 'Charge of unconsciousness unconditionally withdrawn.'

Peter, as might be expected after extending his resources to the limit at Leeds, slightly faltered in the last weeks of a momentous season. At The Oval, in the second innings of the fifth Test in mid-August, he suffered the indignity of a duck. The catch off the unlucky bowler at Leeds, Athol Rowan, was this time accepted in the identical leg-trap position. It came too late to dilute the praise. Norman Preston, in his counties summary in *The Cricketer*, wrote that no other player had given students of Test cricket more cause for optimism than May.

May struck nine centuries to head the first-class averages with 2,339 runs at an average of 68.79. Only Jack Robertson, acknowledged at last by a winter tour to India, scored more runs. Robertson, with 2,917, was among the sizeable throng of players, including Denis Compton (runner-up to May), Len Hutton, Tom Graveney, David Sheppard, John Langridge and Bill Edrich who topped 2,000 runs in this season.

May, closely shadowed by Bob Appleyard, who shot to fame as a bowler with 200 wickets in 1951, won the accolade of the 'Young Cricketer of the Year' awarded by the Cricket Writers' Club. Others on the shortlist for the award were Jim McConnon, Malcolm Hilton and Frank Lowson. Lowson, after undergoing an operation for varicose veins at a London hospital, did gain recognition of his talents. He was selected, along with Hilton, for the MCC tour of India and Pakistan under the leadership of Nigel Howard in the following winter. Among others in the party chosen for further examination were Tom Graveney, Brian Statham and Roy Tattersall.

There was yet another tribute to bolster the hopes of Peter May when he was named as one of *Wisden*'s 'Five Cricketers of the Year' in 1952. He shared this award with Bob Appleyard, Tom Dollery, Jim Laker and Eric Rowan, the South African tourist of the previous summer. Reg Hayter provided a glowing citation. 'Schoolboy prodigies,' he wrote, 'do not always justify predictions but, by the end of the 1951 season, Peter May had achieved sufficient to prove the judgement of those who had proclaimed him as the most promising batting prospect in postwar cricket.'

May maintained his inexorable progress towards high estate when he returned to Cambridge for his last term in 1952. He again passed 2,000 runs and was second to Sheppard in the national and university averages. His overall tally of 2,498 runs included 938 for Cambridge and another 804 for Surrey at the start of their championship reign.

The hostility of his cricket carried an unceasing threat; in a run-chase against the clock, the university came within 12 runs of victory over Essex. May and Sheppard both scored centuries and Marlar recorded a hat-trick. The succeeding match against Yorkshire was watched by the biggest post-war crowd for a county match at Fenner's. May trounced the Yorkshire bowling to such a tune that his 171 included 96 in boundaries. One of the major surprises of the university summer was that such a strong Cambridge team, considered one of the best in their history, achieved only two victories and were held to a draw by a defiant Oxford. Cambridge fielded six current and future Test players – May, Sheppard, Warr, his new ball partner McCarthy, Subba Row and Alexander, who later achieved distinction as the West Indies wicket-keeper and captain.

The betrayal of the Cambridge talents was disappointing, but May was able to harness the power of his batting to the exciting surge towards the title at The Oval. Peter, captaining Surrey for the first time after coming down from Cambridge, hit an unavailing 143 in the shock defeat by India. There was also, for the young deputy captain, a shock of another sort. It was the no-balling of Tony Lock by the umpire, Fred Price, the former England and Middlesex wicket-keeper. Price, from square-leg, no-balled Lock in one over and twice in another. An angry Oval crowd goaded Price with incessant cries of 'no-ball'. The umpire stopped play and lay on the grass until the noise subsided. It needed an imperious appeal by Brian Castor, the Surrey secretary, over the loudspeaker to silence the barrackers.

May asked Price for an explanation of his decision. 'We were all amazed,' said Peter. 'Fred was in no doubt that Tony had thrown his faster ball.' It was the first time that Lock's action had been officially regarded as questionable. Lock himself felt that Price should have had the courtesy to give him a warning. The incident was not without precedent that summer. Cuan McCarthy had also been no-balled for throwing while playing for Cambridge against Worcestershire. The issue was to cast a dismal veil over May's last tour of Australia in 1958–59. Peter later said: 'Lock obviously alarmed certain umpires with his quicker ball, which was doubtful at times. But the tendency at that time was to sweep such unpleasantness under the carpet.'

The turmoil of Lock, selected despite his apparent malpractice for the last two Tests against India in 1952, contrasted with the unquestioned mastery of May. At Leicester, he illuminated the proceedings with a classic 197, his highest score of the season. In the match against Hampshire at Southampton, he moved at a swifter rate. His unbeaten 123 contained no less than 92 in boundaries. May and Eric Bedser, newly promoted as opener, added 104 in 80 minutes, and Surrey won by six wickets.

Of all his ten centuries in this season, none surely gave Peter greater pride than his first county century against Kent in a thrilling match at The Oval. It was the cornerstone of Surrey's first innings and the prelude to an adventurous and nail-biting climax. The concluding events unfolded in a frenzy to tighten the nerves of the supporters, perched on the edges of their seats. It was to become a familiar happening in the bold, enterprising days, with Stuart Surridge at the helm. Surrey were set a target of 188 runs in 92 minutes, and won by two wickets. They required 128 in the last hour, 50 with 17 minutes left; and Surridge, having already claimed eight wickets, appropriately made the winning hit on the stroke of time.

Peter May was reunited with his Headingley partner, Leonard Hutton, this time as his rival, in a flurry of Festival runs at Scarborough. They both, in a neat juxtaposition, scored separate hundreds in the match. May's first innings score of 174 took him just over three hours. It was sprinkled with glorious shots, hurtling over and into the boards of this happy little ground beside the sea. There was also the joy of shared success with two others of England's rising young men, Tom Graveney and Colin Cowdrey. Cowdrey, the twenty-year-old Oxford blue, gave a foretaste of his future association with May. The brisk coda of a century stand in forty-five minutes was a gladdening omen.

As a postscript to his years at Cambridge, there are the agreeable testimonies of university friends to the esteem enjoyed by Peter May. One remarked on his scholastic distinctions and studies in Economics and History. He recalled that May had taken a very creditable Honours Degree that would not have disgraced an historian unencumbered by the demands of cricket and football, in the latter as captain of the university eleven.

Another observer in the autumn of 1951 described May's college, Pembroke, as predominantly a post-National Service college. The ex-servicemen of the 1940s had left, but there was still an extra degree of maturity, with undergraduates recovering their own individuality and occupied with their own concerns. The deep affection and respect accorded to May had surprised the writer (who signed himself M. C. L.) on a return visit, since this was now an environment in which schoolboy adulation for sporting heroes was unlikely to be widespread.

'Peter had three reputations,' he explained. 'Of these the most obvious was that of one of the finest games players that [Pembroke College] had ever produced. The second was of a man both intelligent and industrious who was reported, perhaps apocryphally, to do his background reading in the pavilion at Fenner's before going out to bat and then to write his essay in the evening.

'But perhaps the deepest-seated feeling in the college was for a man who in spite of his growing importance to the outside world had no trace of arrogance ... who was likeable, modest and universally approachable. We had every reason to be proud of him.'

Chapter 6
Besieged by Lindwall

'Anyone else would have been totally demoralised.'

Alan Davidson

There is an old and colourful saying in Australia which, in a land of unremitting zeal, divides frailty and fortitude. 'You throw in a player when he is a kid,' is the shuddering command, 'and let him bleed.'

Peter May was the abashed young contender and a marked man when the Australians came to play Surrey at The Oval in 1953. He might well have suffered a double blow to his esteem, having been dismissed for a duck by Ray Lindwall in the first innings. He did escape the pair but his stress was unrelieved as the Australians set an ambush for him in the second innings. It was assuredly a daunting baptism, not one for a faintheart, on this, his first appearance against the tourists.

Lindwall, one of the most feared bowlers in cricket history, prowled like a tiger, eagerly scenting its prey. He moved in, off his smooth, controlled and accelerating run, to deliver a wounding over, expressly designed to humiliate the newcomer. It was, observes another Australian, Alan Davidson, 'one of the most incredible overs I've ever seen'.

The exceptional promise of their adversary had not, of course, escaped the notice of the Australians. Richie Benaud says the offensive plan was quite clear at The Oval. It was a ploy to remove a threat and lay the seeds of doubt in the minds of the England selectors. Lindsay Hassett, the Australian captain, was intent on testing the mettle of May. 'Lindsay wanted Ray to give Peter a going-over, though no one realised what would eventuate,' comments Benaud.

He recalls a 'fascinating experience', immensely relished by him and others in the slip and gully cordon. 'I think five outswingers, perfectly pitched, went past the outside edge and one inswinger between bat and pad.' Lindwall himself remembered what must have been a frustrating

54

episode for a bowler. It was, however, fruitless, a masterly assault on May's morale. 'Each one of the six balls beat Peter,' said Lindwall. 'They were just a fraction over the stumps, some cut back, others cut in. He could have been out – six out of six – but he didn't get out.'

Peter May, looking back on this early menacing lesson, recalled a cloudy, humid morning at The Oval. 'I was one year down from Cambridge and had already had a modicum of success against South Africa and India in the following season. Surrey batted and I was soon at the crease. My first impression was that I was surrounded by little men wearing huge green caps. They clustered around in what was known as a "Carmody field".' This was named after Keith Carmody, captain of the Royal Australian Air Force team in 1945, who instituted the 'umbrella' field settings close to the wicket.

May continued: 'A chap called Lindwall was bowling from the pavilion end. He treated me to an over of six balls which consisted of five late outswingers and one inner – the fourth, I think – and I missed the lot. I kept waiting for the fatal snick or death rattle but neither came. It really was a most brilliant example of the swing bowler's art. Frankly I wondered what the devil I had let myself in for. Of course, typical of cricket, I was bowled out at the other end by a slow straight yorker from Ron Archer. I might say that I nearly retired from cricket that night.'

Alan Davidson spells out the enormity of Lindwall's mentally sapping thrust which could so easily have undermined May. 'For anyone less than Peter, it would have finished him; others would have been totally demoralised. Memory always reminds you. If you can survive such an experience, as Peter did, then you've got to be made of special stuff.' Davidson is in accord with Benaud in the view that the grim joust with Lindwall stiffened the resolve of the 'humble, modest champion'. 'It toughened him up and made him try all the harder,' is the conclusion of two admiring veterans.

In 1953, Lindwall's powers were undiminished; his probing accuracy, now combined with the surprise variation of his faster ball, sorely tested England's premier batsmen. May was again Lindwall's victim, while under inspection by the selectors and in the MCC colours at Lord's. He was not alone in his disarray; the Australian, in his first five overs, dismissed Simpson, Sheppard and Denis Compton, the first two for nought. May, struggling for true form, at last found conviction with a century against Northamptonshire. It was achieved against an attack which fortuitously

55

included Freddie Brown, the chairman of the selectors. May was rewarded by selection for the first Test at Nottingham.

The rarity of shelter in the unaccustomed position of no. 6 in the order was intended to offer comfort and composure. His stay in the pavilion did not last long. The Australians, having been dismissed for 249 (Hassett 115), were on the rampage and England lost three wickets for 17 runs. The conditions were made to order for Lindwall's late-swinging deliveries. In eight balls he overcame Kenyon, Simpson and Compton. May, after an unsuccessful appeal against the light, was caught behind the wicket off the leg-spinner, Jack Hill. The encircling gloom mockingly cast a shroud on his departing figure. Moments later the umpires at last decided it was too dark to play.

The dismal weather at Nottingham did, in the end, deny England a victory earned by the magnificence of Alec Bedser (7 for 55 and 7 for 44). May later said that this would have been a kind of memorial to Bedser's prowess. Bedser's feat in taking 14 wickets for 99 runs in the match has to be measured against the fact that England went into the match with only four bowlers – the others being Bailey, Wardle and Tattersall. Only two Yorkshiremen, Wilfred Rhodes and Hedley Verity, who each took 15 wickets, had dismissed more batsmen than Bedser in the previous matches between England and Australia. Bedser did have the consolation of overhauling the then English Test record of 189 held by S. F. Barnes. Barnes, at eighty, was present at Nottingham, and he was one of the first to pay a deserved tribute to his successor.

Peter May, to his own disappointment, was dropped, for the only time in his career, for the second Test at Lord's. His replacement, Willie Watson, was thus enabled to score a century and enter the hall of fame in his first Test against Australia. He never again matched the heroic dimensions of this innings. It was a triumph of stamina and calm resolve in a perilous situation. England looked doomed to defeat until his match-saving fifth-wicket partnership of 163 runs with Trevor Bailey. It extended over four hours on a nerve-racking final day. Watson's vigil held rapt a thrilled nation as the minutes and hours ticked by to safety. On the next morning he was hailed as a champion in every newspaper throughout the country. The *Daily Sketch* gave up its front page to the achievement. Splashed across the page in jumbo-sized type were the words 'Wonderful Willie Watson!'

May remained on the sidelines for the third Test at Old Trafford. This was the match in which Johnny Wardle took four wickets for seven runs in five overs to humiliate the Australians in a crazy last hour. Australia finished the game in an undignified scramble, losing eight wickets for 35 runs. Until the last phase they had held the advantage but their frailty against spin was mercilessly exploited and their morale imperilled to tip the scales, psychologically, towards England. Leonard Hutton, the England captain, rejected the excuses of several Australians. He was told: 'Don't take any notice of our second innings. We knew we couldn't lose, so we didn't try.' Hutton replied: 'It wouldn't have made any difference either way; 35 runs was as many as you would have made in any case.'

Wardle's remarkable analysis was to remain just a cheerful memory as England, without him, regained the Ashes after an interval of twenty years. The allegiance to Tony Lock, preferred to Wardle in the anxiously drawn Test at Leeds and in victory at The Oval, could not be refuted on figures. The weight of evidence supported the retention of Lock and Laker as a match-winning pair. As a partnership in five home series in the 1950s, the two Surrey bowlers took 130 wickets between them.

Peter May, despite the vagaries in form in a critical summer, headed the Surrey averages in 1953. His aggregate of 2,554 runs surpassed his tally in the previous summer. In Surrey's second match against the Australians at The Oval, he shared a partnership of 128 runs with Fletcher. Lindwall again claimed his wicket, but not before Peter had gained the satisfaction of a half-century. In a late resurgence, he enforced his claim for a recall by England. Conspicuous among his deeds were major innings in Surrey's bank-holiday victory, another brisk scamper, by six runs over Nottinghamshire. He was undefeated on 135 in the first innings and added another 73, again without dismissal, in the second innings.

The accent of his play was firmly attuned to winning back his England place at The Oval. By a happy chance, on the day before the team for the conclusive final Test was announced, he was majestic against Middlesex at Lord's. In his own estimation it was his best innings of the summer. He batted for four hours, offering undeniable proof of the ferocious intensity of his cricket. His 159 (scored out of a Surrey total of 299) was an appetising dish to put before the selectors. The return to the England ranks was a near formality; it was the first in a sequence of 52 consecutive Tests.

May, re-established at no. 3, a favoured position from which he was rarely removed, assisted in the famous sporting climax to the Coronation Year at The Oval. Lock and Laker cast a spinning blight on Australia. By the end of the third day, England needed 94 runs to win their first rubber against Australia in this country since 1926. It was achieved despite the loss of Hutton, who was run out twenty minutes before the close of play. 'Poor Len looked in a daze of disappointment as I passed him on my way out to the wicket,' recalled May. 'I have no memory of being offered a nightwatchman but I would have refused one. It seemed important to stop the Australian bowlers from capitalising on their stroke of luck.'

Australia, on the last day, fought heroically in the attempt to stem the advance towards a coveted triumph. Lindwall was thrust into the fray to mount a ceaseless, fast and accurate attack. The tense battle was watched by a vast crowd, with thousands spilling on to the grass. 'Winning seemed to mean so much to so many people,' said May. 'I can never remember an English crowd in such a state of excitement.' He remembered the reassuring presence of his partner, Bill Edrich. 'There was an indestructible quality about him which inspired confidence.' Edrich and May, embattled in defence for nearly two hours, ground out a precious 64 runs. May was not destined to maintain his vigil until the end; he was caught, dubiously, by Davidson in the leg-trap off the bowling of Miller. It was, though, singularly fitting that the illustrious 'twins', Edrich and Denis Compton, should be together to stroke the winning runs and lay the ghost of Australian supremacy.

In the winter of 1953–54 Leonard Hutton was presented with the near equivalent of a poisoned chalice as the England captain in the West Indies. It was a tour marred by menacing crowds and ill-temper in the torrid heat of the Caribbean. Alex Bannister considered it a 'sheer miracle that with so many distractions and worries off the field, Hutton was able to stand head and shoulders above any batsman on either side and to maintain his consistency and concentration'. Hutton headed the England batting averages, with 677 runs, including a superb double-century to help level the series in Jamaica, and averaged 96.71.

Nearly thirty years later Peter May was still fervent in his admiration for the skills of his mentor in the West Indies. By then he was Chairman of the Selectors. Donald Trelford recalls that he sat next to May at a dinner at the British High Commission in Barbados. May was distraught after watching the annihilation of the team led by David Gower. Trelford tried to console him: 'Nobody could have withstood that kind of onslaught,' he said. 'Normally a mild man, Peter turned to me and said with passion: "Len did. It only needs one man to show the others how to do it. Just one man".' The words trailed off in a gulp of exasperation.

May had ample cause to remember the example of a great cricketer on his own first overseas tour in the West Indies. He was always a ready listener and he assimilated many lessons on that trip. Not least among them was one piece of advice: 'Never let the bowler think he is better than yourself.' At the beginning of the tour Peter had also revealed a weakness on his leg stump. He was trying to force the ball square instead of pushing it in the direction of mid-on. Peter quickly took up Hutton's suggestion that he should take guard on the leg stump – 'as you'll then know exactly where the stumps are, and your position in relation to them.' It was to prove immensely beneficial as a defence against fast bowlers. With his earlier leg-and-middle guard, Peter had found the outswinger a major problem. 'I was feeling for the ball, playing across it, losing balance, and generally making loose contact.'

Agitation on the field was exacerbated by the tumult of the crowds. For young tourists, like May, plainly fidgety amid the constant uproar, a calming voice was needed. Denis Compton, watching the distress it caused Peter, offered words of counsel. 'For your own sake, Peter, you must try to ignore the spectators out there. Otherwise they will affect your cricket terribly.' The soaring decibels even tried the patience of more seasoned campaigners. 'You do become accustomed to the noise,' said Hutton, 'although it was so bad after two hours in the field I was hoarse. I could not make myself heard even from mid-on to mid-off. We had to devise a tic-tac system and Tom Graveney became so good at it that he could get a job at the races at Newmarket.'

Umpires, as well as players, were disoriented by the clamour. Charles Palmer, the MCC player-manager, strongly denied accusations of dishonesty among the home-based officials on the various islands. He did, though, feel that a panel of umpires should have been appointed to serve all the venues. 'This was a domestic problem,' he diplomatically declared. 'But it should be remembered that it is extremely difficult to concentrate for five or six days in the sun before noisy, volatile and intimidating crowds.'

The rumpus rose to a deafening pitch during the third Test at Georgetown in pre-independent British Guiana. Extra police had to be brought to the Bourda ground in an area only recently under strain through political demonstrations. They were recruited to protect the Indian umpire, 'Badge' Menzies, who was also the home groundsman. Angry spectators had thrown hundreds of bottles and broken beer crates on to the field. The dissension arose after Menzies had given a run-out decision against Clifford McWatt, the local hero. 'It was like setting a spark to a gunpowder barrel,' reported one observer, Peter Ditton. Alex Bannister, another witness of the hooliganism, said the hysteria was really attributable to the cheapness of rum and Guianese betting habits. 'It also sprang from the practice of clapping in anticipation of an individual century, or when a partnership was in striking distance of a similar total.'

McWatt and the injured John Holt, batting with a runner, had stepped into the breach after the West Indies had lost seven wickets for 139 runs, following England's total of 435. Peter May, as the fieldsman on the leg-side boundary, was the unwitting cause of the disarray. The West Indians' stand had reached 98 when McWatt, having taken one run, foolishly attempted another to hoist the century partnership. May's throw, fast and true, ran him out by at least two yards.

Peter Ditton said the decision against McWatt was the last straw for the enraged fans. It mattered little that McWatt later frankly admitted that the umpire was right. It could just as easily have been twenty yards rather than two. Ditton considered that two of the earlier batsmen, Weekes and Christiani, had to shoulder some of the blame for the disturbance. They had, he said, stayed at the wicket overlong after being ruled out. Christiani appeared to question the legitimacy of a catch by Watson off Laker. His hesitancy produced a feeling in the crowd that he had been the victim of a bad decision. Weekes, less culpable, was bowled by Lock six runs short of his century. He was not immediately judged out. A bail had gently fallen to the ground and a section of the crowd decided that Godfrey Evans, the England wicket-keeper, had kicked it off. The umpire at the bowler's end, E. S. Gillette, was unsighted by the batsman. He deferred to Menzies whose late ruling from square-leg provoked further confusion.

Tom Graveney recalls the extraordinary scenes at Georgetown. 'It was raining bottles and the poor old umpire was absolutely terrified.' Johnny Wardle, in clownish mood, helped to defuse some of the tension by picking up one of the bottles. He gulped down the imaginary contents and swayed like a drunk. The temper of the crowd did not lessen. An intrepid group of boys had gone on to the field to clear some of the bottles. Another missile narrowly missed the head of one of them. 'This boy turned round,' says Graveney. 'He had a beautiful left arm, plenty of ammunition, and he peppered the people in the stand. They scattered in all directions under his barrage.'

The match was held up for ten minutes during which time W. S. Jones, the president of the British Guiana Board of Control, left the pavilion to go out and speak to Hutton. 'This is getting dangerous; you really must come off,' he said. Graveney remembers the unswerving commitment of his England captain. 'Len replied: "No, we're staying on. I want another wicket tonight because we mean to win this match."' Sonny Ramadhin, the next man in, said: 'You can have mine,' whereupon he was bowled by Laker and just as quickly ran off to the sanctuary of the pavilion. Hutton, after his courageous act, on the next day enforced the follow-on. England were subsequently the winners by nine wickets in what had been, until the pandemonium, a fine cricket match.

The mental strain of coupling his batting with the cares of captaincy in the West Indies did not prevent Hutton from assessing the future. He was already looking ahead to the composition of the England team in Australia in the following winter. Hutton constantly impressed on his young tourists, May included, the golden opportunities within their grasp. One Saturday evening in Grenada he invited Peter for a discussion over drinks. He had earmarked May as his successor. 'You are now twenty-three and, as a potentially great batsman, you should be producing big scores regularly,' he told Peter. The wise warrior added: 'Lad, you must toughen up. If the situation is strange to you, or the bowler ties you in knots, you must grit your teeth harder and fight your way out of your problems.'

Peter did ultimately weather the frustration of a gruelling first overseas tour. Reg Hayter, writing in *Wisden*, applauded his advance in the Caribbean. 'After allowing himself to be confined to crease-tied defence in the earlier matches, May eventually gave rein to his attacking strokes and began to fulfil his rich promise.' May's 414 runs in the series included 135 on the jute mat at Port-of-Spain, Trinidad. This was a match which yielded 1,528 runs in six days and was destined from the outset to end as a draw. It did enable England, then trailing 2-0, to regroup and discover a unity of purpose. May and Compton both hit their first Test centuries since 1951. Their partnership of 164 was restrained in manner, but it effectively checked any hopes of a West Indian victory. Graveney failed by eight runs to become the sixth batsman in the match to score a century.

In Trinidad Peter once again profited from Hutton's counsel. He was urged not to waste needless energy in hitting the ball hard when intent on defence, and not to try to force the ball on the on-side, but to play with his left shoulder pointing to the opposite wicket. As another part of the tutorial, Peter was exhorted to cultivate the habit of determining the exact location of each fieldsman. Hutton cited the example of Bradman, who checked the field before each ball, exploring the vacancies, and said that this explained the accuracy of the great Australian's stroke-play.

At Sabina Park, Kingston, in the final Test, Trevor Bailey was in inspired mood. He took seven wickets for 34 runs in 16 overs. The figures were then a record for England against the West Indies. 'Madness,' shrieked the *Jamaica Gleaner*. 'This can be the only reason offered for a West Indies batting side accepted as the best in the world scoring only 139 on a perfect wicket.' Bailey's feat set the stage for England's victory by nine wickets which levelled the series. The West Indies lost four wickets, three of them to Bailey, for 13 runs in under an hour. Clyde Walcott, the lynchpin of the home batting throughout the series, almost alone saved his team from ignominy. He scored 50 in a fifth wicket recovery stand with Atkinson; and then hit 116, his third century of the series, in the second innings to raise his aggregate to 698 runs.

The decline of the West Indies after their earlier dominance demonstrated an exuberant indiscipline. 'The West Indians are cricketers of nature,' commented a writer in the *Gleaner*, Jamaica's principal newspaper. 'But this virtue is at once a fault, preventing them from attaining perfection.' This extravagance, almost brazen in its effrontery, was an expression of delicious freedom. The keynote of the West Indian batting, before it became immersed in rigorous professionalism, was an often eccentric adventure. It could topple from enchanting heights to absurd lows. The invigorating cricket of Brian Lara today posts a message of entertainment. Everyone will hope that it is not stifled by staleness.

Hutton's double-century, only marred by one escape off Ramadhin, in the final Test at Sabina Park once again granted him exclusive status. He batted for just under nine hours and shared century stands with Evans and Wardle. The inscrutable Yorkshire general emerged triumphant though not unscathed; at one stage when he was not in the best of health, as Alex Bannister reported, he lost caste as a captain. Hutton was charged, it now seems implausibly, with tactical weaknesses. He was also accused of being less than severe in his censure of recalcitrant members of the MCC party.

The worst aspect of the vilification was that he was assailed by the stigma of being a professional. 'To a section of people in the West Indies the idea of England being led by a professional was apparently repugnant as it is to a minority in England,' commented Bannister.

Jim Swanton, as another observer in the Caribbean, believes that Hutton's stern assignment would have been rendered easier with a stronger manager as his guide. Swanton recalls a pre-tour meeting with Hutton during the Roses' match at Bramall Lane, Sheffield. Harry Altham, the MCC Treasurer, had asked Swanton to seek the England captain's view on a manager acceptable to him. Hutton said: 'I would like the colonel.' The colonel in question was Billy Griffith, who had been player-manager to Gubby Allen on the previous tour of the West Indies and also vice-captain to George Mann in South Africa in 1948–49. Hutton, as a colleague on both tours, had had ample chance to assess him and judge his capabilities. 'When I told Len I thought that he had named the best possible man it scarcely occurred to me that MCC would decide differently,' says Swanton.

The availability of Griffith ought to have silenced those critics on the MCC committee who were opposed to the appointment of the first professional captain to take a team overseas. Swanton says that a decision to relieve Hutton, as England's leading batsman, of the burden of a strenuous and taxing tour would have created a public outcry. Such an affront to a stout and respected campaigner on the wave of success would have been unthinkable. He believes that it was incumbent on the MCC committee to choose the best man as manager, especially since they knew that Griffith was Hutton's own nomination. 'If ever there was a "natural" for the managership it was Griffith.'

In the event, the committee decided that Griffith, then an assistant secretary at Lord's, could not be spared for the tour. 'The most extraordinary part of the business,' says Swanton, 'was the decision not to provide Hutton with a manager at all, but to appoint Charles Palmer, the Leicestershire captain, as player-manager. He did not know the West Indies and had not played in a Test match. He was put in a contradictory situation of being under the jurisdiction of Hutton on the field, yet otherwise responsible to MCC for the administration and discipline of the team, presumably including even the captain.'

Swanton considers that even with the full status of manager Palmer, for all his personal virtues, would not have been the first claimant as a disciplinarian. 'In the potentially volatile atmosphere of the West Indies, a firm hand was the first requisite. Swanton is fervent in his praise of Hutton as a superb technician. 'Len had plenty of instinctive dignity but he was by nature inclined to be shy, withdrawn, introspective, not the sort to wear authority easily. Nor was he physically robust as he approached his fourteenth, and most difficult, Test series inside eight years.'

When the question arose of the following tour, to Australia in 1954–55, David Sheppard, then preparing for his ordination at Ridley Hall, was the

Establishment favourite. He had deputised for Hutton in two Tests against Pakistan in the home series that preceded the tour. Sheppard recalls the air of conspiracy as the selectors deliberated on the choice of captain. Secrecy even dictated that meetings were held at the home of Ronnie Aird, then MCC Secretary, rather than at his office at Lord's. Soundings were taken as discreetly as possible on Sheppard's availability for the Australian tour. The overtures could not, however, be concealed from the press. Within a short time the captaincy issue was being furiously debated in the newspapers.

Sheppard remembers his dilemma and the unappealing development, which called upon him to break his training for the ministry for two terms. The other consideration involved offering himself as a rival to Hutton, whom he regarded as a friend and honoured as a master cricketer. After consultations with older friends and a meeting with his college principal, he decided that he would undertake the tour if presented with the captaincy. 'This was an altogether different contribution to make to cricket than simply going as a member of the team,' says Sheppard.

One of the most intriguing discoveries is that Sheppard was actually pencilled in as England captain as early as 1952. Before his own appointment was confirmed, Hutton conveyed the news to Sheppard at Cambridge during the match against Yorkshire. 'Len came round to my room one evening and said: "I think they're going to ask you to captain England, and I hope you'll accept".' Sheppard believed that, later in 1954, after his arduous tour of the West Indies, Hutton would have been glad not to carry the burden of the captaincy as well as being England's premier batsman.

Jim Swanton, writing in the *Daily Telegraph*, thought that the appointment of Sheppard was a short-term prospect, but maintained that the impending ordination (in 1955) did not necessarily mean the end of his cricket. 'No one,' he said, 'apart from Hutton himself, has such strong intrinsic qualities for the post.'

The tide did turn in Hutton's favour. Sheppard, as the caretaker captain against Pakistan, sensed the changed climate of opinion almost as soon as he stepped on to the field for the second Test at Nottingham. One of the selectors, Walter Robins, apologetically confirmed this a few days before the announcement of the team for Australia. 'I feel we've been unfair to Len. He was in a very difficult position in the West Indies,' he said. Sheppard did not express dissent at the judgement. It was clear that he was out of the reckoning. By the time of the rain-ruined Test at Manchester he knew that the position was resolved. 'For the only occasion I can think of in Test cricket I breathed a sigh of relief when I was out of it after that match.'

Jim Swanton somewhat ruefully noted the omission of Sheppard, reflecting that it was a 'loss indeed at a time when character and integrity of conduct were never more needed both on and off the field'. He observed: 'No inconsistency can be deduced from the fact that he has been acting as Hutton's deputy. Sheppard was no doubt at one with the selectors in considering the captaincy in Australia was, from a cricketing point of view, an end in itself.'

At the last, the weight of the argument was probably slanted towards the fitness of Hutton, then aged thirty-eight, and whether his resources could withstand the pressures awaiting him in Australia. His illness, a combination of physical and mental fatigue, had impelled an enforced rest for a month during the summer. Hutton expressed his relief at the decision to renew his appointment. 'I am very pleased that the MCC have thought I'm the right chap to take an England team to Australia. Physically, I know I can stand up to it.' There was, to complete his satisfaction, a congratulatory telegram from David Sheppard.

Peter May, not given to overstatement, was immensely cheered by the presence of Hutton in Australia. He declared his allegiance in one conversation with Geoffrey Howard, the MCC tour manager. 'What a good job we've got Len out here because David would never have done it.' May's appointment as a vice-captain was a signal that he was on trial as Hutton's successor. He was chosen, to surprise in some quarters, ahead of his respected seniors, Trevor Bailey and Denis Compton.

Leonard Hutton masked his shyness beneath an enigmatic smile. The sudden, brilliant gleam of his striking blue eyes meant that you had intruded upon his private thoughts. Despite their vastly different backgrounds, he and Peter May were kinsmen in manner and temperament. The voyage to Australia was well advanced when Hutton decided the time was ripe for a consultation with his young lieutenant. Peter was deep in meditation, leaning on the ship rail on deck one night. Len walked over and tapped him on the shoulder. 'I've been looking for you,' he said. He prefaced his remarks with an earnest glance around the deck apparently to ensure no one was in earshot. His hand then cupped his mouth for even greater privacy.'

'I want to tell you how to get on in Australia,' he began. Peter felt a tremor of excitement as he waited for the words of wisdom from the master. 'You walk out slowly to the wicket,' continued Hutton. 'Mind

65

you, at your pace and in no rush. Then you look around and get used to the light. It's pretty sharp out there. At the wicket, you take guard, as I've explained before. Take a little stroll and give the bowler a glare, just to show you're not frightened of him. Then you check your guard and have another look round to inspect the field.'

Len sighed deeply and stopped to allow the drift of his comments to take root. Peter waited attentively for the final telling conversational thrust. 'What next?' he asked. Len said: 'You just keep buggering on.' It was, as Peter reflected afterwards, sound advice. But, for it to count, you had to digest the nuances of the speech and fill in the words unspoken.

Colin Cowdrey, another of Hutton's bright young men in Australia, recalls another fascinating seminar at the first press conference on their arrival in Australia. 'Len had worked out the role he intended to play and sitting there, tanned, superbly fit, lightweight suit immaculate, he played it so superbly that his character dominated the whole room. After about a dozen answers Hutton had the press corps rolling in the gangways.'

The England captain's replies were punctuated by thespian pauses worthy of another scene-stealer, Laurence Olivier. Hutton once slyly confessed that there was more than a little of the actor in his make-up. He was centre-stage, blinking in the spotlight, and milking the applause on this occasion. He adopted his broadest Yorkshire accent. 'Noo, we 'aven't got mooch bowlin'. Got a chap called Tyson, but you won't 'ave 'eard of him because he's 'ardly ever played.' 'Ah, yes, Lock and Laker. Aye, good bowlers, but we 'ad to leave them behind.' 'Batsmen? Well, we 'aven't got any batters really. We've got these two lads, May and Cowdrey, but we 'aven't got any batters really.'

The preamble was followed by another dream-like silence. He seemed to fumble for words, then concluded his commentary with a rueful smile. 'What it comes to,' he told the awe-struck assembly, 'is that we're starting all over again. We're 'ere to learn a lot from you.'

Hutton, like the wariest of card players, was not going to reveal his hand. His droll catalogue was designed to keep Australia guessing. The comic turn was not entirely a pose. The sheepishly cryptic ad-libs contained essential truths. He was exploring the possibilities, even as he talked to the battalion of correspondents. This was a new beginning. The young guard from England was about to take over. Before long a quartet of newcomers, batsmen and bowlers, would thrillingly come of age and take a giant leap into ascendancy.

Chapter 7
Daring Young Men Down Under

'There was every reason to settle for defence, as he could have done, but that wasn't his temperament.'

Richie Benaud

The nobility of his driving on a treacherous wicket at Melbourne pulsed with aggression. Peter May did not linger in the shallows of uncertainty; the thunder of his strokes rendered the Australian bowlers as impotent as juveniles. 'By all the established usages of post-war batsmanship this was not novelty, it was treason,' declared the *Sydney Morning Herald*.

Ray Lindwall, the tormenting examiner in England in 1953, was treated with disdain on this January day in 1955. May's fearless assault exacted ample revenge for the duck presented to him by the Australian in England's first innings, inopportunely on his twenty-fifth birthday on New Year's Eve. Lindwall was not only compelled to strengthen his off-side field; he withdrew them ever deeper in an attempt to stem of the flow of runs. 'When an Englishman does that to the greatest fast bowler of his time,' wrote Alan Ross, 'it registers, if nothing else, an exchange of dominations.'

May's 91 at Melbourne is recalled by one Australian correspondent. 'I had never before, and seldom since, seen such powerful and stylish driving of fast bowlers.' Keith Miller, the other arm of a famed combination, sportingly applauded two separate fours driven sizzlingly past him to the boundary. Lindwall's own acknowledgement was an adjustment of the field in the afternoon. 'Both of these great bowlers sought containment with a straightish mid-wicket, mid-off, mid-on and extra-cover deep – and still May drove off the front foot, again and again, through the field.'

As a privileged young boy in the members' enclosure at Melbourne, my correspondent had earlier watched, with awe, May's unbeaten 105 against Victoria. 'He quite destroyed our fast men, John Power and Sam Loxton. I was close enough to the dressing-rooms afterwards to note that his bat was unmarked except for a vivid red circle, grapefruit size, in the middle of the blade.'

Richie Benaud also recalls the wonderful innings in the Melbourne Test. 'There was every reason to settle for defence, as some players might have done, and he could have done, but that wasn't his temperament. Peter was very often at his best in difficult batting conditions.' There were, in Benaud's view, other factors dictating Australia's defensive strategy: 'Peter batted magnificently and certainly got on top of the bowling. But it was also obvious that the pitch could be a horror strip for the side batting last and, quite rightly, our captain [Ian Johnson] was endeavouring to save runs. It was just as much a tactical matter as batting domination.'

Benaud's measured analysis puts the matter in neat perspective without spoiling an undeniable truth. May's innings gave notice that the baton of English command had passed to a new generation. 'Petty wrangling,' in the words of Norman Preston, Editor of *Wisden*, had almost deprived them of a caring leader. Leonard Hutton had almost reluctantly been given the honour of captaincy, by the margin of a single vote. He more than justified the choice, as he nursed and nurtured a quartet of aspiring young men.

Peter May, as his vice-captain, was one beneficiary. Another was Colin Cowdrey, the Oxford University captain of the previous summer, who was destined to become May's most celebrated partner. Their friendship prospered as cabin companions on the voyage to Australia. Cowdrey was regarded as a 'hunch' selection, but he did possess credentials to rival those of May. He was a member of the Tonbridge School first eleven at thirteen and the youngest player to appear in a Public Schools' match at Lord's. In five years, the last two as captain, Cowdrey held sway as an all-rounder at Tonbridge; he scored 2,894 runs and took 216 wickets. At seventeen, in 1950, he made his first-class debut for Kent at Derby and was awarded his county cap during the Canterbury Festival in the following season. This was followed, in 1952, by another honour, the presentation of his Blue, after only three matches, by Peter Blake, the Oxford captain. One year later, he surpassed all his previous performances in scoring 1,917 runs, including four centuries.

Cowdrey pointedly excelled in the right surroundings, notably at Lord's in 1953 when he hit two half-centuries for the Gentlemen of England against the touring Australians. Lindwall and Miller were on hand to try to bounce him among the also-rans; but his mature calm banished such thoughts. Cowdrey's faltering form in 1954, partly explained by a wet summer and his university examinations, was happily disregarded by the discerning selectors.

Jim Swanton regarded the selection of another young contender, Frank Tyson, after only one full season in county cricket, as to some extent 'a shot in the dark'. 'But,' he added perceptively, 'it may prove to be a very penetrating shot.' The menace of Tyson and his lacerating pace had earlier been noted by one observer at Sheffield University. It was the occasion of the Universities Athletics Union semi-final against Durham University. 'I wondered what sort of a fellow he would be,' said this rival, as he waited to greet Tyson in the hall of residence allocated to the visitors. 'Here was a bowler who had wrought havoc among club and university cricketers in the north country; and for whom an England captain had prophesied an interesting future. The Sheffield host discovered him stuffing a 'Combined Services' cap (a souvenir of Tyson's army days) into his cricket bag. 'He was tall, well-built, with a strong but cheerful face, and his hair was thinning and receding. He looked a person of determination.'

At that time, Tyson had failed his BA examination at Durham – a lapse he remedied at the second attempt. It was in English that he had been unable to satisfy his tutors. 'A pity,' his mother said, 'for he likes English.' Tyson reputedly murmured couplets of Wordsworth as he walked back to his mark, and as he stuttered his feet and moved in to bowl.

'After the first over,' said the Sheffield man, 'I reflected that Wordsworth was decidedly inappropriate for the meditation of a man of iron. Far too romantic. He punched the ball into the pitch from whence it leapt eagerly to the bat's edge, as one endeavoured to thrust it down from under the armpits. Adding to the discomfort was a "Carmody" field of short-legs and slips, all in fearful symmetry, waiting to clutch the flying ball.'

Frank Tyson was adjudged 'a quiet fellow but a solid character' by his team mates in Australia, but it was exceedingly strange that so knowledgeable a coach as Harry Makepeace had not spotted his potential as a bowler. Makepeace said, 'He dips at the legs', when Tyson, as a gangling sixteen-year-old, travelled from his Farnsworth village home for a trial at Old Trafford. Northamptonshire presented no obstacle when Tyson, by then a mature student at Durham, gave the county the opportunity to recruit him.

The fourth member of the young guard in Australia was another sterling character, Brian Statham. Lancashire's folly in rejecting Tyson must, even with hindsight, be regarded with wistful regret by Red Rose partisans. It prevented a county alliance of two bowlers born within a few miles of each other. Statham, virtually uncoached, was a natural bowler; his arrival at Old Trafford in 1950 came just in time to reinforce an attack soon to be depleted by the retirement of Dick Pollard. Statham entered the Lancashire fold as almost a stranger, straight from National Service in the Royal Air Force. Harry Makepeace did not repeat his mistake with Tyson. Within two weeks of reporting to the Lancashire coach, Statham, on his twentieth birthday, made his debut against Kent at Manchester.

It is now a matter for wry amusement that Statham's action was at first slighted by the purists, who considered it lacked rhythm. The criticism did not affect a remarkable advance into Test cricket. Statham was called up, along with his Lancashire colleague, Roy Tattersall, to reinforce the MCC party in Australia in 1950–51. Young in years at twenty-four, Statham had already completed two other tours – to India and the West Indies – by the time of his selection for Australia in 1954.

One important figure was missing from Hutton's team in Australia. He was Fred Trueman. His absence was regretted by Ray Robinson: 'A speed attack without Trueman is like a horror film without Boris Karloff.' Peter Loader, another emerging paceman was, it seems, considered a safer ambassador. Trueman, like Surrey's Laker and Lock, had to wait four more years before he first toured Australia in 1958–59. Wardle, Appleyard and McConnon were the spinning choices in 1954. One of the ironies of that year was that, after being passed over for the tour, Laker and Lock suddenly found rampant form. In their last ten championship games they took 103 wickets between them, Laker securing 59 and Lock 44, both for an average of less than nine runs apiece.

Geoffrey Howard, the MCC manager, reflected upon the narrow divide between the two teams in Australia. 'We were a very good side, but Australia were not really inferior.' Before the tour Jim Swanton considered that the England party possessed greater potential than any preceding team in the postwar years. He thought it was weaker in batting but more dangerous as a bowling force.

England, going into the first Test at Brisbane without a spinner, did not make a propitious start to the series. Australia, put in to bat, were aided by a horrendous epidemic of missed catches. They scored over 600 and won in a canter by an innings. The humiliating reverse seemed to rebuke Hutton for placing the emphasis on pace. Douglas Jardine, another avowed disciple of speed, had once before left out his key spinner, Hedley Verity, in Australia and lost. Swanton observed: 'In brutal truth, the game had been bungled by England from start to finish.'

The cloud of despair broke to reveal a silver lining in the second Test at Sydney. For the first two days, there was no change of fortune. Arthur Morris, the acting Australian captain, also exercised the option of giving his opponents the first innings. It appeared a profitable gamble, as England were dismissed for 154. The position might even have been worse. England had lost nine wickets for 111 runs before the merry intervention of Johnny Wardle. Wardle, top scorer with 35, was associated in a last wicket stand with Statham which added a precious 43 runs.

Wardle's blazing assault was particularly directed against Bill Johnston, the fast-medium left-arm bowler. He took 18 runs off one over. His innings had a shattering impact on the Australians, who cowered in areas not indicated in the fielding manual. At length Morris was forced to ask Johnston to take his sweater. 'Bill, however, begged for another over, and it became sheer disaster,' said Morris. 'Johnny hit him over the slips, over cover, over mid-on, everywhere but places guarded by the fielders.' Wardle could not manage another act of piracy in the England second innings, but Statham did, this time in company with Bob Appleyard. The last-wicket pair more sedately added 46 telling runs in fifty minutes.

The real turning-point at Sydney was the fourth-wicket partnership between May and Cowdrey in England's second innings. Theirs was an immense responsibility; if they had stumbled, as Jim Swanton reported, 'England would have been as good as beaten inside three days'. He added: 'The Ashes would then have gone up in smoke and Hutton's captaincy would have been written off as a failure. It was as close as that. Of all their triumphs ahead, none exceeded in value this redeeming partnership.' May and Cowdrey came together after England had lost three wickets, those of Hutton, Bailey and Graveney, for only 55 runs. 'Slowly but surely against bowling and fielding that gave nothing away they righted the ship,' wrote the *Cricketer* correspondent. 'Their magnificent partnership of 116, spread over three-and-a-quarter hours, brought England back into the game with a vengeance.'

'England's "baby" cricketers showed their veteran team-mates the kind of poised, shrewd and patient batting that can win Test matches,' enthused the *Sydney Morning Herald*. 'The umbrella fieldsmen, so close together on other days, scattered to distant parts as if they had quarrelled in committee.' Alan Ross observed: 'May split the air with the noise of his strokes, Cowdrey, the field with the ease of his timing. There was little to choose between them in the correctness of technique, the natural assertion of their breeding.'

71

Bill O'Reilly also paid tribute to one of the most stirring partnerships he had seen in Test cricket. 'The concentration of the two young men was the outstanding feature of their remarkable performance.' O'Reilly, with glad memories of his own duels with England, said the batting of May gleamed with the purpose of an old campaigner of pre-war days. 'His strength has been his resourcefulness in footwork and his splendid on-side play. The innings stamps him as one of the leading players of this era.' May, en route to his first century against Australia, lost Cowdrey just when the pair appeared certain to remain undefeated.

'Poor Cowdrey!' commiserated the *Sydney Morning Herald*. 'His was a valiant innings. Like the boy on the burning deck, and not very much older, he fell victim to his own devotion to duty.' Cowdrey, after his earlier sparkle, was dragged down after tea into a defensive attitude that locks up heart and spirit. He succumbed more from inaction than anything else, mishitting a foxing and highly flighted googly from Benaud. Archer took the catch at long-off. It was a sickening and needless dismissal at the end of a long hard day. Tom Graveney recalls: 'Colin cried his eyes out. He thought he'd lost the Test match.'

Cowdrey's distress was swiftly dispelled by a devastating bowling thrust. Australia were set a target of 223 and, in truth, should have won, with the brilliant but unsupported Neil Harvey as their anchor. Australia, it was thought, would be home and dry by tea-time. The crucial development was the decision by Frank Tyson to cut short his strength-sapping run. Tyson was at pains to make amends for his profligacy at Brisbane, where he had conceded 160 runs and taken one wicket. It was not a new idea, rather a return to the steadier distance he had bowled from in Staffordshire League cricket with Knypersley. He had also belatedly recalled the advice of one mentor, Alfred Gover, who recommended a shorter run before the tour. In the preceding state match he had reverted to the old principle: six shuffling steps followed by ten deliberate raking strides.

Now, heaving into the attack and swept along by half a gale behind him, Tyson was a man of fury. His determined bullet-like yorkers dipped unnervingly into the Australians' stumps. None of the batsmen, excepting Harvey – forlornly isolated on 92 not out in one of the finest innings of his career – knew how to counter Tyson's speed. 'Few bowlers – fast, medium or slow – have ever dominated a match as Tyson did this one,' commented Bill O'Reilly.

Hutton's mission to achieve victory by pace was gloriously fulfilled. Tyson bowled unchanged through the closing ninety minutes of a fluctuating match. 'Throughout that long period,' wrote O'Reilly, 'he plugged away at the stumps with such inspiring intent that one tried in vain to remember the last time that an England side had looked so formidably certain of victory.' The margin was, though, perilously close, a mere handful of 38 runs. Tyson's six wickets in the innings brought him ten in the match; and he became only the third fast bowler, after Larwood and Farnes, to achieve this aggregate for England against Australia.

Tyson's success could not have resulted without the unflagging support of his partner, Brian Statham. His contribution, 'holding up the upwind end over and over till it seemed he could give no more', would, on other occasions, place him in England's debt. Statham was always the immaculate foil, not to be confused with playing second fiddle, for his allies of more spectacular pace. As one writer neatly put it, Statham was so accurate that on a yielding turf the marks where the ball pitched were grouped like rifle shots around a bull's-eye.

In the third Test at Melbourne a chanceless century of astonishing maturity was paraded by Colin Cowdrey. 'Everyone else fell apart,' says Tom Graveney. 'But Colin got a hundred. It was a remarkable knock.' The innings came as a welcome tonic for the captain, Len Hutton. Geoffrey Howard recalls that, after the Sydney Test, Hutton was 'absolutely drained'. So intense had been his mental involvement that a case full of congratulations on his victory remained unanswered. Howard, anxious not to offend the well-wishers, organised stereotyped replies and asked Hutton to 'top and tail' the messages. For the rest of the tour, in order to help the England captain to conserve his energies, Howard and Peter May took on the tasks required off the field.

It is a widely held view that Colin Cowdrey never surpassed the brilliance of his cricket as a twenty-two-year-old in Australia. One writer said of him in his years of eminence: 'He is technically without peer or fault; but he is too sensitive a person, too much of a theorist to destroy mediocre bowling. He bats well only when the situation demands it, when there is a challenge to exercise his fertile mind.' In the view of one contemporary, Dennis Silk, the difference between Cowdrey and Peter May was that one 'sometimes saw dangers that weren't there' whereas the other 'played every ball on its merits'.

There can, however, be no gainsaying that Cowdrey, as a young tourist in Australia, displayed exemplary fortitude. He first had to overcome the hugely distressing blow of the death of his father. A telegram announcing the bereavement awaited him when the MCC party arrived in Perth.

Cowdrey recorded: 'I went to my room, unpacked and stayed there on my own for the rest of the afternoon. When I went down to dinner Len Hutton said nothing. It was only after the meal, when I was having coffee in the lounge, that he came round the back of my chair, put his hand on my shoulder and said: "I'm sorry." There were tears in his eyes.' Cowdrey added that Hutton never made reference to his father again. Hutton did, however, ensure that for the rest of the tour his junior was not allowed to brood in his grief.

Neville Cardus rejoiced in the largesse of Cowdrey's batting in Australia. This included two centuries in one match against New South Wales, achieved before Cowdrey had reached three figures in a county match. They were just a gathering of fruits before the windfall at Melbourne. 'This wonderful innings began a terrible ordeal for him,' related Cardus. 'Keith Miller bowled at his most demonically improvisatory, on an ill-behaved pitch. For four hours he mingled defence and offence perfectly. This was a veteran's serene spirit and technique. It was Cowdrey's finest hour.'

Keith Miller, returning to the Australian team after injury, had expressed his doubts about bowling in a pre-match conversation with Sir Donald Bradman. With his right knee heavily bandaged, he did bowl, unchanged, for ninety minutes before lunch. England lost four wickets for 41 runs. Miller took three wickets for five runs in a spell of nine overs, which included eight maidens. His prized victims were Hutton, Edrich and Compton, while Lindwall, at the other end, dismissed May. Cowdrey's 102, out of a total of 191, dragged Hutton out of his lethargy. Geoffrey Howard recalls: 'Len was miserable after getting out so quickly. He did not take his pads off and just sat in the dressing-room, staring glumly at the wall. His mood changed when he realised from our excitement on the balcony that Colin was playing so well. Before long he had joined us to share our enthusiasm.' As a postscript to Cowdrey's feat, Tom Graveney incredulously recalls that, in the following year, his colleague was experimenting with a new grip. 'Having played one of the greatest innings I ever saw, Colin was worrying about how to hold the bat.'

Ian Johnson, not normally a big spinner, finally dismissed Cowdrey with what was described as a 'freak ball'. Cowdrey, padding up, was bowled behind his legs. It was an ominous event. One observer, who examined the wicket after the match, said the cracks and patches were so pronounced as to defy belief that cricket could be played on it. The controversial allegations of a watered pitch, vigorously disputed by the Melbourne club,

74

actually aided England in their second innings. Jim Swanton related that, over the intervening weekend, a hot north wind blew and the heat grew increasingly intolerable. 'After Melbourne had experienced the hottest night in its history, England, going out to field on the Monday morning, were amazed to find evidence of moisture in the pitch. They had left it desiccated and friable; now the sprigs on their boots, which had slid over the baked, shiny surface, cut lines in the turf.'

The artificial refreshment, added Swanton, suited England well, for it gave them the truest surface of the match for their second innings. Frank Tyson, who with his fast shooters was to cut a swathe through the Australian batting, said: 'Had the curator not acted, there can be little doubt that there would have been hardly any wicket left by the Monday.'

Jack House, the Melbourne curator, was steadfast in defence of his stewardship. He said the Test pitch had not been touched by water since the start of play on the Friday. The wicket, he declared, had not been left unattended during the day, and watchmen had camped beside it at night. His explanation was that, in the humid weather, the tarpaulins covering the pitch had a tendency to draw moisture and close the fissures.

Jim Swanton related how the rout of Australia on an extraordinary morning at Melbourne began with a phenomenal catch by Godfrey Evans, which dismissed Neil Harvey, the major threat to England's hopes of victory. Evans has since described this as perhaps the finest catch, from a genuinely fine glance, he had ever taken standing back. Swanton said: 'He moved across to the leg side not by a prearranged plan but on a hunch that Harvey would play the stroke, and he took the ball after the most prodigious leap at the fullest stretch.'

Australia, with eight wickets left, needed 165 to win before the dramatic last stages of the match. 'Tyson blazed through them like a bushfire,' reported *Wisden*. In 79 minutes the match was over, the eight remaining wickets falling for 36 runs. Tyson took six wickets for 16 runs in 6.3 overs; and Statham captured the other two wickets for 19 runs. Neil Harvey, as the astonished victim of Evans's athleticism, today remembers the explosive qualities of Tyson. 'Frank, along with Wes Hall, was the quickest bowler I ever faced.'

Bill O'Reilly, watching Tyson's demoralising spell, said: 'He rode roughshod over our full batting strength. Batsmen whom we regarded as sanely practical had no answer to offer the English speedster. Not since the eight wickets fell for 35 runs at Manchester in 1953 had Australian cricket

75

been so dreadfully humiliated as it was today. Butterfly backlifts have never looked so ludicrously incongruous as they did facing Tyson and Statham.'

C. B. Fry, the octogenarian sage, presented his summary in the *Cricketer*. He reflected that there was little to compare with the hurricane handicap of real speed. 'The genuinely fast bowler is on to you too quickly. You have to be as keen as a razor and as swift as a snake in order to counter him. The batsman who does not lift his bat from the block-hole in good time, who does not stand tall and commanding, finds himself snatching at a save-me-somehow stroke, edging or missing the high-riser and too late in stopping the one that keeps low.'

Fry, from his standpoint as an Edwardian cricket gladiator, concluded on the heroics – the alert determination – required to counter the dynamics of the human catapult in a hand-to-hand battle. 'No wonder the young Australian batsmen found the need of more study when they had to face Tyson and his mate on the tricksome creek-soil.' He added: 'As for our "Typhoon", he is a young treasure we shall do well to nourish with much pleasure and with no silly adulation.'

England now kept their supporters on tenterhooks at Adelaide before resisting Keith Miller, bowling with characteristic fire, to win by five wickets. The retention of the Ashes cleared the stage for Johnny Wardle to spring into back-handed action in the final rain-curtailed Test at Sydney. Exceptional downpours – the worst experienced in New South Wales for fifty years – held up play until two o'clock on the fourth day. Australia were all out for 221 in their first innings and followed-on 150 runs behind England's 371. Harassed and bewildered by Wardle's beguiling mixture of spinning all-sorts, Australia ended the match 32 runs short and with only four wickets standing, narrowly avoiding the indignity of an innings defeat in less than three days.

Leonard Hutton was vindicated in his recipe of speed, as England won their first series in Australia since Douglas Jardine's controversial triumph twenty-two years earlier. The joyful events, communicated to followers at home, were not discordantly cheered by the banner-waving hordes of today's globe-trotting 'barmy army'. Only two Englishmen, apart from the press corps, were present in Australia to sing the praises of the team. They were Sam Stott, a friend of George Duckworth, the MCC scorer and baggage master, and one long-standing Lancashire member. Accompanying them was an American, seventy-two-year-old Henry Sayen, a member of the Philadelphia team in England in 1908.

The demands of a tense, low-scoring series were surmounted by the tactical acumen of Hutton. Bob Appleyard, denied at least one match-winning opportunity at Melbourne, had to accept a subordinate role in the series. Geoffrey Howard believes that Appleyard, together with Trevor Bailey, did much to control affairs at key stages. Appleyard was in sympathy with the strategic plan adopted by his Yorkshire senior. 'Len believed that quickies win matches in Australia and that others, like Bailey, Wardle and myself, were there to support them. Tyson and Statham opened and then, if they hadn't made a breakthrough, he introduced us. As soon as we took a wicket, we were off.'

Appleyard admits that he would have welcomed a bigger share of the workload in Australia: 'Len was, though, a great captain and his tactics were right. He was able to keep a check on the game with his adopted attack. He couldn't afford to give runs away. He always had the quickies on against a new batsman.'

Richie Benaud does, however, contend that Hutton over-ran the bounds of caution. 'Unfortunately, Len was the one who started the business of slow over-rates.' In fact, this restrictive practice, as Les Ames once told me, was beginning to develop in England towards the end of his career in the early 1950s. Ray Robinson, the Australian writer, referred to the irritation of the crowds during Hutton's frequent talks with his bowlers. These briefings, coupled with the long runs taken by most of them, reduced play to below 60 eight-ball overs a day.

Hutton, in his later retirement, might have had cause to ponder on the deterioration of over-rates. It is estimated that the rates in Australia, taking account of shorter playing hours, in the 1954–55 series would not be very different from the current ICC minimum. This is 15 overs per hour less reductions for interruptions and changes of innings. It would also be better than the over-rates prevalent in Test cricket before the ICC systems of minimum overs and fines were instigated. A general judgement is that Hutton's tactics in Australia might have been slow by contemporary standards, but probably not in present-day terms.

In the 1954–55 series, reported Ray Robinson, 58 overs were bowled in Brisbane and Adelaide and 54 in Melbourne. On the Saturday of the Melbourne Test all except two of the 27 overs from the higher end were bowled by Tyson and Statham. The batsmen were allowed little respite from fast bowling, though Hutton contrived to give each bowler half-hour rests between turns of three or four overs.

The emphasis on slow over-rates, says Benaud, was a deliberate ploy to 'frustrate our batsmen and make them wait for ball after ball'. Hutton was

77

not unaware of the accusation. At the end of the tour he apologised for the restricted overs and thanked Australian crowds for their patience. His remark, 'Fast bowlers must take time over their overs', has a familiar ring in the context of the modern game. Of his own battery of pacemen, he said: 'I felt that as youngsters they needed my help in placing the field.' Geoffrey Howard acknowledges that Hutton's basic objective was to keep Tyson and Statham in prime condition. 'But the slowing tactic did deprive the opposition of the chance to score more runs.'

The grand design was also, perhaps even more significantly, part of a psychological warfare waged against Australia. Colin Cowdrey said that he was conscious throughout the crucial Test at Sydney that Hutton was manipulating a campaign as though playing a tight and ruthless game of chess. One adroit ploy involved Richie Benaud. Johnny Wardle was just about to bowl to Benaud. The over was halted as Hutton moved within conversational distance of the batsman. Seconds passed while he apparently deliberated on some devious scheme. 'What's going on?' asked the perplexed Johnny. 'Put your sweater on,' said Hutton. He then briskly clapped his hands, looking over towards Tyson, fielding in the deep. 'Come on, Frank, have a bowl. Richie's in.'

This message of tough leadership was to become the keynote of the captaincy of Peter May, Hutton's young successor. The *esprit* of the team, naturally nourished by success, said Jim Swanton, was greatly helped by May's conception of his role as vice-captain in Australia. The harmony of his partnership with Hutton was especially reflected in his awareness that the Yorkshireman should be spared, as far as possible, the chores off the field. It was a commendable act of courtesy, and a sign that May was addressing himself to the responsibilities which were all too soon to be thrust upon him.

England and Yorkshire jointly lamented the retirement of Hutton after the Australian tour. Jim Kilburn, the Yorkshire historian, said: 'He left first-class cricket with a feeling of relief rather than regret. He had completed an exhausting journey.' Hutton, in three gruelling years and over four series, had shepherded England back to a commanding plateau. He bequeathed a legacy which Peter May was to build upon and endow with increased lustre in his own distinguished reign.

Chapter 8
The Ferocious Conqueror

'His physical strength was immense and it was backed up by an astonishing determination.'

Sir Colin Cowdrey

It was a trusting friendship which auspiciously began with two young men, on their first tour together, hauling England back from the precipice of disaster in Australia. They were to become as inseparable and twinned in resolution and purpose as were their great predecessors, Denis Compton and Bill Edrich.

Colin Cowdrey markedly recalls Peter May as a man with a 'gracious, gentle streak', but easily the toughest cricketer with whom he was associated throughout his career. Theirs was a close and enduring alliance, supportive in spirit. May and Cowdrey rejoiced in each other's triumphs. 'I am most proud of the fact that we were not jealous or ever concerned with rivalry,' says Sir Colin. 'There was never a hint of a row. No hang-ups at all.'

Measuring the enormous talent of these companions, discussing which of them occupies the role of prince or consort, exercises the minds of many contemporaries. Peter Richardson, as a Test and county colleague, believes that Cowdrey was more naturally gifted as a player. 'Peter prospered through his determination, allied to his own considerable skills, to establish his credentials as a great batsman.' Richardson highlights the criterion of dedication handsomely met by both men. 'They both scored runs when they had to get them and when they were needed.'

The balance of advantage is slanted in the gain of May's equable temperament. Doug Insole, another former England player and Essex captain, describes May, along with Denis Compton, as a dazzling force whose dismissal produced a germ of regret at Chelmsford or Southend. As an opposing captain, he reflects that the pleasures of May's batting,

79

however wounding, set standards for them to follow in respectful obedience. 'Peter was a modest man,' says Insole, 'but he was never in awe of bowlers. He was always prepared to take them on.'

Cowdrey, endowed with a similar array of shots, fluctuated in mood from day to day. He could be strangely subdued against bowlers hardly worth a second glance. One writer said that because Cowdrey regarded cricket as a civilised pastime, he tended to correct the shortcomings of bowlers rather than emphasise them. 'The possessor of an immaculate technique, he batted as though he wished to establish Canterbury in high summer in all parts of the globe.' Doug Insole observes: 'Colin, when he wasn't absolutely on song, tended to allow bowlers to dictate to him. He was a little circumspect and unsure of his tremendous ability, but that was in his character.'

Cowdrey himself concedes that, at Test level, the slim divide in superiority separating him from May meant that he was often cast in a supporting role. 'When we were both going well, Peter would need to maintain his momentum more than I did. It would have been wrong of me to hog the strike; you could sense that he was getting itchy. I didn't worry about hanging around.'

Cowdrey's batting technique – the precision timing using the pace of the ball – served him well on fast wickets. It was in complete contrast to the explosive style of May whose shots scorched across the field like tracer bullets. Godfrey Evans welcomed the respite of batting with Peter. 'I didn't have to run so much because he was bombarding the boundaries. With Colin, we had, perhaps, scampered three before the ball sneaked over the ropes.'

Towering strength was indeed the keynote of May's play but without the recklessness of another brutal striker, Ted Dexter. Cowdrey compares, in another example, his own small hands with the large ones of Peter, which permitted such massive swinging leverage. 'In a match against Surrey at The Oval I once saw him loft David Halfyard into the pavilion. It was sheer power. If I had played the same shot, it would probably have risen in a gentle arc and fallen well short of that target. I would have been criticised for being so stupid.' Even so, he maintains that, if he could play his career over again, he would seek to weave threads of May's style within his own batting design.

Alan Ross said the immediate impression May made on coming out to bat was of an exhilarating freshness. 'He had a fine presence at the wicket, his stance full of naval command. When he ran between the wickets he

Peter May.

Peter's parents, Howard and Eileen May, and his aunt Edith May (*left*).

His first bat. Peter with his cousin Richard Robinson.

Peter and his brother John Guernsey, 1936.

Leading the field – Sports Day at Marlborough House School, Reading.

Sir Robert Birley,
Headmaster of Charterhouse
during Peter's schooldays in
the Second World War –
'an enthusiast for life and
bursting with ideas'.

Cricket on Charterhouse Green, the scene of Peter's early triumphs.

Peter with George Geary, the Leicestershire and England all-rounder and the influential cricket coach at Charterhouse.

The School XI in 1945: (*back row, left to right*) I. W. Lynch, J. H. Perry, H. Le Bas, J. L. Harvey, J. M. L. Prior, J. B. Spargo, T. J. Aitchison; (*front row*) O. B. Popplewell, P. B. H. May, A. J. Rimell (capt.), R. L. Whitby, S. A. N. Raven.

The Charterhouse team for Eton Fives, 1947, including both Peter and John May:
(*back row*) J. W. H. May, M. J. Perkins, T. R. H. Savill; (*front row*) P. G. Nathan,
P. B. H. May, S. E. A. Kimmins.

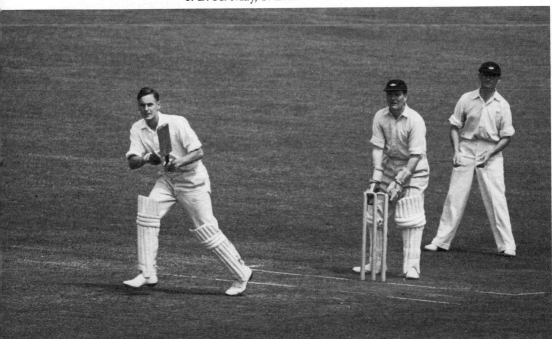

Peter batting during his innings of 162 not out for the Royal Navy v. Royal Air
Force at Lord's, July 1949.

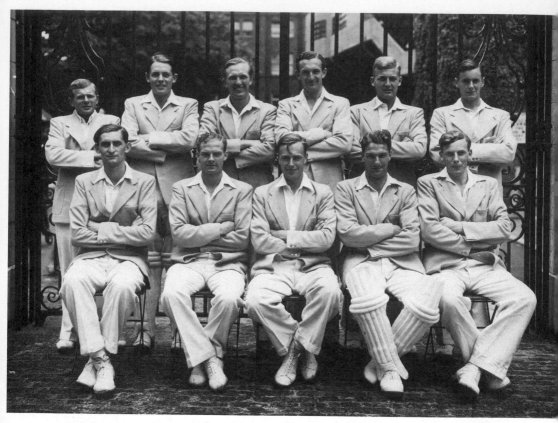

The Cambridge University team of 1950: (*front row*) J. J. Warr, A. G. J. Rimell, G. H. G. Doggart, J. G. Dewes, O. B. Popplewell: (*back row*) T. U. Wells, D. S. Sheppard, M. H. Stevenson, P. A. Kelland, W. I. D. Hayward, P. B. H. May.

THE WHITBREAD BEST BITTER CENTURY MAKERS

Nº34

IN A SERIES OF 40

PETER MAY

1 3 8

V

SOUTH AFRICA

HEADINGLEY 1951

His first Test innings, joining a handful of England batsmen who scored a hundred on their Test debuts.

COLLECT 10 DIFFERENT CARDS. YOU COULD WIN £1,000. SEE DETAILS OPPOSITE.

P. B. H. MAY

Trade cards, issued to celebrate Peter's Test debut against South Africa at Leeds in 1951.

E. NEWS picture to-day of Alec Bedser (left), now almost "a "veteran" in the English Test side, and Peter May, the Cambridge University batsman, who will be taking part in his first Test to-morrow, arriving at Headingley.

Photo   "Cambridge Daily News"
Peter May, the England, Cambridge University and Surrey batsman, who has been voted the best young cricketer of 1951 by the Cricket Writers' Club, with the Club trophy.

Arriving with Alec Bedser at Headingley for his first Test, 1951, as recorded by the *Yorkshire Evening News*.
(*Right*) Honoured as the Cricket Writers Club's 'Young Cricketer of the Year', 1951 (*Cambridge Evening News*).

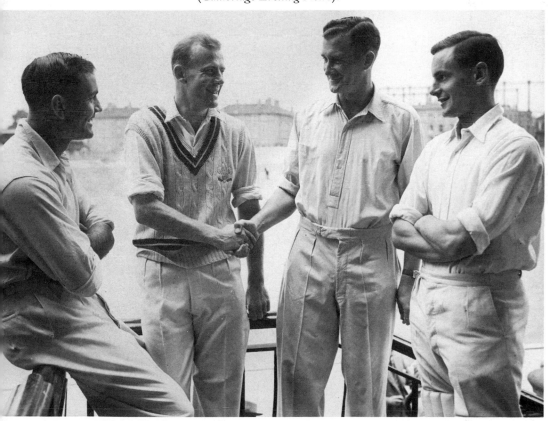

For the Test Match against India at The Oval in 1952, four Surrey cricketers were chosen – Alec Bedser, Lock, Laker and May.

Leslie Compton, of Middlesex, caught by Stuart Surridge, Surrey's captain, in the leg trap.

The Gentlemen's XI v. the Players, 1954.

was a shade ungainly, his over-large pads prone to flap like goose's feathers. As the bowler approached he tensed slightly and then anything overpitched would ricochet off the sightscreen with a bang. His effortless placement of the on-drive was a stroke for which he had no equal, but his straight driving was truly thunderous.'

Alf Gover, as one of May's early mentors at The Oval, presents a picture of exceptional physical command. He remembers the deceptively slim appearance. 'Peter was bigger than he looked on the field; he was broad-shouldered, with wide hips and good strong legs.' Gover enthuses about a 'mighty hitter', spellbindingly assured off the back foot and comparable, in his view, with Wally Hammond.

Another wise observer, Herbert Strudwick, also kept a watchful eye on the young Surrey master. The revered 'Struddy' was one of the finest of the Oval stalwarts. His career with Surrey as a player and scorer spanned sixty years. He shared a memory with Gover of one stupendous strike by May against Nottinghamshire. Arthur Jepson, armed with the new ball, was the plainly disbelieving bowler. For Peter, as Strudwick related, a boundary off his first ball was the best possible tonic to make him feel at home and relaxed.

May's six-hit was struck unerringly off the back foot and over the bowler's head into the Vauxhall Stand. The next ball was also driven for four to compound the audacity. 'Jeppy couldn't believe it,' says Gover. 'It shattered him for the rest of the day.' The verdict of Strudwick was that only a class player – 'standing up straight and ready to hit the first ball if it wanted hitting' – could have produced such a magnificent assault. It was by no means an isolated event. John Woodcock remembered another example of May's power at Lord's. 'From the middle of the ground he hit a medium-pacer high into the Mound Stand over extra-cover, and off the *back* foot.'

Alf Gover, in less demanding circumstances, was the wry recipient of another trenchant blow in a charity match in Wiltshire. Gover was then in his early sixties, but still in good trim through bowling at his Wandsworth cricket school. 'I bowled the old swinger and he hit me for six over mid-on and beyond the adjacent railway line.' Gover, his eyes twinkling, looked inquiringly down the wicket at the young aggressor. Peter was suitably contrite and immediately apologised. 'I'm awfully sorry, Alf; I didn't mean to hit it so far.' Gover replied: 'But, Peter, you've lost the ball and ruined the game.' Peter did then see the fun of the situation. A flicker of a smile passed over his concerned face.

Peter May is unreservedly given by his fellow players exclusive status as the best batsman to be produced by England since the war. Don Kenyon does not dally in his praise; he uses the word 'great', and says that others of his or the present time require a lesser billing. For Richie Benaud, May heads his rollcall of England batsmen. It is a telling statement from an observer whose experience as a player and commentator extends over forty years. Benaud's list also includes seven other quality contenders – Dexter, Cowdrey, Barrington, Graveney, Boycott, Gower and Gooch.

Ted Dexter receives a high ranking in Benaud's estimation. 'No one played any straighter than Ted and yet he could murder a bowling attack.' Peter Richardson, a fervent admirer, says the Sussex batsman played great innings which riveted the attention. Dexter's birthplace was Milan and there was an Italianate extravagance and bravado in his play. But the derring-do approach, exciting in remembrance, carried its own inherent flaws. Discretion was not, especially in his formative years, a priority. Peter May applied his power with greater certainty; unlike Dexter he sought to eliminate risk.

Two other Australians, Alan Davidson and Neil Harvey, give pride of place to May; his distinction as a premier batsman, they explain, lay in the fact that he excelled on all wickets at home and overseas. Harvey couples May with Hutton and Compton as the best of his rivals in a career which began with his own triumphant entry on the Test scene in 1948. As an amateur in category and breeding, May was the exemplar of unremitting professionalism. One close friend, John Warr, in a neat juxtaposition, considers him the supreme professional among the ranks of the amateurs just as Denis Compton was the supreme amateur among the professionals. Trevor Bailey, in his book *The Greatest of My Time*, underlines this point, describing May as 'The Amateur with the Professional Approach'.

Enhancing May's esteem was his mastery on uncovered wickets, the yardstick of technical prowess in his time. In the 1950s there was a galaxy of spinners to test his resourcefulness on spiteful pitches. The ranks of wily practitioners included leg-spinners, Doug Wright, Bruce Dooland and Eric Hollies; left-handers, George Tribe, Jack Walsh and Johnny Wardle, who each combined orthodox and unorthodox spins; and off-spinners, Bob Appleyard, Robin Marlar and Roy Tattersall.

The exploits of Shane Warne have rebuked those who declared that the leg-spinner is a luxury in the modern game. His acclamation as a folk hero in Australia gives rise to hopes of a general revival of a bewitching art. Warne offers a compelling reminder of the old sorcerers, tormenting opponents on bad wickets in their heyday. John Warr, in a mischievous aside, ponders on how current players would have fared amid the perils. 'I would like to see our boys in opposition to George Tribe on a turner.'

Peter May did need to be adept to maintain his authority in such conditions. Very often, as on one daunting wicket at The Oval in 1954, he prospered, while others less endowed groped towards their execution. Peter Richardson and Don Kenyon were members of the Worcestershire team overwhelmed by the spin of Laker and Lock. The match lasted just over five hours and was concluded by 12.30 on the second day. Worcestershire were dismissed for 25, losing their last seven first-innings wickets for five runs, and 40. Surrey batted for only 24 overs, but still won by an innings.

Stuart Surridge, with a glance at the baleful skies, quickly assessed that batting was an untenable proposition. He dispensed with unnecessary runs. His declaration came at 92 for three wickets. May, to his astonishment, was called in, having scored 31. Richardson recalls the farcical conditions. 'We shouldn't have been playing on that wicket. Everyone else was in disarray, edging or gloving catches; but we never missed the middle of Peter's bat.' Of his own dismissal, he says that he attempted to raise his bat high out of harm's way. The ball kept on climbing and it rose to such an extent that he was still caught at the wicket off Laker.

Don Kenyon also remembers the severity of May's batting in a one-sided contest. 'We had a left-hander, John Ashman, a Yorkshireman. The ball was turning alarmingly. Peter came in, sighted him for a couple of balls, then, before you knew what was happening, he was hitting Ashman over cover, extra-cover . . . it was magnificent to watch.'

Doug Insole has dwelt upon May's ability to thrive in difficult circumstances. It was a product of intense concentration. The passion of his commitment held him as if caught in a vice of self-hypnosis. 'You could almost see the flames bursting out of his nostrils,' says Colin Cowdrey. Peter's business hours at cricket permitted no intrusion. The current emphasis on prolonged pre-match bouts of physical training would have mystified him. His fitness was exemplary, but such a needless drain on his energies would have been rejected with disdain. 'Don't ask me to do that,' would have been his response. 'I've got to make a hundred today.'

He was also puzzled by the weight of bats used by modern players. His own bats did not exceed 2lb 4oz; those of Denis Compton were even less; and he was constantly surprised how batsmen such as Ian Botham, and others less strong, could cut with bats of up to 3lb 4oz. Peter was also at odds with the current practice, also condemned by Sir Donald Bradman, of standing at the crease with the bat raised. Great batsmen of other days had made thousands of runs without adopting this style. The weight of modern bats were, he thought, the reason why players of today prefer to pick it up before the ball is delivered. 'I think that when they play fatally across the line, although well in, it is often because they are tired and late on the stroke.' John Warr expresses the view that it would not have been possible to play with the heavier bats on the uncovered and wet wickets of the 1950s. 'It was possible to adjust with the lighter bat. If we'd used a heavy bat against balls which stopped on pitching, we would have holed out at mid-on or mid-off almost every time.'

May invariably avoided practice on the morning of a match, especially if he was likely to be engaged in a long sojourn at the crease. Before he went in to bat the action was studiedly ignored. He did not want to prejudge the happenings on the field. The sketch of his innings was already constructed in his mind as well as possible. He had done his homework on the opposition and was mentally prepared for the examination of the day. 'It wasn't easy to get much sense out of him during this pregnant period,' recalls Doug Insole.

Arthur McIntyre, then the Surrey coach, shared changing accommodation with May in the amateurs' dressing-room at The Oval. He remembers the quiet ritual of letter-writing which often preceded an innings. At the fall of a wicket, he would tap the intent correspondent on the shoulder and say: 'He's out, Peter!' A huge sigh would greet the announcement. 'Oh, dear,' was the usual response. The dismissal, so it seemed, had disrupted May's plans for the morning. He snapped shut his briefcase; took up his bat; and, head down and brows furrowed, hurried out to the wicket. 'Once he got down there and within a short time I could tell that he meant business,' says McIntyre. 'Watching him, I would think: a hundred is guaranteed today.'

Peter Richardson presents another view of May's application, well demonstrated after the batting vigil in tandem with Colin Cowdrey in the marathon stand against the West Indies at Edgbaston in 1957. May had batted for nearly ten hours to help England save the game. On the following day, he travelled to Rushden and scored 96 to pilot Surrey to another victory. 'If I'd just batted as he did in that Test match, the last thing I would want to do is go and play in a county match next day. It was a tremendous reflection of his dedication.'

'Make sure the bowlers can see the maker's name,' was the constant call between May and Cowdrey, as they sought to impose their rule. The

technical command of both players was founded on displaying a monumentally straight bat. John Warr comments: 'Peter rarely played square of
the wicket. He was not an especially good cutter. If the ball was short, he
would be hitting it off the back foot through extra-cover, or similarly on
the other side, wide of mid-on.' May, like Hammond and Neil Harvey,
removed the hook from his armoury. He never regarded it as a 'business
shot' in serious matches. It did mean, as Ray Lindwall recalled, that he was
impervious to the bouncing, short-pitched ball. 'It was a waste of time
bowling bumpers at Peter,' said Lindwall. 'He just ignored them.'

May did negotiate many passages of aggressive fast bowling, but there is
a persistent view that he might have struggled against the more sustained
and venomous barrage of the vintage West Indian quartets. Alan Davidson
considers that Peter would have been able to deal with their thrusts
because of the surety of his back foot play. Lindwall's recollection indicated
that the West Indians would have had to ration their short-pitched
deliveries. May would have compelled them to pitch the ball up. Colin
Cowdrey, though, believes this is a grey area for a player with such a high
back lift. May might have been vulnerable to a line of attack consistently
directed on or above head height.

Tom Graveney points to the positive element in Peter's character,
which carried him through critical situations. 'With Peter, you always felt
that he could cope with any problem. He was very strong-minded. His
attitude was: "If there's something wrong, I can put it right".'

John Warr complements these thoughts with a technical analysis of
May. He names Vivian Richards as the nearest modern counterpart. 'They
both appeared to favour the on-side but in fact any bowler attacking them
on or outside the off stump would find plenty of strokes in the repertoire
in that area. They both had the unerring foot movement to position
themselves for the intended shot, keeping batsmanship as one-dimensional
as possible. They also had that extra sixth sense which seems to anticipate
where the ball is going to be bowled.'

Warr further explains that Peter's security as a batsman was vested in his
adeptness at quickly picking up the line of the ball. 'If it didn't suit him,
he wouldn't play at it.' In addition, and unlike most modern players, he
played with a 'monumentally straight bat'.

The glories of May's on-driving, invested with resonant perfection,
arouse special commendation among his Australian contemporaries. This
fluent and productive stroke was played with a perpendicular bat. Peter
rarely strayed across the line of the ball. Alan Davidson recalls: 'I used to

bowl from over the wicket at his off peg, otherwise you were just giving him runs.' May's deployment of the closed bat, held with his bottom hand, was a defensive counter against the short-pitched ball. 'As a left-hander, slanting the ball across him,' says Davidson, 'I did have a chance of getting him out, caught at third slip or gully.'

Peter himself acknowledged that the pick-up of his bat, starting in the direction of the second slip, did not find favour with the purists. But when it came down and forward it was straight enough. Blessed with strong wrists, he also discovered that by turning his top hand right round the handle of the bat, as he played forward defensively, with the back of the wrist facing him, he was best able to kill the spinning ball. 'With this left hand serving as a "brace" and the handle inclined towards the bowler, I have fashioned a forward defensive stroke which has served me well.'

In his individual batting thesis, written in the mid-1950s, May also stressed that cricket had developed into more of an on-side game. 'In the nature of things, I have found many of my runs on this side which has meant bringing my right hand into play. In fact, I would say that I am essentially a right-handed player. That inevitably means a slight occasional dragging of the bat from off to leg, and hitting across the ball a shade. Probably this has got me out a few times – but it has also brought me lots of runs.'

Alan Davidson remembers the composure of his English rival at the crease; the upright stance; and the evidence of an intelligent mind with a batting script in immaculate order. 'Peter was adept at "working the ball". As in the serve in tennis, you are bowling where you want to bowl. But great players make you change. You think you've got them and then you realise they've rumbled your tactics.'

Other witnesses like Don Kenyon and Arthur McIntyre endorse this batting orchestration. They appraise the razor-sharp reflexes which gave May the precious fraction of a second, enabling him to pre-select his shots and score in areas at his own dictation. McIntyre remembers batting with May against the MCC at Lord's. Frank Tyson was the bowler. He had elected to dispense with a fieldsman at mid-off. 'We had lost two or three quick wickets and I had to go in,' says McIntyre. 'Frank was rather sharp and I was just fending him off, just trying to keep my wicket really.' Peter was not prepared to allow Tyson the luxury of a yawning space in his field. It was an irresistible challenge. He raised himself, as erect as a guardsman, and, off the back foot, punched the ball through the gap.

Roy Tattersall provides another instance, amazing to him at the time, of May's lightning reflexes and ability to realign his strokes. In a match against Lancashire, 'Peter played two shots off me, neither of which I had ever seen before. I had my usual leg-side field. I was bowling very well. The second before I delivered the ball he adjusted his stance, turned round completely, and hit me square through the covers.' Tattersall shook his head in disbelief. Peter looked down the wicket at the mystified bowler. 'It's a good wicket – and I'm seeing it quite well today,' he explained. May then repeated the stroke to show it wasn't a fluke.

This audacity was also noted by Simon Raven, the novelist and a fellow pupil at Charterhouse. 'So far from being a robot programmed to select and play the most efficient and possible stroke, Peter had an individual brilliance which often led him to play the most satisfying and beautiful, even spectacular, stroke possible in the given circumstances – and sometimes in direct defiance of them.'

Bob Appleyard enthuses about May's special brand of cricket. He says that Peter always looked so good. He was never encountered in an ugly position. The excellent timing enabled him to hit a good-length ball on the middle stump through mid-off without any danger when the pitch was in his favour. Appleyard always found bowling against good players a challenge to relish. There was an extra swagger in his stride when he came to The Oval to bowl on wickets supposedly prepared for Lock and Laker. If it helped them, he concluded, there were spoils for him, too, as an off-spinner. 'So I wasn't nervous about bowling at Peter in such circumstances.'

He did, though, have qualms on one occasion. Surrey won the toss and batted on a wicket which shimmered with batting delights. Appleyard, in his medium-pace style, opened with the new ball. May, after an early reverse, was intent on recovering the position. 'Quite early on, I bowled one ball which pitched on the off stump, then cut back, and went over the top of the middle stump. Peter looked down the wicket with a grin and characteristically said: "Well bowled." He knew that he had been morally defeated.' The escape was a grim omen for Yorkshire. The incident was now closed; it was time to renew his attention. 'I don't think I got one past his bat for the rest of the day. It was a plumb wicket and Peter batted beautifully to score a hundred.'

The quality of a true sportsman was revealed in May's unwavering acceptance of umpiring decisions. He did not express annoyance, even when in one Test at Adelaide he was the victim of a dubious catch by Keith Miller off a low skimming drive at cover. Tom Graveney remembered the indignation of the England players watching the incident from the pavilion. They were convinced that the ball had eluded Miller's grasp as he dived to attempt the catch. Frank Tyson says: 'Peter asked Miller if he had taken the catch. Keith said, "Yes", and Peter walked. There was no dispute.'

Wilf Wooller, the Glamorgan captain and an adroit tactician, once won one battle of wits to outsmart May at The Oval. Peter, seemingly content that Bernard Hedges had taken a fair catch at mid-on, turned without ceremony for the pavilion. Hedges, however, signalled that he had dropped the ball. Wooller recalls: 'By this time May was almost passing Barrington at the non-striker's end. May was well out of his ground, so I shouted for the ball to be thrown to the 'keeper and he was run out.'

It was an act of effrontery stretching the bounds of good manners. May was invariably polite in provocative circumstances. He did concede that Wooller had played within the rules, if typically hard in practice. There was a flurry of interest in the press box. The scribes scented a controversy. Reports began to be filed accusing Wooller of duping May. Alf Gover, also on newspaper duties, alerted the Glamorgan captain to the situation during the tea interval. May was also made aware of the imminence of feverish headlines. He approached his cunning rival and delivered an olive branch. 'Don't worry, Wilf,' he said, 'there was really a single there and Ken should have run. He was the one to blame. If he hadn't been watching the ball, we'd have been all OK.' It was a droll response calculated to assert his authority and claim a hold on Wooller's conscience in the affair.

May never neglected to express his debt to his England seniors for their part in his development as a cricketer. Denis Compton, Bill Edrich and Len Hutton, each in their turn, helped him to draw up his batting blueprint. One important lesson he learned and profited from was the placing and timing of the ball. 'I always used to think it is no use hitting fine shots at fieldsmen,' he once told me. 'Basically, what batsmen are trying to do is miss them. To score runs you have to do just that. The best players, like Len, Denis and Bill, hit the gaps.'

Evidence that May was well-schooled in this is presented by Peter Richardson. 'Many times, when batting with Peter, I would look at the scoreboard and think: "Where has he got those 30 runs from?" He had not been hitting the ball particularly hard.' Richardson, as an opening batsman, had, at this stage, diligently accrued 20 or so runs. He was quite pleased with his labours until he contrasted his own perseverance with the ease of his partner.

Admiringly, he would be inclined to take a count of the fieldsmen to establish whether there was a full complement on patrol. Their attempts to staunch the flow of runs all seemed ridiculously futile. 'The fielders *had to move* – and smartly – because Peter hardly ever hit the ball at them.' Richardson says these skilful manoeuvres made him feel thankful that May was on his side. Reinforcing this was the knowledge that there were very few bowlers of whom it could be said that they stood on the same level as May as a batsman.

Tom Graveney enjoyed the harmony of May's friendship in his apprentice years. Expectations were high on the tour of the West Indies in 1953–54 that they were both embarking on brilliant careers. 'Peter was nice and relaxed; we were both finding our feet on our first tour together. We had our fun times, drinking rum and enjoying ourselves as young men do.' Graveney was a logical contender for sustained Test recognition. His infectious spirit did subscribe to the tenets of enjoyment. A gregarious man, he was never happier than when swopping banter with his rivals, on and off the field. But he did, by his own account, err in indulgence as a batsman, perhaps succumbing to joyous expression too freely on the field. He was rated a liability under pressure and less than secure against fast bowling.

Graveney belatedly discovered self-assurance and responsibility after exchanging the slow wickets of Bristol for conditions more attuned to his stroke-play at Worcester. All doubts as to his pedigree were resolved in his late flowering as an England batsman in the mid-1960s. He was recalled against the West Indies at Lord's in 1966, on his thirty-ninth birthday, and he celebrated with a magnificent 96 against the fiery pace of Hall and Griffith. This achievement preceded a run of 24 consecutive Tests over four seasons before his retirement.

There is now a cheerful recognition that he was overshadowed by May. 'Peter was a mature player from the outset. He is the best postwar batsman by a street, head and shoulders above anyone else.' One instance of May's supremacy is rooted in his memory. The episode was an 'afternoon bunfight' – a 20-overs' exhibition match played to entertain a Saturday crowd after the end of a Test against New Zealand at Lord's in 1958. 'I had scored around 20 when Peter came in. He totally embarrassed me. He lofted the offspinner over extra-cover, an unusual shot in those days, into the Mound Stand. I decided that the best course was to concede my wicket and leave the stage to him. He was making me look like an idiot.'

May's domination against the New Zealanders in 1958, the last of his ravenous summers in England, was expressed in three innings in that year. It was first shown against the tourists on a fiery pitch at The Oval. He scored 165, more runs than those gathered by the visitors in both their innings. He was at the crease for just under four hours, little more than half the time required by Surrey for victory. Loader, with eight wickets, routed the New Zealanders for 74; and Lock spun another tale of woe, taking five wickets for nine runs, as the tourists were dismissed for 51 in the second innings. The next highest scorer in the match was Stewart, with 25, and only Miller, for the New Zealanders, reached double figures in both innings.

Ted Dexter, making his England debut in the fourth Test at Old Trafford, was May's companion and able to witness at first hand another batting feast against New Zealand. Heavy rain had delayed play until mid-afternoon on the Monday. May then hit four sixes and seven fours in a fifth-wicket stand of 82 runs with Dexter in an hour. Dexter recalls their partnership which illuminated a gloomy day at Manchester. 'Tony MacGibbon, Johnny Hayes and Bob Blair were big raw-boned bowlers, the pitch was damp, the light not good and the ball was moving about. Peter played and missed a few times, and I certainly did. The situation was quite awkward.'

Dexter wryly conveys his impression that the England captain considered him something of a young scallywag. 'He was probably right, but he offered me plenty of encouragement. He had been very kind and welcoming, as he always was, but I did not yet feel that I knew him very well. Suddenly he walked down the pitch and said: "There's nothing for it, I think they've got to go." The next thing I knew the ball was whistling over extra-cover and to all parts as he simply took the attack apart.'

The spectacle of conquest was revealed in perhaps even more withering style against Lancashire at Old Trafford later in the month. It is remembered by many observers for the absorbing duel between May and Brian Statham. Ken Barrington, in typically obdurate mood, scored 74 in a fourth-wicket stand of 145 runs. His resistance was the spur for a great innings. Statham and Higgs had opened up a wide and ominous breach. Surrey lost three wickets for 64 before May and Barrington came together. They did save Surrey from ignominy as is shown by the remarkable statistic that nine other batsmen scored only 63 runs between them. May's scintillating 174 (out of a total of 314) shone forth like a beacon amid the disarray.

Denys Rowbotham, in the *Manchester Guardian*, graphically described the innings. 'But for May, Lancashire's bowlers might have proved irresistible. When he came to the crease he looked as if already he had been batting for an hour. The pace of the wicket and fitful slight lift were as powerless to deceive him as Statham's whipped movement off the pitch. His judgement seemed well-nigh infallible. His feet moved so swiftly that he was positioned perfectly with time to spare for every shot. Howsoever Statham cut the ball repeatedly away from him, May's front foot was flawlessly planted. It seemed as if the ball's movement had been plotted clairvoyantly and the middle of the bat found by some mysterious act of magnetism.'

From the start of the innings, wrote Rowbotham, 'the majestic young man was attacking. Let Statham only once drop slightly short and the right foot was back and the stroke through the covers was punishing to see. The room and the time which May had to play these shots was as astonishing as it used to seem with Hammond.

'May could no more be hurried than he could be moved fatally into error. He lay back and bludgeoned Statham's few short balls with a suave imperviousness which disguised the degree to which they often lifted. Not until Loader joined him did he once depart from strict, groomed correctness, relinquish an atom of his poise, indulge a single rhetorical gesture, or make an ungrammatical shot.'

The exhilarating innings ended in a carnival of strokes. May opened his shoulders with a vengeance. He drove Higgs mightily over mid-off for six, and then hit him high to long-on for four. The Lancashire bowlers reeled giddily in his wake. Statham stood, hands on hips in bewilderment, as one thunderous stroke, driven scarcely credibly off the back foot, hurtled past him, and over deep mid-off.

Statham, at last, gained the prize which had eluded him throughout a long and challenging day. May drove once too often and was bowled. In five hours of supreme batsmanship, he had unfurled a vintage innings as peerless as any witnessed in this famed cricketing arena.

Another witness of the master batsman on the rampage in 1958 was Tony MacGibbon. He was New Zealand's most successful bowler that summer, taking 20 wickets in the series at 19.45 runs each. He rates May, along with Everton Weekes, as the most dangerous of his rivals. 'Peter was a magnificent driver, always controlled and in the correct position, and very severe on any loose ball. But he was such a pleasant person that, even if you got him out, you felt sorry to see him go, even after he had hit me for six over extra-cover off the back foot.'

Chapter 9
First Without Equal

'If there was not a Saint Peter already, all the Surrey professionals who played with Peter May would press for his instant canonisation.'

J. J. Warr

The Oval class in which Peter May registered in the early 1950s was on the brink of unparalleled distinction. Its audacious headmaster was the champion optimist, Stuart Surridge, who was to bully and cajole Surrey to five of their seven successive championships in the unlovely but lovable Kennington arena.

Surridge bequeathed a legacy of glorious adventure to May, his successor as captain. Micky Stewart is another of the graduates in this distinguished academy. 'Everyone from the most senior to the lowliest of juniors had huge respect for "Stewie" Surridge. He had his limitations as a cricketer, but he took useful wickets and made runs at the right time. Above all, he set the best possible example in the field.'

Douglas Jardine reflected on the influence of Surridge, which enabled Surrey to assume the ascendancy in 1952. Surridge was aged thirty-four when he acceded to the leadership. He followed Michael Barton, a fine tactician but a gentleman of milder temper. The gain in authority dealt Surrey a winning hand and the first title to be held outright by them since 1914. 'There was a world of difference between the good, workmanlike stuff served up before Surridge and the dynamic current with which he charged it for the next five years,' said Jardine.

Alec Bedser regarded Surridge as the last true amateur, an independent spirit who, whatever the odds, always thought that Surrey could win. There was a collective spread of endeavour. 'Every day, under Stewie, we tried to make things happen,' says Bedser. One example of his whirlwind captaincy belongs to the championship year of 1953 when Surrey completed their programme by beating Warwickshire by an innings in a day.

Members rose in unison to acclaim the team. The last and only time that a first-class match had finished in a day was at The Oval in 1857. Warwickshire were dismissed for 45 and 52. Bedser took twelve wickets, including eight for 18 in the first innings, and Laker performed the hat-trick. Twenty-nine wickets fell in the day. Testifying to the brilliance of the fielding was the fact that not one of the visiting batsmen was bowled. Warwickshire, in their second innings, were all out in seventy minutes, five minutes fewer than in their first innings.

Alfred Gover remembers that Surridge, as he lifted his team to world-class status, was unmistakably the leader. At the beginning of his reign, one of his gifted followers, Jim Laker, went up to the amateurs' dressing-room to see his newly appointed captain. Laker said that he and his colleagues would be only too pleased to ease his path with advice. 'No thank you, Jim,' said Surridge. 'I'm the boss.'

In the ensuing years Surridge, driving his team with taunting expletives, showed why such aid was unnecessary. Peter May was not excluded from the withering rebukes. 'He didn't understand Stewie at first,' says Gover. 'The skipper used to chase him like blazes.' Peter never forgot one valuable maxim which became an abiding rule in his own cricketing philosophy. 'Remember, Peter, it's no use being second,' stressed Surridge. 'You must be first.'

It was a lesson which Surridge himself had committed to memory. His own adviser had been Brian Sellers, the Yorkshire captain in their great years and briefly at the helm after the war. Surrey had held the initiative for most of one match against Yorkshire, only to lose in the end. Surridge, in some despair at an unexpected reverse, spoke to Sellers after stumps. 'We were winning easily yet you turned it round and beat us,' he said. There was a certain irony in that Surridge took the bold route set by the Yorkshire navigator. It was the basis of his conquests when he relegated Yorkshire into second place in his own special era.

Micky Stewart has referred to how Surridge eliminated the gulf between amateurs and professionals at The Oval. Peter May, in his turn, recalled that Surridge was wholeheartedly pledged to his players' welfare. 'He insisted that we all shared railway carriages and stayed at the same hotels, which had not previously been the custom.' May also noted the 'boundless energy' of their engaging pilot. 'With his drive, impatience, often unconventional approach and touch of irascibility, he was regarded with profound respect, trust and indeed affection. His style of captaincy was unusual, but it worked – and we all knew it did.'

Arthur McIntyre has dwelt upon the percipient trait in Surridge's buccaneering leadership. 'No one read the game, or a given situation, as well as Stuart. He believed that it was easier to chase runs than get wickets.' Surridge's manifesto was direct to a point of simplicity. 'If you get 200, the other side has to score 201. We didn't get a lot of runs. But we got enough. Besides, if we'd scored many more, I wouldn't have known when to declare.' Doug Insole, as one of Surrey's opposing captains, says Surridge was completely confident in his own judgement. 'Stewie was a great character and some of his declarations were a little bizarre. He wanted to win matches in one day if possible. But he did have the standby of a second innings if matters went awry.'

Sir Leonard Hutton endorsed the verdict of others that the Surrey team was powerful enough to bear comparison with the famed Yorkshire team of the 1930s. Essentially, it comprised one of the finest bowling attacks in the history of the game. It had an envied balance of Test bowlers to thrive in all conditions: Alec Bedser and Peter Loader to provide the opening thrust, complemented by Tony Lock and Jim Laker in spinning harness. Behind the wicket was Arthur McIntyre, whose England appearances were restricted by the brilliance of Godfrey Evans. 'Little Mac', as he was known, was quietly efficient, unfussy and always dependable. He was accounted the equal of Evans in standing up to Bedser's accurately delivered inswingers. His deftness in taking them on the leg-side was an illustration of his fine art.

McIntyre recalls one match against Sussex during the immediate postwar captaincy of Errol Holmes. Bedser untypically lost his temper when Holmes refused to allow him a gully fieldsman for Jim Langridge. 'Alec and I both knew that Langridge was a candidate for a catch in that area. Alec was red-faced with anger. I was standing up to him as usual. He felt he bowled better that way. He pounded in to bowl and the ball fairly hurtled into my gloves, rocking me back on my heels. Alec had really got his dander up.'

Peter May recalled that these were 'exciting times in which to play cricket'. One of the great strengths of Surrey, he told me, was that they had such a good second team. 'We often had at least four players on England duty. Those chaps who deputised when we were away were quite happy to play in the seconds. They considered it an honour to represent Surrey.' The batting abilities of one loyalist, Eric Bedser, who opened for Surrey on occasions, gave him first-team status as an all-rounder. But his off-spinners were only fully employed when Jim Laker was absent. Geoffrey

Howard, the former Surrey secretary, remembers the assessment of another county stalwart, Bob Gregory, who played from 1925 to 1947. Gregory had no hesitation in advancing the view that Eric Bedser had the potential to become an England bowler. With any other county, Bedser would have been assured of the 'double' (100 wickets and 1,000 runs) each season.

The conflicting personalities of Surrey's match-winning spinners, Laker and Lock, required constant attention. Peter May must have looked on with more than cursory interest as Surridge released their animosity to the profit of Surrey. He was provided with a salutary lesson in the management of temperamental players. 'Stewie was a great disciplinarian. He transformed the team, drove the buggers and swore at them. Locky used to bowl dripping with anger,' recalls Doug Insole.

Alfred Gover explains the psychology adopted by Surridge. There was invariably a velvet-gloved approach in his dealings with Laker. 'He used to butter-up Jim: c'm on, I'll give you another short-leg.' The accusatory method worked better with Lock. 'I've never seen such (expletive deleted) bowling. What are you supposed to be . . . doing? Now, c'm, for God's sake.' Gover adds: 'Locky would shake his head in disbelief at the Gaffer, redouble his efforts and probably take a crucial wicket.'

Insole eavesdropped, to his considerable delight, on one vigorous conversation between the Surrey captain and his embattled spin bowler. Eric Bedser was bowling in tandem with Lock in one match against Essex. Insole was at the striker's end and facing Bedser. Surridge and Lock stood shoulder to shoulder in the leg-trap. Between balls their opponent became aware of a fractious exchange of views. 'Stewie was accusing Lock of not being able to spin the ball.' Lock indignantly pointed to his gnarled spinning finger. 'What do you know about it?' he responded. Insole listened to the talk with mounting rapture. He told Surridge: 'I want to get runs off Eric, but I'm enjoying your conversation so much that I'd rather stay at this end.'

As with their counterparts, Johnny Wardle and Bob Appleyard in Yorkshire, there was a turbulence in relations between Lock and Laker at The Oval. But, pursuing the analogy, the Surrey bowlers fitted each other like two well-worn gloves. The gauntlets, to stretch the metaphor, were at times quarrelsomely raised; but they hunted voraciously as a pair. Stuart Surridge, as the wily ringmaster, ensured sharpened appetites in the pursuit of wickets.

There are insistent claims that the Oval wicket was expressly tailored for Surrey bowlers. Certainly it did possess demons unknown in the pre-war groundsmanship of 'Bosser' Martin when the wickets were as unyielding as concrete and overwhelmingly in the batsman's favour. After the war and the use of The Oval as a POW camp, it became a different kind of beast. Martin's successor, Bert Lock, was regarded malignly in some quarters as Surrey's twelfth man.

Peter May exonerated Lock in defence of his home ground. He said that the Surrey bowlers were incensed at the charges that the pitches were prepared for them. 'These implied a subtlety, a prescience and a deviousness that Bert and his staff did not possess.' May recalled that the Surrey team were often assured that a splendid pitch was at their disposal. 'The promise left us rather mystified when we found ourselves, or our opponents, on the rack at 43 for 7.'

Arthur McIntyre even more pertinently stresses that the Oval wicket aided both teams: 'We had to bat on it as well as the opposition.' Micky Stewart was one of the home batsmen confronted with its perils. 'The Oval wasn't the easiest pitch to bat on in the 1950s. It used to break up either before noon on the first day, or before tea on the second day. I fielded for Surrey for three years before we faced a total of 300.' If the Oval wicket could be a preposterous terrain, then there is statistical evidence to deny its overriding value in Surrey's successes. The figures (given in the statistical appendix) conclusively reveal that Lock and Laker in championship matches obtained more wickets away from The Oval.

A weary Surrey, having retained the title, collapsed against the spinning wiles of Roy Tattersall and Malcolm Hilton at The Oval in September 1956. Prolonged celebrations to mark the fifth championship and the retirement of Stuart Surridge were probably a factor; but the downfall did indicate the opportunities to be grasped by visiting bowlers. Tattersall and Hilton shared 16 wickets for the Rest of England eleven; the champions were unexpectedly dismissed for 71 and 72, and lost by 128 runs.

Doug Insole, the Rest captain, snatched a leaf out of Surridge's book when he applied a second-innings declaration at 79 for three. Frank Tyson, as Tattersall recalled, was relaxing in the bath at the time and had to emerge swiftly to join his colleagues on the field. Arthur Milton, another superb and fearless close fieldsman, was a member of the Rest team. 'Art was taking 'em off the edge of the bat in that match,' says Tattersall. Milton regularly vied with Surridge in the catching lists. It was a moment to relish for him, if not the Oval crowd, when he captured the wicket of his challenger. On his last appearance at the Oval, Surridge was applauded all the way to the wicket and back again after Milton clung on to a catch in the leg-trap.

Roy Tattersall takes the well-supported view that he, along with other bowlers of his stature, could be just as menacing as the Surrey spinners on the Oval wicket. 'It did suit their attack, but it also benefited ourselves from Lancashire.' Lancashire, ill-favoured by the weather at Old Trafford, were close contenders for the championship in 1956. They lost two matches, three fewer than Surrey, and took part in fourteen drawn games. A few days before the Rest's overthrow of the champions, they came to The Oval, needing to beat Surrey to retain any interest in the title quest. Tattersall and Hilton were again in command, taking nine wickets in the first innings. Surrey were bowled out for 96, but rain intervened and there was no play on the last two days.

There was, though, except on rare occasions, an inevitability about Surrey's rampant progress in the 1950s. It led to one seemingly extravagant expression of confidence by the pre-war Surrey amateur captain, Monty Garland-Wells. He was so impressed with Surridge's prediction that Surrey would win five consecutive titles that he placed an accumulator on seven in a row. After four years he accepted a settlement from the bookmaker and, with the proceeds, threw a celebration party for the victorious team.

Emulating the traditional Roses rivalry were the contests between Surrey and Yorkshire in this period. So close were the encounters that they exercised a fascination as compelling as the most intense Test match. Watching the combatants, almost literally on tiptoe, were massed crowds, totalling as many 60,000. The narrow divide between the teams can perhaps best be judged from the fact that they jointly supplied thirteen players to England in one season. In 1955, the Surrey representatives were May, Barrington, Lock, Alec Bedser, Laker, Loader and McIntyre. Yorkshire contributed six others: Wardle, Appleyard, Trueman, Lowson, Close and Watson.

Yorkshire made Surrey fight hard for their fourth championship in this summer of glorious weather. The feast had only twice previously been accomplished under the same captain. Yorkshire, led by Brian Sellers, were the champions in three seasons immediately before the Second World War and for one season afterwards. Alfred Shaw captained Notting-hamshire in their run of four titles from 1883 to 1886.

Surrey, fielding probably the finest team in the club's history, were just as imposing in their rule. They set up a new record for championship points since the system of awarding 12 points for a win, and 4 points for a lead on the first innings, was introduced in 1938. Surrey recorded 23 victories out of 28 games to total 284 points. Yorkshire, in fierce but unavailing pursuit, won 21 games. An aggregate of 268 points beat their previous highest total of 260, achieved in 1939.

Significantly, Surrey held their catches, 383 in all, and three players – Surridge, Lock and Micky Stewart – shared 156 of them. Stewart was a key figure in the close fielding cordon which contributed so much to Surrey's triumphs. His agility and enthusiasm sprang from his youthful admiration of the West Indian all-rounder, Learie Constantine. Stewart stills holds the Surrey record of 604 catches; his tally of 77 in 1957, including seven in one match at Northampton, is the second highest by a non-wicket-keeper. It is only one short of the record established by Wally Hammond in 1928.

Of his fielding to the exuberant Tony Lock (another amazing pick-pocket at short-leg) he once said: 'If Locky is bouncing them, I ought to be able to "cop" them off the splice.' Stewart was only one of many vigilant performers who, brave and helmetless, crouched unflinchingly beneath the batsman's gaze. He was a trusting accomplice, encouraged by the mean accuracy of his bowlers on the uncovered wickets of the time.

Peter May gloried in the gladiatorial struggles with Yorkshire. The North-country pundits were scandalised by his treatment of Johnny Wardle in one match. Wardle recalled: 'Peter was a tremendous player and he sorted me out on a bad wicket at The Oval. I don't think Surrey got many more than 180 and he scored a hundred of them. He refused to move away from me. All he did when I pitched it up was to hit it as hard as he could. He was dropped three times, twice at slip off thick edges. But they were sharp chances.'

Jim Kilburn, the *Yorkshire Post* correspondent, watched the assault. 'May is among the great batsmen of any age,' he reported, 'and he illustrated his quality with every over he played. His innings was not flawless; the incalculable behaviour of the ball left him helpless occasionally, but he was never less than magnificent. He exposed erratic length and increased its incidence by square cuts, drives and leg-hits of thrilling power and beauty. One over from Wardle summarised the whole character of his deeds. It contained a late cut for two, an off-drive for four, an edged boundary that might have been a slip catch, an uninhibited six over mid-off and a despairing appeal for lbw.'

The hurricane display was a typically robust response from a player who knew his responsibilities as the lynchpin of the Surrey batting. 'When Peter was in prime form it was entertaining to be at the other end,' says

Micky Stewart. 'You learned much about batting in his company. He was very attentive to his partners, encouraging them all the time. Essentially we batted as a pair, although, like all great players, he was a good counter of balls in an over. Of course, everybody was willing to run for him.'

There was, however, one occasion when Stewart failed to discharge this duty. It happened against Middlesex in one of his early seasons at The Oval. 'I was one of the few people who ran him out, but it was his fault anyway. I could have sacrificed my wicket, but it didn't enter my head. I sent him back.' Stewart, following his first innings duck, now had to make amends. The game was played on a fiery, green wicket, well exploited by Warr and Moss in the heavy atmosphere in Surrey's first innings; and then crumbling to allow the spin of Lock to work its wonders. Surrey were the victors by 39 runs. Before this was achieved, Stewart, without May, had to provide runs as a ballast. His 60 was of inestimable value and did much to relieve his conscience.

Stewart recalls May's good, dry sense of humour, called upon notably in his cricket dealings with Ken Barrington, his redoubtable fellow townsman from Reading. The business of running was quite hazardous with Barrington. The cadences of his calling – a kind of pleading whine – had canine origins. 'Peter was often on the receiving end of "Yes, no, wait" situations with Kenny.' As Barrington, smiling weakly, regained his ground, May would imitate his confused chatter. 'Woof, woof,' he would call out to his rueful partner.

May never considered himself beyond reproach. Stewart, as a good hooker and cutter, once heedlessly surrendered his wicket in a match against Hampshire at Portsmouth. He was in the nervous nineties, but his partnership with May had built up well in Surrey's cause. 'Peter came in at tea and gave me some stick,' remembers Stewart. May went out after the interval and, sighting a juicy long hop, holed out in identical fashion. At the end of the day Stewart and May exchanged companionable smiles. 'Don't say anything, Micky,' said Peter. 'Just try and remember, word for word, what I said to you at tea. It will teach me a lesson.' Peter was mentally lashing himself in this dilemma.

John Warr alludes to the 'barmy theory' advanced by others that May was fallible against leg-spin. One exponent, judged supreme in the art, was Bruce Dooland, the Australian, who was then playing for Nottinghamshire. May countered his critics in scoring 135, 74 and 211, all not out, against his Midland rivals in three successive innings. The second of these scores was achieved in an exhilarating race against the clock at Trent Bridge in

1955. Dooland had to view a less than satisfactory concession of 178 runs. Surrey were set a target of 188 in two hours. One local wag accused Reg Simpson, the Nottinghamshire captain, of 'throwing the match'. Arthur McIntyre, after his first innings century, joined May in the helter-skelter surge to victory. They added 149 in 57 minutes and Surrey won by eight wickets, with 33 minutes to spare.

McIntyre remembers the bewilderment of Arthur Jepson, one of the Nottinghamshire bowlers. As the boundaries mounted, a distraught Jepson could be heard complaining: 'Bugger me, bugger me!' So violent was May's bombardment of the covers that Freddie Stocks, one of the hapless patrolmen there, approached Peter between the overs. His hands were seared with bruises. Stocks had just been paid and he pulled out a bundle of notes from his hip pocket. 'What's it worth to get out?' he jokingly asked. 'We're fed up with you in the covers.'

Between 1952 and 1956, the years of Stuart Surridge's reign, Surrey were victorious in 86 matches, with winning margins in the championship ranging from 16 to 32 points. Lock, Laker, Alec and Eric Bedser, Loader and Surridge between them took 2,163 wickets, all but two of them with averages of under 20. One Yorkshire player paid his tribute to the inspirational Surridge. 'If we had had Stuart as captain during those five years, we would surely have done just as well.'

When two more titles were garnered under the captaincy of Peter May, there were other wry words of praise in the *Yorkshire Post*. 'Here we are plucking our forelocks in humble acknowledgement of a feat, which every county said could not be done. Every county, except Surrey, of course.' The correspondent added: 'If we allow this to continue, it will become harder to convince the rising generation that Surrey don't own the championship.'

The duels between Surrey and Yorkshire in the 1950s prompted one writer to reminisce and select a combined team representative of Yorkshire in the 1920s, and Surrey thirty years later. It was a distinctive array of talents. He chose: Holmes, Sutcliffe, May, Rhodes, Kilner, McIntyre, Laker, Lock, Bedser, Macaulay and Surridge. Separating the opening pairing of Hobbs and Sutcliffe is not credible; but Holmes, along with Surrey's Andrew Sandham, would have graced any opening assembly. The nostalgic selection discounted the giants of other ages, not excluding those opposed to Surrey in their greatest years.

'Man for man,' said one New Zealand writer in 1954, 'the Yorkshire eleven was the equal if not superior to Surrey, but the better moulded team won the championship.' Surrey, in this season, appeared unlikely title aspirants. At the end of July they were eighth in the table, trailing 46 points (96 to 142) behind Yorkshire. The sequel was a remarkable transformation. In their last ten matches, Surrey won nine outright, including five in two days, and claimed 112 out of a possible 120 points. Yorkshire, in their remaining twelve games, beginning on 10 July, could only muster 52 out of a possible 144 points. They were ultimately consigned to second place, 22 points behind the leaders. Coinciding with Surrey's triumph was another event which brought immense satisfaction to Peter May. His brother, John, was a member of the Berkshire eleven which won the Minor Counties championship. 'The family felt very proud of having a finger in two championship pies,' said May.

The writer Gordon Ross recalled Surridge's reaction when the odds seemed insuperably stacked against him in 1954. Motoring home from The Oval one evening, he said: 'Stewie, you honestly don't believe you have any chance of winning the championship this season, do you?' For a moment he thought Surridge was going to stop the car and order him out. 'What are you talking about?' he replied. 'Of course, we shall win it.' Ross added: 'I never asked him any more silly questions.'

Surrey's efficiency in all departments of the game ensured their tenure as champions. Yorkshire – and their grieving supporters – had to accept that they no longer had an inalienable right to the championship pennant. Yet they clung on grimly to gain second place four times and were third on two occasions. The emphasis on the futility of a secondary role now dictated the governance at The Oval.

The sequence of five victories over Yorkshire in the 1950s included the first double for thirty-six years. Yorkshire recklessly squandered an opportunity in Jim Laker's benefit match at The Oval in June 1956. The match was dominated by the bowling of Lock and Appleyard, who each took nine wickets. It was completed in two days. At the last, Yorkshire, set a modest target of 124 runs, tumbled from 60 for two to 100 all out.

The defeat was replicated in another fluctuating battle in the return fixture at Bramall Lane, Sheffield. Yorkshire gained a first-innings lead of 61, a commanding advantage in a low-scoring game. Peter May, top scorer in the match with 68, and Barrington added 94 for the third wicket in Surrey's second innings; but Yorkshire's position seemed unassailable when they began the last fresh and breezy morning, needing only 67 runs, with eight wickets in hand.

'Yorkshire,' wrote Jim Kilburn in stern admonition, 'devised a crisis with incredible simplicity. They descended to one of the most miserable, unrealistic displays of batting they can ever have presented. It had neither strength nor sense; it invited disaster and humiliation.'

Tony Lock had been held in reserve because Surrey did not consider the pitch was ready for his spin. He was not called upon until Yorkshire had laboured to 50 for 4. A position of stalemate threatened. Lock swiftly bowled Close to give Surrey a faint prospect of victory. In the end, Lock and Loader were almost contemptuous in their mastery. Lock furiously swept aside the Yorkshire tail. His final figures were five wickets for 11 runs. Surrey, against all expectations, were the victors by 14 runs. 'The unbelievable story had become reality,' wrote Kilburn. 'Yet neither Lock, nor Loader, nor Bedser, nor the pitch made Yorkshire's scourge. They fashioned their own.'

Surrey, urged on by Surridge, could scarcely believe their luck. Opposed by frail batting, they became increasingly convinced of their own invincibility. For an hour-and-a-half Yorkshire defended like slaves in chains; and then abandoned hope in the madness of a wild counter-attack. Alec Bedser remembered the fusillade of cushions, pitched on the ground by the disgruntled Sheffield partisans. The adjacent factories fashioned their protest at the impending defeat. Plumes of smoke belched forth from the chimneys as a signal of distress to reinforce the old legend. Micky Stewart recalled: 'After we had taken three or four wickets, the smoke was so dense I thought they'd set the stadium on fire.'

The rivalry between Surrey and Yorkshire had never been more intense than in the previous year, 1955. The two counties traded success with success; at times they were bracketed together at the top of the table, but significantly for only four days during the summer did Surrey yield first place. The major turning point occurred in Arthur McIntyre's benefit match at the beginning of June. On a treacherous pitch Surrey won by 41 runs, but not without being given a fright. Yorkshire finally succumbed within twenty minutes of the safety of a draw. Appleyard, making his off-breaks rise wrist-high, took seven wickets in Surrey's first innings. His challenge was met by the double thrust of Lock and Loader with four wickets each. Yorkshire's lead of 47 runs on the first innings became a deficit of 216, as May and Fletcher built up their match-winning partnership.

One Surrey supporter, with mingled loyalties, expressed his compliments to Yorkshire on their resistance in the fraught climax to the game. Bill (W. H. H.) Sutcliffe's valiant 40, an innings of fine defensive skills, lasting two hours and twenty minutes, did not go unnoticed. 'How lovely it was to see young "Herbert Hobbs" [Sutcliffe's second and third Christian names] standing up to Bedser and Lock. His old dad would have been proud of him.' The measure of Yorkshire's standing in the south was revealed in a postscript to the message. 'May I thank you, Yorkshire, for that wonderful game at The Oval,' continued the correspondent. 'It was electric – real Surrey versus Yorkshire. You know we have a deep respect for you down here. It was a pity one of us had to lose. We have learned very thoroughly that nobody has beaten Yorkshire until the last Tykes' wicket has gone down and the stumps pulled up.'

Two weeks later, at Headingley, another thrilling contest drew a crowd of over 60,000 people. Surrey were beaten by six wickets. It was their first defeat in sixteen consecutive games, denting a record which stretched back to July in the previous season. The gates were closed on the Saturday when Surrey staged a spectacular recovery after losing eight wickets for 119 runs. By a combination of misfortune and misjudgement Yorkshire surrendered their advantage. Lock, at no. 9, scored 55; Loader, at no. 10, scored 81; the ninth-wicket pair added 96 runs, the tenth, 53. 'Some of them were lucky runs from the edge of the bat and some were skied hits to untenanted parts of the field,' reported the *Yorkshire Post*. 'Once or twice the ball missed the stumps by those margins that lead bowlers to premature old age.'

Jim Kilburn conceded that the spirit in the batting was of 'such stuff as champions are made on . . . Lock and Loader were fortunate in the origins of their transfiguring stand, but they were brave and deserving in the development of it. The hitting was hard but selective; Yorkshire were outmanoeuvred as well as outfought.'

Yorkshire trailed by 102 runs on the first innings, but they forced their way back into contention in near darkness on the Monday evening. Street lamps were burning brightly when play ended after a furious bowling assault by Trueman and Mick Cowan. One observer commented: 'It was dark enough to make Aunt Edith a menace on the back lawn rather than the two Yorkshiremen hell-bent on destruction.' There were no light meters to ration the dismay of the Surrey batsmen. Peter May said the light was the darkest he could remember as a player in England. 'The umpires stoutly refused to go off – to the delight of a large and noisily jubilant crowd. The light on the scoreboard was described in the Surrey dressing-room as shining like a beacon on the Eddystone lighthouse.'

In an hour and forty minutes Surrey lost seven wickets for 27 runs.

Trueman's figures were three for 18 and Cowan's four for four. The Surrey rout was encompassed in alarming conditions when batting survival demanded physical courage in disproportionate relation to technical skill. Tony Lock was a survivor in such circumstances. He was battered from foot to shoulder, but he displayed exceptional tenacity as the unbeaten nightwatchman. His heroics were in keeping with the compliment paid to him by one Yorkshire player. 'Locky would be the man you would want alongside you in the trenches.'

Before a third-day crowd of 17,500 – the biggest at Leeds for many years – Yorkshire completed a cherished victory. It did, as one writer observed, prevent a revolution in the broad shires! Yet another defeat at the hands of Surrey would have sorely rankled. Yorkshire's target was 178 in three-and-a-quarter hours. The winning hit was made by Willie Watson with only ten minutes to spare.

Peter May, in Surrey's triumphant years, exuded authority as the exemplar of batting security. Gordon Ross said that watching him standing tall in the sunlight at The Oval could even make the gasholders appear to be covered with a resplendent sheen. 'Peter became as great in the minds of the Surrey habitués as Rad Hobbs in his day.' Attesting to May's mastery is the fact that out of all the batsmen, including Hobbs, Hayward, Sandham and John Edrich, to have scored over 10,000 runs for Surrey, he is the only one to have achieved an average in excess of 50.

May was also cherished for his integrity and unfailing courtesy. Testimonies abound to his civilised command. He would stride into The Oval, an umbrella tucked beneath his arm, like a City gent with an urgent appointment. Waving his greetings to everyone, not excepting the adoring gatemen, he would disappear into the pavilion, later to emerge as a god in whites.

Micky Stewart relates two stories which provide insights into May's personality. The first concerned a meeting with Brian Castor, the doyen of county secretaries, and the signing of his professional contract with Surrey. This was at a time when professionals were still expected to show deference in dealings with their amateur superiors. As late as 1963, when Stewart became the Surrey captain, he was allocated the huge amateur's dressing-room and had his own valet in attendance. The isolation did not suit him; after a few weeks he moved downstairs to join his fellow professionals.

Stewart remembers the earlier signing ceremony and the courtesy accorded to him by May. It was the renewal of an acquaintance, which had begun some years earlier. They had been rivals in a match between a Public Schools' XI and a Combined Services team at Lord's in 1949. Peter, from that time, had shown considerable interest in the progress of the former Alleyn's School captain. Stewart, despite their narrow gap in years, could be regarded as May's protégé. He was given a cordial welcome at The Oval office. 'Thank you, Peter,' was Stewart's response to May's congratulations at the ceremony. Brian Castor frowned sternly and interjected: 'You mean, Mr May.' May turned to the Surrey secretary and said: 'Peter will do nicely, Brian.'

May's care and understanding was also demonstrated on the occasion of Stewart's wedding. 'I was playing professional football with Charlton and they wouldn't give me time off to get married,' recalls Stewart. The cricket and football seasons overlapped and Stewart was committed to a final match for Surrey, as champions, in the Scarborough Festival. It immediately preceded his call-up for soccer training at the Valley. 'Sheila and I were married on the Saturday and travelled up to Scarborough on the Tuesday. Peter, with every good intention, had arranged separate hotel accommodation for us.' The hopes of a quiet retreat for the newly married couple were abruptly banished. 'As we walked into the reception area, we met one of the cricketers. He said: "Is this where you are staying? It's a great place; no one goes to bed till five in the morning."' The honeymoon interlude, so kindly nominated by Peter, had to be postponed. Stewart and his wife instead joined in the revelry following Surrey's victory over the Rest XI before travelling back by sleeper to London.

May was fortunate, when he succeeded Stuart Surridge as captain in 1957, in the inheritance of a richly endowed team. It contrasted with the less favourable circumstances of his friend, Colin Cowdrey, at Kent. Cowdrey says: 'Peter did have an advantage in that he always played with good sides whereas I had to contend with poor sides.' It was a transitional period for Kent; and Cowdrey, captain at twenty-four, had to bolster a struggling team. Cowdrey says it was a benefit rather than an imposition. Holding the reins in precarious times enhanced his cricket wisdom and taught him how to deal with men. 'I was born to cope with failure. In my three years as an undergraduate at Oxford we never won a match.' A similar situation prevailed in Kent in his formative years. Many good and experienced players were nearing or had passed into retirement. 'In my first five years as Kent captain we won only about three or four matches a year.'

It is a matter for conjecture as to how the career of Peter May would have progressed in such a situation. What is certain is that he maintained the disciplinary rule fostered by Surridge at The Oval. He had been brought up in a hard school, but it is a measure of his intelligence that he kept a team of seasoned professionals under civilised control.

By his side were two encouraging men, Alec Bedser and Arthur McIntyre, who succeeded Andrew Sandham as the county coach in 1959. Peter, often away on Test duty, paid Bedser the honour of appointing him vice-captain. 'Alec was splendid in every way,' said May. 'So much depended upon him. He and I ran the show, including team selection.' McIntyre was another link in the chain of continuity. Blessed with a strong sense of responsibility, he was able to support May with his own censure when players became lax in their behaviour.

There was another strand in May's maturing leadership: the adoption of an unremitting approach to cricket. In this he followed the example of Leonard Hutton. 'Len did not believe in sparing the opposition once he had got them on the floor,' says John Warr. Doug Insole maintains that Hutton and Surridge, although totally dissimilar in temperament, were driven by an identical competitive urge. 'Stewie was, though, much more demonstratively belligerent.' May, by contrast, was quietly assertive, never unpleasant, but just as strict in his own way. His players knew what was expected of them. The politeness was deceptive: there was a hard and unforgiving streak; and a bright mind combined with an inner steel. Trevor Bailey, in his assessment, says: 'Peter, at his best, combined some of the drive of Surridge with the tactical tightness of Hutton. His considerable personal charm tended to camouflage his toughness on the field.'

John Perry, his close friend from Charterhouse days, endorses the picture of a resolute captain. 'Peter was so gentle, courteous and polite, but he was never a soft touch. Every decision he made was just and fair, and with explanation. It was all done with the minimum of fuss. He was stern when necessary and *better* with difficult men, who could win him the game.'

Micky Stewart intriguingly makes a final comparison in the captaincy styles of the two conquering leaders at The Oval. He disputes the image of Stuart Surridge as the implacably hard captain. 'Stewie was really just like a big, cuddly teddy bear. It was the quiet, traditional English gentleman, as represented by May, who had the iron-clad personality. Peter, straight and sincere, was the harder man.'

Chapter 10
The Record Reign

'Peter was never off-hand or aloof. You could talk to him. There was no
"us and them". In the team he was unmistakably one of us.'

Fred Trueman

The calm of the young leader brought allegiance from those who might
have proved enemies. The boyish appearance of Peter May, England's
most successful postwar captain, concealed an unyielding command. 'He
was a quiet, not a shouting captain,' observes one Test partner, Peter
Richardson. 'But he had a presence about him which was unusual. You
always watched him.'

The disarming manner tended to dissolve quarrels on and off the field.
Fred Trueman, one of his bowling lieutenants, remembers that May did
not slip into arrogance. 'The bull-at-a-gate, say as I do, approach was not
Peter's style.' He was also, as Fred and others maintain, an approachable
man, who mingled with his team after play. Roy Tattersall recalls that his
skipper 'liked his pint of beer as much as anyone', and Peter Richardson
describes May as a 'steady supper'. During his bachelor days, Peter liked to
relax on the dance floor. As the England captain on tour, he had to take
the lead in social events. One of his ballroom partners, after an uneasy
quickstep, offered a polite inquiry. She asked him: 'Tell me, are you a
dancer?' Peter replied: 'No, but I like the sensation of the room going
round me.'

The essence of May's captaincy combined an unswerving dedication
with a sensitive awareness of the need to harness the talents of his team. It
was not in his nature to act the tyrant. His way was to encourage, not to
rule by coercion. Vernon Pennell, a Fellow of Pembroke College,
Cambridge, wrote: 'The burden of captaincy might well have daunted
anyone older than Peter. It was only his supreme tact and delightful

personality which enabled him to captain a team, in which he was far from being the oldest member, and yet retain his run-scoring abilities.'

The qualities which were to carry May to the zenith of distinction were foreshadowed in one early test of his authority. The encounter was with Johnny Wardle, a Yorkshireman of unpredictable temper. Peter recalled: 'When I first captained him I realised that I'd given him the wrong end. So I took him off after four overs.' Wardle, outraged by the decision, angrily snatched his sweater. He was not a happy man. Peter quickly saw he had to sort out an impending conflict. He said: 'I'm sorry, Johnny, but I am your captain; if I take you off, that's it.' It was a timely intervention. The gulf in their ages could have been an obstacle had May then meekly given way to a senior professional, who was to become one of his favoured bowlers. 'Johnny did recognise that although I was young I was going to be the boss. He was never any trouble after that little spat. We had a very good relationship.'

The unexpected withdrawal of Leonard Hutton thrust May into the captaincy spotlight against the South African tourists in 1955. Hutton had initially been confirmed as captain for the series, but was forced to concede that his great career had run its course. The first symptoms of his flagging health came when he led the MCC against the tourists at Lord's in May. An attack of lumbago compelled his retirement from the match after the opening day. The ravages of his illness were also reflected in his declining form. Two ducks, one against Sussex and another against Surrey at The Oval, were followed by two more batting failures in the return fixture against the champion county at Headingley.

'Test cricket demands a high degree of physical fitness,' said Hutton. 'In addition to my back trouble, I have been troubled by my left arm.' This was a legacy of a wartime accident. After his tour of Australia, Hutton, never a robust man, was also disconcerted by the English chills. 'Coming back to our climate has not helped my back problems, either.' Peter May, as Hutton's vice-captain in Australia, was thus presented with an onerous task. 'Len's retirement,' he said, 'was a melancholy event because it seemed so abrupt and premature. Yet I had realised that he was no longer enjoying his cricket.'

At twenty-six, May became the youngest player, other than David Sheppard in a caretaker capacity in 1954, to captain England for nearly thirty years. Percy Chapman, at twenty-five, and another Reading townsman, had famously won his first laurels in the Ashes triumph of 1926. May's promotion brought renewed distinction to Pembroke College. He was the fifth member of the college to lead England in a Test series. His predecessors were Chapman, Arthur Gilligan and Frank and George Mann, the latter two then the only father and son to have captained England.

Alan Gibson was among those who thought that May had been pitched into the captaincy too soon. 'Another couple of years without the responsibility might have given him the confidence to be more adventurous.' May, in 1955, had not yet succeeded Stuart Surridge at The Oval; at Cambridge, his university peers had cast their vote for David Sheppard, whose more extrovert personality did advance him as a candidate to succeed Hutton. As late as his sabbatical year of 1962–63, Sheppard, who toured Australia under Ted Dexter, was earnestly pressed to take over the captaincy. Bearing in mind these intentions – and the status Sheppard evidently held within the MCC hierarchy – it is quite likely that May would again have been overlooked had his former Cambridge rival not chosen to go into the ministry.

As events unfolded, it became apparent that May was far from being a mild, alternative choice. He had, as Alan Gibson put it, 'crammed himself into the mould of Hutton'. Jim Swanton confirmed May's understanding of and affection for the professionals who played under him for England. 'The purest of amateurs himself, he never forgot that their livelihood depended very much on his consideration and his personal performance. He was the antithesis of the legendary carefree amateur.'

Peter was unfailingly loyal to his team. 'A good day for the boys,' he would say, even when he knew the reverse was the case. He did not wield the big stick, which may have led to accusations of leniency; but no one was more severe on irresponsible players. He was quietly scathing about batsmen who played recklessly in a crisis. Bowlers, too, were rebuffed if they gave less than their best.

Tom Graveney remarks on another characteristic which May shared with Wally Hammond. There was an austerity about Hammond, whose rigorous upbringing was a major cause in the rift between him and the lesser lights in Gloucestershire. 'Great players don't always appreciate the frailties of others not so talented,' says Graveney. 'Wally couldn't understand the disparity and he was very hard on people.' May, brought up in another stern home regime, upheld equally high standards. His temperament normally excluded feuds, but he could be sharply unforgiving in his relations with those who disappointed him.

Graveney recalls one rebuke, almost telepathically conveyed to him by

May at Trent Bridge in 1957. He had been recalled to the England team in the previous Test against the West Indies at Lord's. Having just reached his century, he pardonably relaxed. As he acknowledged the applause, he looked up to the pavilion. The greetings, as far as May was concerned, were premature. He was standing on the balcony, his hand rapping an urgent tattoo on the rail. Graveney instantly translated the code of his captain's message. 'Peter was telling me to get my bloody head down.' The sequel, as Graveney resumed his innings, amply justified the reprimand. He went on to his highest first-class score of 258, sharing, along the way, partnerships of over 200 with both Richardson and May.

On another occasion Peter Richardson was the target of this brusque style of command. 'That's the way Peter gave his rockets.' Without recourse to words, the frown of dismay communicated a warning to be heeded: 'Now, come on; smarten up and play properly.' The signals, discreetly but firmly expressed, were the mark of a great disciplinarian. 'Cricket wasn't a pastime with Peter,' Graveney points out. 'There weren't too many smiles on the field. He knew what he wanted to do and tried to make it happen.'

David Sheppard is at variance with Jim Swanton in his view that May established better relations between England and Australian players. 'When I first played against Australia in 1951, most of their side would not look at us on the field and there was a minimum of contact off the field, except by friendly individuals. "Do you think you can learn to hate these Australians for the next six months?" did not represent the whole atmosphere in which the games were played.' Sheppard does, however, maintain that these were the words used by a senior England player before his first tour of Australia in 1950–1.

When he returned to Test cricket in 1956 he expressly noted a change in the climate. 'The game was played just as hard, but in a new atmosphere of friendliness. May and Ian Johnson were the captains in 1956 and much of the credit must go to them.'

Swanton declares that the policy of non-fraternisation, instituted by Leonard Hutton, persisted under May's captaincy. He remembers that he was invited by the West Indies Cricket Board to take his first team to the Caribbean in 1956 in order to help normalise relations after the troubles of the previous England tour. He views with distaste what he considers was a serious blot on three MCC tours: to the West Indies (1953–54); to Australia (1954–55); and to South Africa (1956–57). On the latter tour he remembers that on the Wanderers ground in Johannesburg, where the

110

home and visitors' dressing-rooms adjoined, the connecting door had been locked on the MCC side.

'An unfriendly impression was created in the respective countries because of the deliberate policy of non-fraternisation followed by Len and also Peter.' Hutton's attitude to the opposition was, he believes, derived at least partly from a patriotic reaction against England's failures in the early postwar series in Australia and the West Indies.

Swanton recalls that Alec Bedser, who always enjoyed the congenial companionship of Australians, was once asked by Hutton not to mingle with them. Bedser retorted that, so far as he was concerned, hostility ended when stumps were drawn for the day. Tom Graveney was another similarly cheerful mixer. Both of them enjoyed the cut and thrust of repartee after working hours. It was not in their nature to refuse to take a glass of beer with their rivals after the close of play.

Swanton accepts that touring players do need to keep their own *esprit* high by sticking together. 'But there is a balance to be maintained requiring considerable managerial skills.'

Peter May later looked back nostalgically on the golden years of the 1950s. England did not lose a Test series for eight years. May led his country in a record 41 Tests (35 in an unbroken sequence) until 1961 and he was victorious in 21 Tests, another record. Eleven of his victories over South Africa, Australia, West Indies, New Zealand and India were by an innings. He suffered only nine defeats, including four in one series in Australia in 1958–59. The caution, which some of his critics thought impaired his captaincy, proved uncommonly fruitful. His instincts as a captain only once failed him – in the crucial match at Durban in the series in South Africa in 1956–57.

Doug Insole, his vice-captain on that tour, comments: 'Peter wasn't one to give chances to the opposition. He did not give too many runs away, or make foolish declarations. But he didn't have to be indulgent; with Surrey and England he had bowlers of the highest calibre.' May himself was politely dismissive of his critics. 'I was well aware that although I was an amateur – and a genuine one unsupported by sponsors or advertisers – I did not always play in the obviously light-hearted way which had been associated with some amateurs in the past.' He did not really need to make this reservation. The suggestion that he had only to throw the ball up to allow one or other of his eager bowlers to catch it implies a robotic control. May would not have been so successful had he just been a puppeteer routinely pulling the strings.

It is true that he did have an almost embarrassing choice. Any selection able to dispense on occasion with such bowlers as Trueman, Wardle, Les Jackson, and Laker and Lock, seems to enter the realm of lunacy. May recalled: 'Some of our longest selection committee meetings owed their length to painful decisions which had to be made to leave out bowlers of proven class just because others might be more effective on the type of pitch expected, or were thought to be fitter or in better form at the time.'

There were similarly disadvantaged batsmen. Peter Richardson, who came to the fore in May's time, observes: 'I couldn't afford to fail. There were so many others waiting to take my place.' It was not so disquieting as to quell his ebullience, for Richardson, an enormously confident left-hander, was one of the finds of the period. He occupied one problematic vacancy at the top of the order left by the retirement of Hutton. Colin Cowdrey, because of his prowess against fast bowling, was briefly a reluctant convert as an opening batsman. His partnership with Richardson prospered in one season in 1956.

Other opening permutations included Kenyon and Graveney; Bailey and Lowson; Ikin and Close; and Milton and M. J. K. Smith. England sorely needed Richardson as a dependable bulwark. He had no fewer than eight partners – Cowdrey, Close, Don Smith, Sheppard, Bailey, M. J. K. Smith, Milton and Watson – in five series between 1956 and 1958–59. Some were tactical selections, or forced by injuries, but they do illustrate one prolonged England dilemma not satisfactorily resolved amid the harvest of talents.

Peter May did not waver in his own batting empire. David Sheppard, on his England recall in 1956, noted an increased toughness. 'Peter had come through the fire of great Test matches and he was even hungrier for runs than he had been before. There was an intensity of concentration only matched by Hutton and Barrington among England players.' Louis Duffus, the South African writer, watched May in the previous season, his first year as England captain, at Lord's. 'May was the maestro of the day, with a power and timing that was a joy to behold,' he enthused. 'He looked on that day the most accomplished batsman in contemporary cricket.'

May ascended the heights of batsmanship for four years in the 1950s. So engrossing were his majestic exploits that one six o'clock newscast was delayed in order to announce the arrival of another century. In seven Test innings he failed only twice. Four home series between 1955 and 1958 produced a yield of 1,861 runs. Twice he averaged over 90, once against Australia

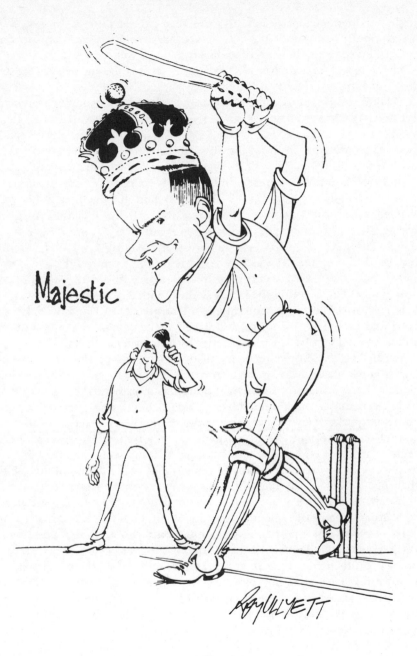

Majestic

while his opponents floundered on less than perfect pitches. In two series against South Africa and Australia he scored over 1,000 runs and in only three of his sixteen innings was he dismissed for fewer than 40.

The renewal of his rivalry with South Africa, against whom he had shown valour as a Test trialist four years earlier, brought equal satisfaction for May in his debut as captain. Jackie McGlew, one of his opponents in England in 1955, today acknowledges an astute captain and a fierce competitor. 'Peter was born to win,' says McGlew. 'He was always totally focused on the job in hand. It was his relentless concentration which ensured that his reign as England captain was such a gigantic success.'

In 1955, South Africa made history by winning two Test matches to fulfil the highest expectations of their compatriots. England, who were plagued by a crippling spate of injuries, were narrow victors in a see-sawing series. Louis Duffus said there was little to choose between the teams. The key factor dividing them was the batting supremacy of May and Denis Compton. May's two centuries, complemented by two other innings of 97 and 89 not out, gave him an aggregate for the series of 582 runs. They were accomplished, said Duffus, with a 'judgement, power and polish that marked his artistry among the aristocrats of English cricket. So much did he mean to England as a batsman and captain that without him South Africa might have won the series by four matches to one.'

South Africa's spirited recovery from two-down produced a series of high drama. Peter May was generous in his praise of the Springboks' fielding. They maintained a vigilant tradition upon which the spotlight has again been thrown in recent times. 'I don't think we'll ever see a better outfielding side,' May told his opposing captain, Jack Cheetham. 'Eight or nine of your team ran like stags and threw like bombs.' At the last, in the decisive match at The Oval, the South Africans were betrayed by frail batting. They were beaten by 92 runs. Lock and Laker countered the challenge in another tumble of wickets on their home ground.

It was, as Cheetham said in his congratulations, 'very nice for Peter to start his international captaincy on the winning side'. But a fluctuating series never at any time permitted complacency. South Africa possessed in Peter Heine and Trevor Goddard two young cricketers who grew in strength on their first overseas tours. Heine, the son of a Natal farmer, was a powerful man, standing over six feet four inches. His hostility and endurance gained him the acclamation of the England captain. May rated Heine as South Africa's most dangerous bowler. The left-handed Goddard was considered to have matured into the best all-rounder since the far-off days of G. A. Faulkner. His accurate and economical bowling, mostly directly at the leg-stump from over the wicket, was a persistent thorn in England's side. The decision by England to play five left-hand batsmen at The Oval was an attempt to combat the tightness of his attack.

The constancy of Tayfield's off-spin was another outstanding feature, as the tourists held winning sway in their pilgimage through the England counties. Ray Robinson, the Australian writer, provided an informative pen picture: 'Trousers billowing in a toes-out run, Tayfield mostly lands the ball in line with the off-stump, mixing straight top-spinners with off-breaks that turn enough to require careful watching. Making batsmen play forward ball after ball, he gnaws at their patience. He has the stamina of a Grand National winner, though only half the number of legs to keep him going.'

The tall and elegant Tayfield was a leading figure in the postwar renaissance of South African cricket. He was known as 'Toey' because of his habit of stubbing his toe into the ground before bowling. He followed spectacularly in the footsteps of Athol Rowan to become the highest wicket-taker in his country's history. His tally of 26 wickets in the 1955 series was unequalled by a South African in England and his overall total of 143 was the highest number earned by any bowler visiting England since the war. At The Oval, he took his 100th Test wicket in only his twenty-second Test. He bowled unchanged for five-and-a-quarter hours to return figures of five wickets for 60 runs in 53.4 overs.

The economy of another great bowler, Johnny Wardle, enabled Peter May to release Frank Tyson at his fastest on a rain-freshened pitch in the first Test at Trent Bridge. Tyson's conquest of the Springboks in the second innings was as comprehensive as any of his feats in Australia. He secured his 50th Test wicket after only nine Tests, and took six wickets for 28 runs in the innings. In his last spell he clean-bowled Cheetham, Tayfield, Winslow and Adcock. He took five wickets for five runs in 7.3 overs. South Africa were all out for 148, beaten by an innings and five runs.

Motoring back to London after the victory, Peter May was charged with anticipation. 'I remember thinking that if Frank could do it on a slow pitch, there must be a great future ahead for him and any side for which he played.' In the event, Tyson's success at Nottingham signalled the end of his short, meteoric Test career. He was fit to play in only one more Test that year, and in only the last match against Australia in 1956. 'Plagued by injuries,' recalled May, 'Frank lost the extra yard of pace and some of

115

his accuracy. He was never again the matchwinner of those few months.' Tyson played in eight more Tests, spread over four years, and took only another 24 wickets.

Brian Statham, with the finest bowling performance of the series, took seven wickets for 39 runs at Lord's. South Africa, set a target of 183, lost by 71 runs. Statham bowled unchanged for three hours and ten minutes; his spell of 29 successive overs was broken by a rest of two hours enforced by bad light and the tea interval. May recalled: 'He started again refreshed while the batsmen were correspondingly unsettled. McLean, Waite, Endean and Keith all fell to him in a wonderfully sustained piece of bowling.' Geoffrey Howard, then the Lancashire secretary, had mixed feelings about Statham's marathon. 'He came back to Old Trafford drained of energy. We were obliged to leave him out of the next county match.'

Roy McLean stormed the ramparts with a glorious century at Lord's. It was a cavalier display of unrestrained delight. It rose to a stirring crescendo of assault. Before he was bowled by Statham with the second last ball before lunch on the second day, he had scored 142 out of 196. It was a thrilling spectacle and his mastery in the end compelled Trueman to bowl with only a single slip. The rest of the fieldsmen were withdrawn in a deep circle. McLean was blessed with good fortune. He was missed six times. The lapses were heartbreaking for England and yet his batting was so enthralling that Arthur Gilligan said: 'What a beautiful innings! Thank goodness they didn't catch him.'

The most thrilling match of the series, conspicuous for uninterrupted sunshine, was the third Test at Manchester. May, with his second century in successive Tests, and Compton were associated in a third-wicket stand of 124 in England's second innings. Compton's demoralising 158 in the first innings was the highest of the series and he followed this with an irresistible 71 which Jack Cheetham regarded as the most destructive in the series. Colin Cowdrey recalled that Compton's car had broken down en route to the match. His kit had to be left behind, apart from a pair of boots. Denis was ferried to Manchester in a light aircraft piloted by a friend.

'On the morning of the match he wandered round the dressing-room collecting odd pieces, rather like a star who has just opened a Christmas fete.' The borrowed bat was pillaged from the bottom of Freddie Titmus's bag. It was, said Cowdrey, 'a grubby and well-seasoned object, which might well have been on exhibition at Lord's as used by W. G. Grace.' Denis was unconcerned by its condition. 'He proceeded to play two of the greatest innings I have ever seen,' added Cowdrey. 'The strokes poured out of this old bat with a mellow ring; it might have been Yehudi Menuhin at his special best.'

A display of vintage batting by Compton was desperately needed. England trailed by 237 runs on the first innings. Jim Kilburn related that Compton was the leader in the stand with May. 'He directed the ball along the path of his choice with the perfection of timing that eliminates all appearance of effort.' May found inspiration in the presence of his boyhood hero. 'Their batting was magnificent,' reported Kilburn. 'It raised itself above the match in which it was a part, transcending the situation and the statement on the scoreboard. It was batting beyond the saving or winning of the game.'

Three South Africans, McGlew, Waite and Winslow, had hit centuries in what was to prove a matchwinning first-innings total of 521. It was the first of two totals of 500 or more in the series. Louis Duffus, in a reflective postscript, said the fact that his country were twice able to reach such prominence against a formidable array of bowlers was due to their determination in adversity. At Manchester, South Africa required 145 for victory in two-and-a-quarter hours. They achieved the target, not without a few alarms, and won by three wickets. The chase for runs was a nail-biting affair. The clock had ticked on to leave only three minutes to spare in an exciting climax to the match.

At Leeds, England, with a much-changed team, lost the initiative after first reducing South Africa to 38 for five wickets, and then prising out two more batsmen before the total had reached three figures. England fared little better and Compton's 61 almost alone ensured a slender first-innings lead of 20 runs. Their decline was hastened by stout-hearted bowling by Heine and Tayfield in oppressive heat.

A crowd of 25,000 on the Saturday was speedily made aware of the pleasures of batting. South Africa, like penitents sworn not to repeat the sins of the first innings, took command of the game. The Headingley partisans, groaning with dismay, grew red-faced by the hour, in more than one sense. The temperature soared to 89°. It was the hottest at a Yorkshire venue since the war. It was serenely attuned to the gloating batsmen. McGlew and Goddard established a South African first-wicket record of 176 runs. Wardle, playing in his only Test at Leeds, and Lock shared the spinning duties for England. Between them they bowled 89 overs, toiling in unison through the long hours of the innings. There was never a hint that they might falter; their rivalry, on this occasion, was committed to a common cause.

South Africa drove home their advantage. McGlew, as acting captain, psychologically did not declare on the Monday morning; he elected to push the score up to 500. It was South Africa's highest second-innings total. England were given eight hours and twenty minutes to score 481, and at an unrealistic rate of 57 runs an hour. The mission was the security of a draw to preserve their lead in the series. But despite the resistance of May and Insole before lunch on the last day, England were unequal to the task. At one stage the score was 204 for three; and they looked hopefully towards a mirage of salvation.

Crowning several moves that proved successful, McGlew refused to take the new ball. It was a decision forced upon him because of the risk of injuries. The footholds at the Kirkstall Lane end had given trouble since the first day, first damaging Adcock's foot, and then restricting May's use of Statham. Heine attempted a trial run at the start of the play, but decided that the foothold was too hazardous and withdrew from the attack. South Africa effectively won the match, by 224 runs, with two bowlers. Goddard bowled unchanged for four hours to achieve remarkable figures of five wickets for 69 runs in 62 overs. Tayfield took five for 94 in 47.1 overs.

The turning-point was the downfall of Peter May, three runs short of another century. His going, reported Louis Duffus, set a torch to the zeal of the South Africans. May was lbw to Tayfield to the last ball of the morning. It was the fourth time in eight days that this wily bowler had dismissed him. Tayfield had twice taken May's wicket in the victory over Surrey at The Oval. Jim Kilburn said that May's uncertain back stroke, with lunch beckoning, was an error which must have made him the most distressed man in England at that particular moment.

'His consolation must be to reflect upon an innings of superb technique and fine spirit over four hours,' commented Kilburn. 'Half his skill and heart would have won the match for England in the first two days.' Peter, recalling his own disappointment said: 'The ball from Tayfield certainly turned an unexpected amount but this was one of those occasions when I bitterly reproached myself for getting out.'

South Africa, resilient and increasing in buoyancy throughout an exciting summer, could not seal their recovery in the final Test at The Oval. At the topmost rung, said Duffus, they slipped but in their ascent they had raised a blaze of Springbok glory.

★

The encores of the celebrities returning to Test cricket in 1956 would have graced a Royal Command performance. Wilf Wooller, one of the esteemed selectors in that year, recalls an invigorating chapter of events. The 2–1 victory over Australia, captained by Ian Johnson, holds pride of place in his memory as one of those series 'when we were walking on water'. It was a summer of inspired selections, including the recalls of David Sheppard (at Old Trafford) and Denis Compton (at The Oval). Another choice, heavily criticised and taken against the wish of Peter May, was that of the forty-one-year-old Cyril Washbrook. Washbrook, himself a selector, returned to the England team after an absence of five years. 'Surely the position is not as bad as all that,' was his response when Gubby Allen, the chairman of the selectors, advised him of the selection.

Washbrook confounded the sceptics in an epic swansong to his Test career. It was given impetus by a doleful start to the England innings. Ron Archer, deputising for Miller with the new ball, took three wickets for three runs in nine overs. His victims were Richardson, Cowdrey and Alan Oakman of Sussex. The England score was just 17 runs when the Lancashire veteran joined May at the wicket. Wooller remembers one of the finest pieces of psychological cricket he had ever seen. The old Red Rose warrior for once had a Yorkshire crowd on his side. He strutted out, his cap at the familiar rakish angle. 'Cyril took guard quietly, then he stood back and memorised the field. He looked down again, checked his guard, and signalled that he was ready. He played out the first over and the crowd settled down. It was as though he had given them a bromide.'

The challenge of a crucial innings was one to be relished. Washbrook and May added 187 runs for the fourth wicket to turn the tide in England's favour. The partnership only stumbled once, and not fatally. When Washbrook was 44 and the total exactly 100, he drove Johnson hard and shoulder-high to cover. Miller misjudged the hit against the background of spectators and spilled the catch. 'An innings with a chance is a diamond flawed,' wrote Jim Kilburn. 'But this flaw was a small detraction from the gleam and value of this gem. With half the higher criticism of cricket scorning his selection, Washbrook returned to the Test scene to magnify his reputation. He stood firm in the gravest of crises and played beautiful cricket.'

Washbrook recalled the splendid reception of the Yorkshire crowd. 'There is no doubt that did help me. I got off the mark fairly soon and felt at home in a short time.' There was, he insists, no anxiety as he approached what would have been a deserved century. He failed by two runs. He went for the hook in characteristic style; the ball from Benaud might have been dispatched on other days; but he was fractionally late as the ball struck his pads. 'I wasn't nervous, just beaten by a good ball and given out lbw,' says Washbrook. 'In fact, I was pleased to get as far as 98.'

Peter May, along with his veteran partner, was at his most businesslike as England climbed the long hill to recovery. It was a painstaking struggle against tight bowling. 'At ten minutes past six, the sun beamed a belated benediction,' reported Kilburn. 'Mackay pitched short outside the off-stump and May crashed the ball through the helpless covers. The next ball was a half-volley on the leg-stump and the inevitable and immaculate on-drive gave him a century so worthily earned.

'Delight and disappointment breathed almost the same breath. Ten minutes before the close Johnson bowled a slow head-high full toss down the legside.' May could not resist this tasty morsel. He swung at it and struck it fiercely down to fine leg. Lindwall was waiting there to swoop and claim the catch at his ankles. 'An innings nobly conceived and bravely constructed was over in the very moment of its triumph,' concluded Kilburn. May, as he relaxed afterwards in the pavilion, did not forget Washbrook, his ally, in the England revival. He turned to Gubby Allen and said: 'I'm so glad that I listened to you and accepted your advice.'

The seeds of the ensuing triumph were sown by May and Washbrook. Lock and Laker, with 18 wickets between them, zestfully flourished on a turning pitch. Neil Harvey battled vainly to avert an innings defeat. His valiance ended when Lock acrobatically took a return catch. At the end, thousands raced across the ground to the pavilion and the players ran the gauntlet of congratulatory hands. For Peter May, proud and smiling above the exultant multitude, it was another day to savour. He had captained England to their first victory over Australia at Headingley. 'Peter captained England magnificently that summer,' says Richie Benaud. 'He did it, remember, mostly with only a four-man attack.'

At Manchester, with the series poised at one-all, the selectors made another significant choice in bringing back David Sheppard. Sheppard, after going into the ministry, had almost completely severed his connection with first-class cricket. He had played only four innings for Sussex before the Test at Old Trafford. One of the curiosities of a famous match was that the first five England batsmen – Richardson, Cowdrey, Sheppard, May and Bailey – were all amateurs. The last time this had happened against Australia was in 1899 when Fry, MacLaren, Ranjitsinhji, C. L. Townsend and Jackson comprised the top order.

There was the fanfare of an opening stand of 174 between Richardson and Cowdrey. It was England's best start against Australia since 1938 when Hutton and Barnett began with 219 at Trent Bridge. The adroit and brisk runs paved the way for a resplendent century by Sheppard. It was an innings of unquenched mastery; a precise sermon in batting which gave no hint of lack of match practice. Before the end of the first day there were ominous signs of a crumbling wicket. Accusations were made that the pitch had been specially prepared for England's spin bowlers. These were naturally and swiftly rejected by the Lancashire authorities, but no acceptance of blame could have diminished one of the historic bowling performances in Test cricket.

Jim Laker was the avenging bowler, intent on erasing the memory of his disastrous match against Australia at Leeds eight years earlier. 'Ten little Aussie Boys Lakered in a Row' was the joyous headline in the *Daily Express*. Laker wove a spinning plot as cunning as any devised by Agatha Christie. England won the match by an innings and 170 runs to retain the Ashes. Laker's figures will surely never be eclipsed. In Australia's second innings he took 10 wickets for 53 runs, in the match 19 for 90 in 68 overs. On the last day, with bowling of numbing accuracy, he claimed eight wickets for 26 runs in 36 faultless overs. Keith Miller, one of Laker's defeated opponents, said no other bowler, in his experience, could have exploited the dry and breaking wickets of this summer as well as Laker did.

'There has never been anything like it before,' commented *The Times*. 'The Australians came one by one to the slaughter convinced, it seemed, before they took strike that they had not long to live. It was a nasty wicket certainly; but had not England scored freely on it? And the fact, too, that between them Lock and Laker toiled for 18 overs in the first innings before they struck at all shows that it was far from impossible.' Alan Ross wrote that, whatever the speculation, the true result, one-sided as it was, was fairly achieved. 'The toss, which England won, made difference in degree, not kind, and the pitch itself, the villain of the piece, was more one in charade than in reality.' He added: 'It is not often that one can say of a Test that, whichever side had batted first, the result would have been the same. But it was so in this case.'

Les Ames, another of the Test selectors of that year, recalled: 'The Australians were not good players against off-spin. They did rather give up the ghost. The top of the wicket went after the first day. Jim, with his marvellous control, turned the ball at right angles.' At Manchester Laker became the first bowler to take 19 wickets in any first-class match, surpassing Sydney Barnes' 17 for 159 on the Johannesburg mat in 1913. In seven games against Australia in 1956 Laker took 63 wickets, including 46 at a cost of 9.60 each in the Tests. Only Barnes, with 49 in four Tests against South Africa in 1913–14, has exceeded this figure.

One of the mysteries of the match was the failure of Lock to exploit the conditions. It was rumoured that such was his self-disgust that he did not speak to Laker for several weeks following the Old Trafford Test. 'Lock turned the ball too much at Manchester,' said Ames. 'In his frustration he bowled too short. Godfrey Evans was at times having to take the ball shoulder-high behind the wicket.' Laker, nonchalant in his hour of triumph, was the last person to gloat over his achievement. He did, though, slyly take his Surrey partner to task. In a flash of vintage humour, he said: 'Lockie spoilt it by taking one wicket and depriving me of all twenty.'

As a study in greatness, Laker's rainbow summer was stranger than fiction. It was made even more incredible by the fact that he also bowled out Australia on his own for Surrey at The Oval earlier in the summer. Surrey became the first county to beat an Australian touring side for forty-four years. In four-and-a-half hours Laker tormented and teased the Australians. He took ten wickets for 88 runs in 46 overs. Not since 1878, when the left-arm bowler Edward Barratt, another Surrey player, did so, had ten wickets in an innings been achieved by a bowler against the Australians.

Peter May, watching Laker, the supreme inquisitor, find his crock of gold, was a contented man. He had now played in three consecutive winning series against Australia. Not since the days of Grace and Stoddart before the turn of the century had England thrice beaten Australia in succession. 'I did not know as I spent the last days of September preparing to sail to South Africa that very soon I should be regarding a score of over 40 in a Test match as riches indeed,' said May. He was about to learn at first-hand that cricket makes no distinctions in its hostages to fortune. It is, as always, a great leveller.

Chapter 11
Waylaid on the Veldt

'May's run of Test failures were crucial to his side. But they were more an accident of nature or an act of God than attributable to any decline in concentration or power.'

Alan Ross

The batting eclipse startled like an ugly cloud drifting wantonly across the sun. Spectacular catches rocked Peter May on his pedestal in South Africa in 1956–57. One of those alert rivals with magnetic hands was Trevor Goddard, the hailed newcomer in England on the 1955 tour. May was the player who had held him spellbound in 1955; and now in adversity, says Goddard, he revealed his stature as a true sportsman. At the end of a series in which South Africa courageously gained parity, May scorned excuses. 'If you hit the ball into the air against these chaps, you must expect to get caught.'

May's decline in South Africa was freakishly comparable with the unexpected lapses of Denis Compton in Australia six years earlier. Freddie Brown, as the luckless captain in that series, had watched Compton score only 53 runs at the ludicrous average of 7.57. Brown, now as MCC manager, was forced to contemplate another master batsman tussling to regain command. May's misfortunes did, perhaps, manifest a degree of pardonable strain on his first tour as England captain. Yet the omens, in the beginning, were bright with promise.

He began the tour with four centuries in a row, including a double-century against Rhodesia at Salisbury, where he shared a partnership of over 300 with Trevor Bailey. 'The poise and power of May's batting outstripped all else,' reported Jim Swanton. 'He assured himself of a fresh place in *Wisden* by becoming the first player to score four successive hundreds in South Africa.' Of May's 162 against Western Province in the opening fanfare, Swanton declared: 'It was an innings played apparently

123

with a bat about double the prescribed width as the centrepiece.' Everything seemed in place for continued prosperity. In four innings May chancelessly compiled 610 runs. Colin Cowdrey believes that May never played better than in this wonderful prelude to the series.

Swanton notably provided a comparison with Bradman. It was not uncommon for the great Australian to lay down his challenge with a double-century on his triumphant tours of England. 'Here was this great young English player putting to trial his own technique, drawing on his own ample reservoir of concentration. The key to May's batting is his self-discipline.'

A magnificent beginning caused a wave of depression to sweep over the South African supporters. Then, suddenly, it stalled when Heine dismissed May first ball in the match against Transvaal. In ten Test innings, May scored only 153 runs at an average of 15.30, and this was reinforced by 61 in the fourth Test at Johannesburg. It was small consolation that his star seldom dimmed in the provincial matches. Away from the Test scene, as *Wisden* related, 'May thrilled thousands with the quality and grace of his stroke-play'. These were innings to treasure in the memory. Despite his Test reverses, May headed the MCC batting list with 1,270 runs with a more satisfying average of 55.21.

There was, in mitigation of his Test travail, a sequence of remarkable catches. One instance, to haunt him in retrospect, was a stunning one-handed catch taken by Russell Endean in the first Test at Johannesburg. Endean leapt athletically at mid-wicket to cling on to the ball from a wind-swirling hit before he thudded to the ground. 'I thought, as I played Heine off my legs, that it was a certain four,' recorded an incredulous May. He also later maintained that the sluggish tempo of the series induced risks on his part against tight bowling and brilliant fielding. They did, as is the nature of gambling, only add to the sum of his losses.

Superstition, as the dismal chapter unfolded, tetchily disconcerted him. Doug Insole, his vice-captain, remembers that at a reception in Salisbury, the city's mayor presented May with a live duck. He expressed the patriotic hope that it might have a debilitating effect on Peter's future performances. 'From that point on,' says Insole, 'Peter struggled to reach double figures in the Tests. After getting out to yet another magnificent catch late in the series, he came back to the dressing-room, threw his bat in the bag, and said: "That . . . duck!" Peter did not often swear.'

Johnny Wardle was ecstatically happy in his bowling supremacy on the hard, bouncy wickets in South Africa. His impact as England gained a 2–0 lead with victories at Johannesburg and Cape Town, was pronounced. This was his peak series in Test cricket and confirmed his prowess as a wrist-spinner. He took 26 wickets at a cost of 13.80 runs each, and headed the tour averages with 90 wickets (105 in all matches) at 12.25 runs apiece. At Cape Town, at the beginning of the New Year, he claimed seven wickets for 36 runs in the rout of the Springboks for 72. All of Wardle's team-mates remember his artistry in the soothing setting beneath the oak trees at Newlands. Charles Fortune, the South African sports commentator, paid a stirring tribute to the Yorkshireman. 'Had the Wardle who bowled out South Africa at Newlands been on English television screens during his great hours he would have introduced millions to a type of bowling few have so much as seen. Wardle bowled it with rare accuracy and almost uncanny skill.'

Peter May, said Jim Swanton, always subscribed to the prime maxim of captaincy, as set down by Don Bradman. This was to bat on steadily and win every match by as much as you possibly can. Swanton said May was not as coldly analytical as the Australian, but he was mightily keen to win every match if possible. May was, though, judged by one writer to have taken a circuitous route to victory in the second Test at Cape Town. He did not enforce the follow-on after South Africa trailed by 164 runs on the first innings. England extended their lead to 384. It provided the incentive for May to persevere with Wardle's unorthodox spin.

Wardle recalled: 'It was the first time under Hutton or May that I had been given the ball at the start of an innings. Peter realised that I was a matchwinner on that particular wicket. He did spoil it by asking me not to bowl the chinaman stuff at Trevor Goddard. I said: "Look, skipper, let me bowl how I want to bowl and I'll have him out in three overs. I'm not going to bowl orthodox to him. That would be just like giving him a net on this wicket. If I give him a net for half an hour, I'll struggle to get him out."' His persistence won May over. Wardle was allowed to bowl as he wished. 'I did Goddard, as I'd promised, and from then on it was plain sailing.'

South Africa resumed at 41 for two wickets on the last day. Wardle had dismissed McGlew and Keith on the previous evening. Their defeat came much sooner than expected. Eight wickets went down for 31 runs in an hour-and-a-half. Four wickets fell at the same total, 67, and the last six South African wickets tumbled for five runs in twenty minutes. Russell Endean recalled: 'We were aiming to defend and try and save the game. It was a hopeless situation and the circumstances were made for Wardle. But

125

he gave a marvellous exhibition of bowling. He made the ball break by feet.'

Endean was given out 'handled the ball' on appeal in South Africa's second innings. A ball from Laker spun from his pad outside the off stump. It lifted gently straight above his head and might have fallen on his stumps, had he not, his bat held limply by his side, chosen to divert it with his hand in a hockey-style manoeuvre. It completed a unique double. Endean, curiously, was also concerned in another unusual Test dismissal. He was the South African wicket-keeper when Len Hutton was given out 'obstructing the field' at The Oval in 1951. Hutton knocked a ball from Athol Rowan out of Endean's reach in trying to protect his wicket.

Wardle returned match figures of 12 wickets for 89 runs at Cape Town. England won by 312 runs and thus held a governing position after their first-Test victory by 131 runs at Johannesburg. Godfrey Evans, from his vantage point behind the stumps, also enthused about Wardle's bowling. 'Johnny did bowl magnificently. It wasn't a fast wicket at Cape Town. The ball did not come off all that quickly. It you could spin it – and Johnny could – and pitch it in the rough, the ball came off at varying heights, and often kept quite low.'

Roy McLean was one of Wardle's perplexed adversaries in South Africa. 'Wardle tucks his hand away behind his right rump, wheels over his arm, and from the back of his palm, serves up a mixture of curves and spin that made a number of us look like junior-school novices.'

Freddie Brown believed that Wardle, in his unorthodox style, might have clinched the series for England in the third Test at Durban. 'Peter took him off after Funston, with some risky shots, had hit Johnny for three boundaries. It is easy to be wise after the event, but I think that if May had kept him bowling, he would have won the Test for us. But it would have been a close thing as Wardle was tired after a long spell.'

Peter Richardson also considers that this was one of May's rare indecisive days as captain. 'It must be said that South Africa called his bluff. Johnny was bowling like a god. He did miss a return catch when Funston misread his googly. Funston then had a slog, a panic measure really, and struck a few boundaries. Peter took Wardle off and he nearly went berserk. We were winning the match. The rest of us knew it was wrong.'

Peter May won the toss for the third successive time at Durban. It was his eleventh correct call in thirteen Tests as England captain. The prospects for a conclusive victory seemed bright when Richardson and Bailey scored 103 together in the morning session. The opening stand was worth

115 when Richardson departed, lbw to Adcock for 68. May was dismissed by Tayfield to continue his series of low Test scores (6–14–8–15–2). After he was out at three o'clock, England added only 33 runs in 26 eight-ball overs. Tayfield bowled 14 consecutive maidens in the afternoon. Bailey scored 21 in three hours.

Jim Swanton confirms the widely held view that after the opening partnership the stage was set for England to press home their advantage on a perfect wicket. He was appalled by the stalemate and the indefensible tactics adopted by a proven and respected campaigner. Bailey, as at Lord's in 1953, staying in to save a Test match against Australia, was entirely admirable. But it was, he thought, a different matter when Bailey did not exploit a favourable position at Durban, with England on top.

Peter May expressed another view: 'Trevor was an intelligent man who knew perfectly well what was wanted, but he was limited and inclined to become bogged down mentally and technically by good bowling. I think that he saw himself as engaged in a personal duel with Tayfield and became so wrapped up in it that the momentum of the innings slipped away without him realising it. It would have been nice to have been in a position to tell him to attack and not bother if he was out. But the rest of us were not doing well enough for that.'

When bad light ended play twenty-five minutes early Bailey had batted for five-and-a-half hours for his 71. England's earlier advantage had been eroded. At the close they were 184 for four wickets. Bailey's painstaking marathon seemed almost pardonable on the second morning. South Africa were in the ascendant. In 18 overs and three balls they took the last six England wickets for 34 runs. A fourth-wicket stand of 59 runs between Goddard and McLean enabled them to finish the day only 78 runs behind.

McLean went on to record his first century of the tour on his home ground. It did not bear his usual aggressive stamp but it was marked by fine discipline and judgement. After their encouraging start, South Africa were restricted to a lead of 65 runs. Insole's maiden Test century in England's second innings then meant that South Africa required 190 to win in four hours and ten minutes. It was a scoring rate higher than either team had achieved in any previous innings in the series.

Russell Endean believes that if England had had another 100 runs Peter May might have decided on all-out attack and won the match. South Africa, in fact, lost their first four wickets for 49 runs. Endean and Funston added 75 runs for the fifth wicket to give South Africa an outside chance of victory. 'We were going for the target and living rather dangerously,' remembers Endean. 'But one or two catches were put down. Peter perhaps decided that, rather than feed us with a few runs, he could exert more pressure by putting other bowlers on. It was possibly a mistake because the wicket did suit Wardle's unorthodox deliveries. He must have fancied his chances.'

May recalled that Tayfield had taken eight wickets for 69 runs in England's second innings without achieving great purchase for his spin. 'I was not confident that we could bowl them out unless they took risks. In fact, South Africa never worked themselves into a position from which they looked likely to win. In the end, we were doing the attacking, and although we were not successful, a draw seemed not a bad thing in view of our 2–0 lead. But it is a fact that it cost us the series.'

Johnny Wardle had no doubts that Peter May erred on the side of caution. He was convinced that England squandered the chance to win the series at Durban. 'I felt that I could bowl them out with my wrist-spin. Peter preferred to keep them quiet and play for a draw. It did not suit me at all.'

Hugh Tayfield was to expose the folly of England's lack of resolution at Durban. He now marshalled his resources to lead an exhilarating rally. At Johnnesburg, in the fourth Test, England were set a target of 232 runs in a little over seven hours. They lost by just 17 runs. 'Hats went in the air, parasols were flung recklessly about, crowds streamed across the field,' reported Alan Ross. 'Tayfield was embraced, then borne shoulder-high to the dressing-room. No Roman emperor ever had more willing slaves.' Tayfield had bowled throughout the day. His full figures were: 37–11–113–9. No South African had ever taken nine wickets in one innings of a Test before; nor, as Tayfield had done, 13 in a Test against England.

The South African bowler was able to make his off-breaks turn and lift in the thrilling climax at the New Wanderers ground. 'On the last day England's batsmen and the South Africans in the field brought true distinction back to Test cricket,' wrote Charles Fortune. 'England batted in terms of victory or nothing; the response was a full frontal attack unrelenting right through until the last wicket was taken.' Insole continued in rich batting vein, sharing a first-innings partnership of 91 runs with May, who at last found the touch which had eluded him through the series. But he again failed, along with Compton, in the second innings. These were crucial blows from which England could not recover. At tea the match was still poised in the balance. England wanted 46 runs to win, with four wickets left. Brave hitting by Cowdrey and Wardle brought a glimpse of victory. The alliance of the Tayfield brothers appropriately brought the match to an end. Arthur Tayfield, fielding as substitute, took the catch on the long-on boundary to dismiss Loader.

South Africa levelled the series at Port Elizabeth, on the field where, in 1843, the first recorded cricket match in the Union was played. Their victory was achieved on a swiftly deteriorating pitch which led to one batsman telling another: 'Yours was only a carpet-sweeper; mine burrowed through the earth'. Peter May was overthrown by one of the latter variety. 'Had he not received an unplayable ball from Goddard in the last innings he would probably have won the series for England,' commented Alan Ross.

England required 189 runs for victory and lost by 58 runs. Tayfield, supported by superb fielding, took six wickets for 78 runs. Forcing strokes allowed no margin for error; his accuracy on a perilous pitch spelled doom for adventurers. Tayfield's 37 wickets at a cost of 17.18 runs each in the series beat the record set up by his compatriot, Bert Vogler, forty-seven years earlier.

Peter May returned home still undefeated in a series as a captain but chastened by his batting fortunes on the veldt. The hostility of Heine and the deceptions of Tayfield had sorely perplexed him. His technique had betrayed him when faced with the thrusts of Heine. The fast bowler had beaten him most often with balls lifting quickly off just short of a length around the off stump. They had found him pushing warily inside the line of the ball. Alan Ross, in addressing these frailties, remained faithful to a master batsman. 'He stands beautifully, he is a magnificent hitter of the ball, whether short or overpitched. His Test run of failures was more an accident of nature or an act of God than attributable to any decline in concentration or power.'

There was, though, a woeful chuckle in Peter's voice when pressed about his struggles in South Africa. He certainly overstated his batting plight when he suggested that his head might roll. Heady deeds against the West Indies and a memorable duel with Sonny Ramadhin lay before him. He emerged from the gloom to make amends in inimitable style. The iron fist flourished again at Edgbaston.

Chapter 12
Taming the Tormentor

'Ramadhin's finger-spin perplexed almost every batsman who opposed him. Only the best of technicians, prepared to use quick footwork, achieved anything like a solution.'

John Arlott

An eruption of trickery threatened to engulf England at Edgbaston in June 1957. The reign of Peter May was placed in jeopardy for the first time. England were staring over the parapet at impending defeat. Sonny Ramadhin, at twenty-seven, was once again the arch tormentor. His skills honed on the hard overseas pitches gave him a disturbing menace on English wickets where the ball often turned from the first day. He seemed destined to reap another victory harvest.

The stranglehold exerted by the immaculate little man from Trinidad can rarely have been excelled. It is a cricketing tale to tax credulity. His partnership with Alf Valentine – and their sleight of perplexing hands – conjured a web of deception. It is still a source of amazement that the two novices on their first visit to England in 1950 could be hailed as the finest spinning combination since the days of the Australians O'Reilly and Grimmett. Ramadhin and Valentine had not reached their twentieth birthdays and it was said of them before that series that they had only a sketchy idea of the positions on the field.

Ramadhin, born in Esperance Village, Trinidad, was reported to have been discovered playing on a rough clearing near his home. Twelve wickets in two trial matches represented his entire first-class record. Yet during the next five months he took 135 wickets. The unknown and untried East Indian climbed the ladder to greatness. The aura of his invincibility grew as the tour progressed and England – deprived of the services of Hutton, Washbrook, Bailey and Compton at various stages in

130

the series – slipped into a downward spiral after winning the first Test at Manchester.

'Ramadhin's finger-spin perplexed almost every batsman who opposed him and, as the problems he set remained unsolved, so his reputation preceded him,' wrote John Arlott. 'Only the best of technicians, prepared to use quick footwork to counter the spin and subtleties of pace, achieved anything like a solution. Others, less well-equipped, perished amid their doubts.'

Ramadhin bowled always in a cap to keep his wayward hair in place; and with his shirt sleeves buttoned to the wrists. His was a distinctive whirling action, with an almost imperceptible flick of the fingers. 'Trimly neat, almost tiny, he bowled an over in a trice: three quick steps up to the crease and his arm swung over quickly on his delivery skip and, then, immediately, he was eager to bowl again.' Arlott's inimitable words present a portrait so enticing as to put Ramadhin, in the calypso phrase, 'on the ball again'.

Ramadhin and his Jamaican ally, Valentine, each bowled over 1,000 overs on the 1950 tour, taking 258 wickets between them. In four Tests Valentine sent down 422.3 overs and Ramadhin 377.5 overs. It was a perfect pairing which was helped by the fact that the two boys became the best of friends. The bespectacled Valentine, invariably and understandably sporting a huge smile, was a left-arm spinner with immensely strong fingers. Tom Graveney recalls the 'crabby approach' to the wicket. 'Val crouched as he bowled, but he was a tremendous spinner of the ball.' Ramadhin and Valentine, briskly moving through their overs at a rate of less than a minute, operated in the manner of all great bowling combinations. They sought to frustrate with maidens and to compel impatience and often suicidal shots by their opponents.

'The two bowlers,' said the West Indian cricket writer, Tony Cozier, 'cast a spell which left the home team in psychological disarray and the staggering consistency of the West Indies batting, living up to every expectation, capitalised on it.' For the triumvirate of the three 'W's, as they were known, 1950 was a summer of exhilarating conquest. Walcott and Weekes each scored seven centuries and Worrell six. Weekes was avaricious in his pursuit of runs. His contribution included one triple-century and four double-centuries. Of the classic, daring strokes of the West Indians, Harry Altham, the cricket historian, wrote: 'It took me back to 1912. That's how the great players batted then.' The West Indians won 17 (ten by an innings) of their 31 first-class matches and lost only three.

The West Indies reinstated John Goddard, their winning leader of 1950, as captain for the tour of England in 1957. His team again included Worrell, Weekes and Walcott, and Ramadhin and Valentine. The omens appeared bright for a renewal of their mastery over England. There was, however, pause for doubt as to whether the spinners could again carry the burden without the support of recognisable pace. Both Ramadhin and Valentine today recall that it was not uncommon for them to rub the shine off the ball and open the bowling. 'In our time, as spin bowlers, we had too much work to do,' says Ramadhin. 'Two good pace bowlers would have been a great help.' Their confidence, as boys seven years earlier, had been bolstered by the fact that 'our captain believed in us'.

The dangers of over-reliance on them had been demonstrated in the 1951–52 series in Australia. The tactics of John Goddard were criticised in the first Test at Brisbane which Australia won by three wickets. The West Indies opening bowlers, Worrell and Gomez, bowled only 21 overs in two innings. Ramadhin and Valentine were called upon to bowl 130 overs in the match. At one stage, after calling for the new ball, Goddard rendered it obsolete by grounding it in the dust. He then asked his spinners to continue bowling. The inevitable outcome was that their accuracy was diminished and both bowlers suffered a reaction in the following games.

Test cricket returned to the Birmingham arena at Edgbaston after an interval of twenty-eight years in 1957. 'In the four matches Ramadhin played before the opening of the series at Edgbaston,' wrote Tony Cozier, 'the only noticeable change in the cheerful Trinidadian of 1950 was around the waistline. Otherwise, he was still casting the same spell over batsmen and had 38 wickets to his credit when Goddard handed him the ball after an hour's play in the Test.'

Even without Valentine, who had been left out of the eleven, Ramadhin slipped easily back into his well-remembered rhythm. In 31 overs, he took seven wickets for 49 runs (his best return in Tests) as England struggled for four hours to total 186. 'None of us could pick him; he was a real headache,' says Colin Cowdrey. It was Cowdrey's first sighting of this elusive member of the spinners' magic circle. The news, not entirely revelatory, had filtered through that if allowed to monopolise a situation, Ramadhin just got better and better. 'We decided to have a dart at him,' says Cowdrey. The sequel to this 'knocking about', as he ironically confides, 'was that we were all out by twenty minutes to four.'

The West Indies then assiduously built up a lead of 288 runs. The prodigiously talented Collie Smith, later to die tragically in a car crash, was top scorer with 161 in his first Test against England. He added 190 runs with the injured Worrell, who batted through the five hours of their partnership with a runner. Walcott had earlier provided the impetus for the run-spree with a buccaneering 90. During the innings he tore a leg muscle so severely that he collapsed and fainted. He was never fully restored to fitness and did not recapture his form for the rest of the series. It was yet another of the misfortunes afflicting the West Indians on this tour. Weekes, Valentine and Gilchrist, who sprained an ankle at Edgbaston, were also handicapped by illness and injuries.

England, at 113 for three in their second innings, looked to be at the end of their tether on the third day. Ramadhin had taken another two wickets. One of his victims, Peter Richardson, says that defeat appeared so certain that the England team had booked out of their hotel. It was a mountainous task facing them: twelve hours remained for play and there was the dread prospect of Ramadhin wheeling away for over after over. 'The odds, had there been a call-over at eleven o'clock, must have been long against England saving the game,' commented *The Times*. 'More to the point seemed to be the time at which they would expire.' However, Sunday had intervened to allow England a breathing space and a chance to resolve how to counter Ramadhin.

Wilf Wooller, one of the England selectors, detected one ray of hope. He had noticed how Ramadhin tossed his leg-spinner a fraction slower and higher than his normal delivery. 'He always seemed to struggle going round the wicket.' Wooller's advice to the England batsmen was to urge them to get forward as far as possible to Ramadhin when he bowled over the wicket to nullify his off-spin. 'I reminded them that they could not be out lbw if they were a long way forward and that they could recognise the leg-spinner by the change of flight.'

May had also spent much time discussing the situation with Colin Cowdrey over the weekend. 'Colin and I both agreed that we must keep going forward and that Ramadhin must be played as an off-spinner. If it was the leg-break, we just had to hope that it would miss everything.' May said that it was usually possible to assess a deceptive spinner sooner or later, but the quickness of Ramadhin's arm made him unique in his experience. 'Sometimes we would decide that the leg-break was the one which he bowled slightly slower or higher, or from slightly wider of the stumps. But we were never sure.'

The sinister swiftness of the arm, which dealt the spinning puzzles, is also confirmed by Godfrey Evans. Evans's successes against Ramadhin had included a century against the West Indies at Manchester in 1950. His strategy, as a batsman, was to account the ball which looped in the air as the leg-break. 'All the rest I played as off-breaks. It often seemed to work.'

A memorable partnership began shortly before noon on the Monday. The best part of two days lay ahead and England still needed 175 runs to save an innings defeat. It brought together May and Cowdrey who, three years earlier in Australia, had salvaged England's pride. May recalled: 'Ramadhin was unusual with his quick loose wrist, rolled down sleeves and, for a spinner, brisk pace and lowish trajectory. In the English light it was hard to see the ball spinning in the air and no one could read him. He turned the ball just enough to do damage and won himself a big moral advantage by his accuracy allied to the doubt which he created in the batsman's mind.'

Colin Cowdrey reflects on their good fortune in encountering Ramadhin on a slowish wicket in the second innings at Edgbaston. 'Peter wasn't very good at picking him; but he was so resolute and watched the ball like a hawk. I cannot possibly exaggerate this concentration during our early struggles. Peter was very disciplined in restricting his range of shots during a difficult period. This was what made him supreme: knowing what he was going to do and never deviating from his chosen pattern of play.'

The partnership between May and Cowdrey had begun in the guise of two men making the best of a forlorn hope. 'As it developed,' wrote Jim Swanton, 'one felt that its example might at least hearten all due to follow with a determination to sell their wickets dearly and to postpone the moment of defeat.'

By tea-time England had reached 279, having scored exactly 100 runs during the day; and by twenty minutes to five the first milestone of levelling the scores had been achieved. There had been passages of anxiety as one batsman or the other had narrow escapes. May, at times, lived precariously in the short-leg area with strokes which he lifted unintentionally. There was the occasional edge through the slips and not many overs from Ramadhin went by without an appeal for lbw. 'The inscrutable Ramadhin,' reported *The Times*, 'would half-turn his head, raise his eyebrows, and look questioningly at the umpire out of the corner of his eye. But the gentlemen in the white coats must have seemed to him like Russian diplomats as they vetoed his requests.'

The spectators – and others nervously watching the gallantry of the two England batsmen on television at home – started to build their castles in the air. Expectations were given a lift when Gilchrist left the field with a sprained ankle to reduce further the bowling options of the West Indies, already deprived of the services of Worrell. May and Cowdrey could,

134

though, afford no lapse of concentration against the remarkably sustained accuracy of Ramadhin. He had been introduced into the attack shortly before noon and bowled without rest until lunch. At three o'clock, after Gilchrist had all but punctured May's defence with the new ball, Ramadhin returned at the pavilion end. Thereafter, apart from a ten minutes' respite before tea, he bowled for all but half an hour through the evening. In all this time he perpetrated only two full pitches. Cowdrey was so surprised that he mishit the first; the second was struck for four past cover.

'As May and Cowdrey grafted on,' reported *The Times*, 'one thought of that taut match at Sydney in December 1954 when the two of them came together with England facing defeat. Not until now had they shared a comparable partnership and this time, as in Australia, the atmosphere was just as tense.'

The pattern of play was firmly established in these fraught hours for English supporters. 'At one end was Cowdrey, pushing massively forward, his bat and pad tightly locked together,' continued *The Times* correspondent. 'At the other, May was the master of the situation, his bat as clean and white as when he started, his manner as composed. Ramadhin at last was sent empty away.' The unbroken stand had added 265 and England were ahead, narrowly, by 90 runs. May, with 193, had reached his highest Test score; and Cowdrey, comfortably settled in a supporting role, was watchfully secure on 78.

Jim Swanton enthused about the command of May. 'In Australia it was his batting – furthermore with Cowdrey – which made possible the victory of the England bowlers and the retention of the Ashes. Yet I dare say that nothing will have given him more pleasure and satisfaction than this thrashing back of the West Indies when they had all but burst through.'

Ramadhin bowled 48 overs at a cost of less than two runs an over on this day. With the lbw law as it was then constituted, the batsmen were able to pad the ball away with impunity if it pitched outside the off stump. The safety-first policy, so sternly pursued, has been subjected to criticism in English as well as West Indian quarters. 'The ball repeatedly beat the forward defensive stroke and hit the front leg, thrust forward as a shield,' wrote Tony Cozier. 'Soon throats became sore from appealing to the umpires (Charlie Elliott and Emrys Davies). As is customary in England, they were reluctant to uphold them with the point of contact so far from the stumps.'

Michael Manley, another West Indian observer, commented on the justification for the umpires' attitude. He said that it lay in the claim that if the left leg is stretched well down the wicket, a batsman cannot be given out.

135

They reasoned that there was an element of doubt as to whether a fractional deviation in the direction of the ball might have made it miss the wicket. Manley did, however, maintain that May and Cowdrey were not defensive with their pads outside the line of the stumps. 'Much of the time the left pad was in line with balls that seemed to be perfectly directed at the wicket.'

Sir Colin Cowdrey today takes a measured view of the criticisms. 'We knew what we were doing out there.' He says that in his learning curve as a Kent batsman he had profited from a lesson set by his senior, Arthur Fagg, a former England batsman. Fagg had told him: 'When in trouble, you assume that the ball is going to hit the middle stump. If it misses, you're not out.' Cowdrey maintains that the major problem with Ramadhin was sighting the ball. 'At The Oval (in the fifth Test) I got done by Ram. Having got him in my pocket, I couldn't pick him out of the crowd. I went to flick him wide of mid–on and got rolled over by his leg-break.'

Doug Insole, one of the perplexed England batsmen at Edgbaston, confesses that he never fathomed the mysteries of Ramadhin. He does, however, dispute the legend that the West Indian was unfairly deprived of success. 'It was a great game of cricket played fully within the laws.' Other England contemporaries – Peter Richardson, Godfrey Evans and Tom Graveney, who was twelfth man at Edgbaston – all express their sympathy for Ramadhin. 'The ball wasn't bouncing for little Ram; Colin had to be out so many times,' says Richardson. Graveney is even more forthright. 'Colin kicked him to death. He never tried to play him with the bat.' Evans's memory is of an immaculate bowler, who 'sooner or later must have got one pitching on off-stump.'

Sonny Ramadhin recalls his accuracy as a bowler and his line of attack constantly directed at the wickets. 'Most of my wickets were either bowled or lbw because I bowled more off-breaks than leg-breaks.' He retrospectively absolves Cowdrey from blame. 'Colin always played with his pads. But the "kicking", after Edgbaston, went on all round the counties. I was so disgusted that I refused to tour England with the West Indies in 1963.' Ramadhin still regards the events at Birmingham as 'unbelievable'. 'I would have had a field day under the "intent to play" lbw ruling, which applies today.'

The accusations, however sweeping, cannot detract from the size of England's task and a remorseless partnership which brought salvation. It had hardly seemed conceivable that anything could happen to dwarf Ramadhin's bowling in England's first innings. In the end, England could have won the match. They were baulked by three wickets after the West

Indies, left to make 296 in two hours and forty minutes, had staggered to 72 for seven on a wicket frayed by wear.

May and Cowdrey added 411 for the fourth wicket in a match of tumbling records. It was a record England stand and then the third highest in the history of Test cricket. It fell 40 runs short of the 451 by Bradman and Ponsford for Australia at The Oval in 1934. A stand of 413 between Roy and Mankad had been recorded for India against New Zealand at Madras in the 1955–56 series. May's unbeaten 285 was his highest in first-class cricket and the biggest postwar innings, beating Compton's 278 against Pakistan in 1954. It was also the highest by an England captain, surpassing Hammond's 240 against Australia at Lord's in 1938. Cowdrey's 154 was then his highest Test score and his first Test century in England.

The bogey of a bowling maestro was buried at Edgbaston. Two captains, said one writer, helped to destroy Ramadhin – his own, John Goddard, who overbowled him, and England's Peter May, who played one of the greatest of Test innings. Having looked certain winners, the West Indies went on to suffer the indignity of a 3–0 defeat in the series. Frank Worrell, soon to become an inspirational captain, thought his team played shabby cricket. The West Indies were thrice beaten by an innings – at Lord's, Leeds and The Oval, on each occasion inside three days.

Sonny Ramadhin, in his marathon and unavailing bowling performance at Edgbaston, bowled 774 balls, the most delivered in a Test. It beat Hedley Verity's 766 balls against South Africa at Durban in 1939. Ramadhin conceded 179 runs in 98 overs in England's second innings. He also bowled the most balls (588) in any first-class single innings, beating the 555 balls bowled by Ghulam Ahmed for Hyderabad against Holkar at Indore in 1950–51. A mere recital of these statistics induces weariness. After his ordeal, Ramadhin said: 'I was terribly tired. I had a hot bath and, when I got on to the bed, I was aching all over. I couldn't sleep.'

John Goddard had still persevered with Ramadhin, unadventurously affording him only a defensive field, on the eventful last day at Edgbaston. 'The magician had lost his magic,' reported *The Times*. 'No longer was he quite so mechanically accurate. Yet he was always a willing slave.' Ramadhin, said Jim Swanton, went through the motions of bowling, 'floating about for all the world like a sleepwalker'.

Before England's declaration Peter May had relaxed to bisect the field with glorious strokes. By then he was toying with the bowling. He gave a hard chance to Smith at mid-wicket in the first over of the afternoon; and another when he had reached 278. He hooked a long-hop from Smith to

Alexander, one of three substitute fieldsman, who was unable to cling on to the ball at square-leg. Another substitute, Asgarali, eventually caught Cowdrey at long-on to bring a great stand to an end. Cowdrey's last 50 had been scored in less than an hour; and in the final onslaught he outpaced his partner.

Trevor Bailey, in his impressions of a magnificent England rally, remembered his own mentally sapping vigil. He always liked to watch play before going in to bat. The investigative exercise was this time prolonged beyond normal limits. 'I had my pads on for the longest time probably any cricketer has ever worn them. I sat for two days in the dressing-room. In fact, I never did go to the wicket. That's what I most remember about the game – just waiting in the dressing-room.'

There were suggestions, only half-heartedly expressed, that May might have declared when Cowdrey was dismissed. Rex Alston, one of the match commentators, said: 'We all got excited towards the end of the England second innings when we felt that an earlier declaration could have increased the chances of an England victory. But I am convinced that Peter May, still batting in the middle, was too much in a blur to make a clear-cut decision.'

Godfrey Evans was May's partner in the closing stages of the innings. They batted on for another half-hour, adding a further 59 runs before the declaration. May's fatigue was shown by the fact that he had to ask the umpires how far England were ahead. He was told 295 runs and he knew then that his mission was completed. Evans, jaunty and brimming with energy, had earlier shown his intentions. He was eager to follow his captain's instructions to score runs as quickly as possible. Evans recalls: 'My first ball was off Ram and I pushed it towards deep extra-cover. I called out: "Come two", and scampered up and down the wicket. I nearly ran out Peter on the second run.' At the end of the over, May walked purposefully down the wicket. There was a wry smile on his face. 'Godfrey,' he said, 'I do admire the way you have taken my words to heart. But please don't forget, I have been out here for nine hours!'

May, in fact, batted in all for five minutes under ten hours. His match-saving innings began at twenty minutes to six on the Saturday evening and ended at twenty-past three on the Tuesday afternoon. He had come to the crease with the total at 65 for two and left it, still undefeated, at 583 for four. As he left the field, the crowd rose to acclaim him. A moment later, with the calypso band striking up merrily, Collie Smith bowed his way into the pavilion as his team's only wicket-taker of the day.

OFFICAL SCORECARD

THE WARWICKSHIRE COUNTY CRICKET CLUB
FIRST TEST MATCH
1957

ENGLAND – v – WEST INDIES

at EDGBASTON on
MAY 30th, 31st, JUNE 1st, 3rd & 4th

3d.

A new ball may be taken after 200 runs or 75 overs

* Captain
† Wicketkeeper

HOURS OF PLAY
11-30 am to 6-30 pm
each day
Lunch 1-30 pm to 2-10 pm
Tea Interval 20 minutes

ENGLAND	1st INNINGS		2nd INNINGS	
1. P. E. Richardson	c Walcott b Ramadhin	47	c sub b Ramadhin	34
2. D. B. Close	c Kanhai b Gilchrist	15	c Weekes b Gilchrist	42
*3. P. B. H. May	c Weekes b Ramadhin	30	not out	285
4. D. J. Insole	b Ramadhin	20	b Ramadhin	0
5. M. C. Cowdrey	c Gilchrist b Ramadhin	4	c sub b Smith	154
6. T. E. Bailey	b Ramadhin	1		
†7. T. G. Evans	b Gilchrist	14	not out	29
8. J. C. Laker	b Ramadhin	7		
9. G. A. R. Lock	b Ramadhin	0		
10. F. S. Trueman	not out	29		
11. J. B. Statham	b Atkinson	13		
	Extras	6	Extras	39

MATCH DRAWN

Total 186

Total 583
Innings declared

1 wkt for. 32 2. 61 3.104 4.115 5.116 6.118 7.121 8.130 9.150 10.186 1 wkt for. 63 2. 65 3.113 4.524 5. 6. 7. 8. 9. 10.

WEST INDIES	1st INNINGS		2nd INNINGS	
1. B .H. Pairaudeau	b Trueman	1	b Trueman	7
2. G. Sobers	c Bailey b Statham	53	c Cowdrey b Lock	14
3. C. L. Walcott	c Evans b Laker	90	c Lock b Laker	1
4. E. D. Weekes	b Trueman	9	c Trueman b Lock	33
5. F. M. Worrell	b Statham	81	c May b Lock	0
6. O. G. Smith	lbw b Laker	161	lbw b Laker	5
7. D. Atkinson	c Statham b Laker	1	not out	4
*8. J. D. C. Goddard	c Lock b Laker	24	not out	0
†9. R. Kanhai	lbw b Statham	42	c Close b Trueman	1
10. K. T. Ramadhin	not out	5		
11. R. Gilchrist	run out	0		
	Extras	7	Extras	7

UMPIRES
C. S. Elliott
E .Davies

SCORERS
G. C. Austin
W. Ferguson

Total 474

Total 72

1 wkt for. 4 2. 83 3.120 4.183 5.197 6.387 7.466 8.469 9.474 10.474 1 wkt for. 1 2. 9 3. 25 4. 27 5. 43 6. 61 7. 68 8. 9. 10

Bowling Analysis	O	M	R	W	Nb	Wd	O	M	R	W	Nb	Wd	Bowling Analysis	O	M	R	W	Nb	Wd	O	M	R	W	Nb	Wd
Worrell	9	1	27	0									Statham	39	4	114	3			2	0	60	0		
Gilchrist	27	4	74	2			26	2	67	1			Trueman	30	4	99	2			5	3	72	2		
Ramadhin	31	16	49	7			98	35	179	2			Bailey	34	11	80	0								
Atkinson	12.4	3	30	1			72	29	137	0			Laker	54	17	119	4			24	20	13	2		
Smith							26	4	72	1			Lock	34.4	15	55	0			27	19	31	3		
Sobers							30	4	77	0			Close							2	1	80	0		
Goddard							6	2	12	0															

Peter May was earnest in his praise of the contribution made by Colin Cowdrey. 'He was such a great help, never failing to urge patience on me when I passed a landmark.' One stroke which he had ruled out against Ramadhin was the shot wide of mid-on to a ball slanting in towards the leg stump. There was an early instance of unease before it was eliminated. It nearly cost May his wicket. 'Before the next over I made sure that Colin had noticed my mistake. I remember telling him to tell me if he saw me playing it again and not to play it himself.'

May later concluded that his innings at Edgbaston was his best as well as being the highest of his career. 'It was, at that particular time, undoubtedly very important. I had to get going again after my barren series in South Africa. Most important, we had had a feeble first innings, as a result of which the team was very down in spirits. Unless something was done, we were going to start the series with a heavy defeat. Thus its value to the side was probably as great as any other I played.'

The question, in the end, was how the Edgbaston pitch would react to the spin of Laker and Lock. It was also a matter of time and space, and England, as it proved, cut it a shade too fine. May later insisted that the excitement of falling wickets in the last hours of the Test did nothing to persuade him that he was wrong in not declaring earlier. Trueman removed Kanhai and Pairaudeau in the five overs granted to him. The score was then 9 for 2 and Sobers was caught at slip before Laker joined Lock in the attack. In the furious finale the West Indies lost seven wickets for 72 runs. The two Surrey spinners bowled on unchanged except for a couple of overs by Close to enable them to switch ends.

'May brought in more and more fieldsmen to crouch round the bat as the clock went round and they were all kept in a state of continual expectation,' reported *The Times*. Worrell and Walcott were both caught in the leg-side cordon. Forty minutes remained when Weekes was caught by Trueman in the gully, as a ball from Lock reared off the splice of his bat. Goddard, with the aid of Smith, and finally Atkinson, steered his side to safety. The West Indies captain, convinced that the umpires could not rule him out lbw for pad play either, kicked away the threat of spin.

England's dramatic escape at Edgbaston was the clinching factor in the 1957 series. Sonny Ramadhin, manacled by defensive tactics, was brought to heel. The spell had been broken. Yet for a few short and fascinating years he had baffled the best of batsmen. The cunning little man did not allow his opponents to penetrate the secrets of his bewitching art. 'We never fathomed him,' said Peter May. 'But he was never the same force again.'

Chapter 13
The Throwing Masquerade

'It was absolutely terrifying. We just stood there like rabbits.'

Tom Graveney

The seeds of disenchantment were sown in 1958–59, amid the debris of England's worst tour of Australia for thirty-seven years. Peter May, hitherto the acclaimed captain, was capsized in a controversial series. His predecessor, Johnny (J. W. H. T.) Douglas, had gone down 5–0, but his defeat was executed in the wake of the conflict of the First World War. May's men travelled as undisputed champions. They were vigorous in complexion after their overwhelming victory over New Zealand in the previous summer.

By the end of the Australian series they were shown to have been complacent voyagers. Their stars had waned: the great side built by Hutton and May, as one writer recorded, 'was decaying before our eyes; there was a sense of fatalism among those players who wilted under the pressure of tough and determined opposition.'

The batting constancy of Peter May was unruffled in Australia. He paraded his invincibility with more handsome deeds for Surrey and England in 1958, one of the wettest summers in memory. His command was inexorable in the bleak conditions. He led Surrey to their seventh championship; and his eight centuries, including five against the New Zealanders, placed him unassailably as the best batsman in the land.

New Zealand were outclassed at Edgbaston, Lord's, Headingley and Old Trafford and only rain saved them at The Oval. Lock and Laker were rampant and able to please themselves against the hapless tourists. They shared 51 wickets in the series; and Lock's 34, at a miserly cost of only 7.47 runs each, illustrated his menace in propitious circumstances.

Among the batting candidates under inspection for Australia was Arthur Milton, the Gloucestershire opener. Milton, at thirty, played in his first

Test match at Headingley. M. J. K. Smith was his partner, bringing together two double-internationals, one soccer and the other rugby, to open an England innings. Milton became the third England player since the war to hit a century on his Test debut. He shared this distinction with his captain, Peter May, and the feat had also been achieved by Billy Griffith against the West Indies at Port of Spain, Trinidad, in 1948.

Milton's opportunity occurred after New Zealand had been routed for 67. He was emboldened in his quest for recognition by the encouragement of May. Their unbroken third-wicket partnership put on 200 runs. The England captain was in imperious mood. 'His authority and his artistry were as convincing as they were charming,' wrote Jim Kilburn. 'The inadequacy of the challenge diminished its value but not the delight of his performance.' Milton had accumulated around 60 when May joined him at the wicket. 'Peter proceeded to hit the bowlers out of sight, over the top, and in every direction you care to name,' says Milton. 'He overtook me and reached his century before I'd scored 80.'

May then tempered his aggression to coax the newcomer to an important milestone. A declaration was looming but May stayed his hand to give generous support. 'I'll try and give you the bowling now, so that you can go on and get your own hundred,' he said. Milton cherished this comradely act. He batted for nearly five hours at Leeds to establish his Test credentials. 'The quiet, rather self-effacing persistence, the gradual blossoming into firm off-side shots from the back foot and well-timed square-cuts, were brought to Headingley precisely as though they might have been on display at Bristol,' commented Kilburn.

Milton's century ensured his selection for the Australian tour and as a member of an MCC party which was accorded general approval. Richie Benaud wryly remembers the pre-tour publicity which sounded victory fanfares for England. 'At a time when some of his players were on their way down rather than on their way up, May was ill-served by this publicity. Our rivals were listed as the greatest-ever team to leave English shores. They had an enormous amount to live up to and sometimes that kind of adulation can be worse than the fiercest criticism.'

Benaud was soon, tellingly, to be thrust into his first series as Australian captain. But he was not the first choice. Ian Craig, their youngest captain at twenty-two, had led Australia to a 3–0 victory in South Africa in the previous winter. Benaud replaced him as New South Wales captain when Craig was struck down with hepatitis. Neil Harvey, Craig's vice-captain, would have been assured of the captaincy had he not decided to move from Victoria to Sydney. The choice thus lay between Two New South Wales colleagues and Benaud, newly installed as the state captain, was fortuitously given the chance to regain the Ashes.

The reports dinning Australian ears before the tour indicated a walk-over for England. The challenge of Australia was dismissed as puny and there were even suggestions that such a futile contest ought to be scrapped. The declarations were brazenly flaunted in the sporting columns. 'They did produce a certain amount of determination in our ranks,' laconically notes Benaud.

Jim Swanton was more decorous in his overtures. His tone, even so, conveyed an air of patronage. He thought the mission of MCC was to adorn the cricket scene with glamour to counter competing attractions in Australia. 'The poor record of the 1956 side in England – the worst ever by an Australian team – was what chiefly disenchanted their countrymen.' Swanton did, however, urge caution with regard to England's prospects. 'If pressed for a forecast, I would say that the proper odds at this stage must be just a shade in Australia's favour.' He was almost alone in this divergent view.

The misfortunes from the start were foreboding. The voyage of the MCC party – the last by ship – was made on the P & O liner, *Iberia*, then on its thirteenth crossing to Australia. Inauspiciously, for those inclined to superstition, it also landed at Fremantle on the thirteenth day of October. Back in England, before the departure, there had been a saddening conflict in Yorkshire. An unseemly wrangle involving Johnny Wardle had spilled over on to the pages of the national press. The result was his withdrawal from the tour. Peter May, to his own immense disappointment, was deprived of a key bowler then at the height of his supremacy. Wardle was acknowledged, after his earlier triumphs in South Africa, as a master dual-purpose spinner on overseas pitches.

There was, in addition, a troubled episode concerning Jim Laker. It was concealed, in his case, within Surrey circles. Laker, prior to selection, had made it known that he would not be available to tour and then changed his mind. Doug Insole says that Laker made his first trip to Australia in a state of 'high dudgeon'. It was a surprising affair. A great bowler, so often spurned by the selectors, had at last been given a prized opportunity to visit Australia. The scene was set for him to enhance a reputation established in England. It was even reported that a feud had erupted between Laker and May following allegations by his Surrey captain that he had 'not been trying' in a match against Kent at Blackheath. In the course

143

of eight consecutive days' cricket Laker had bowled 175 overs. His spinning finger was beginning to show distinct signs of wear and tear.

Don Mosey recalled Laker's sense of outrage at the accusation made by a revered colleague and with whom he apparently enjoyed a good relationship. 'It is possible that in the middle of that concentration of bowling days Jim might have seemed to his captain to be less than a hundred per cent enthusiastic about the job in hand. But it takes a brave, or a foolhardy, critic to tell a great bowler he is not actually trying.' The quarrel would seem to betray a clash of personalities, unusual in May's temperament since one of his key qualities was tact. But on this occasion he was certainly unforgiving.

The impasse between May and Laker was resolved following a timely intervention by Denis Compton. Compton instigated a meeting between the two players at Lord's which was rapidly followed by another at The Oval. Mosey records the outcome of the second discussion. 'This time May said he had been thinking deeply about the whole affair and suggested Jim should "forget he had said anything" about the match at Blackheath.' Laker did gladly accept the olive branch but then risked a further estrangement. At the start of the voyage to Australia he announced that he would be retiring from first-class cricket after the 1959 season. The reason given was the arthritic condition of his right forefinger. It was hardly the right time to make such an announcement, with an important series in the offing, nor the action of a man intent on the bowling duties before him.

According to Peter Richardson, a fellow tourist, disappointment masked May's anger when Laker withdrew from the England team on the morning of the fourth Test at Adelaide. Don Mosey said that a marathon bowling stint in the earlier Test at Sydney had caused the condition of Laker's bowling finger to deteriorate to a point where he could bend it no more than thirty degrees from straight. After a net in Adelaide Laker expressed his doubts about playing in the match. May, hoping for an improvement, suggested that a decision should be delayed until the following day. As Mosey relates, the MCC management drew up twelve names for the Test. The understanding was that Tyson would play if Laker was unfit.

On the following morning Laker confirmed that he would be unable to play. The late announcement, perfunctorily delivered by the MCC manager, Freddie Brown, produced hostile press criticism. It led to claims that Laker should have played despite the injury because this was a vital Test. It was his duty to play, it was said, no matter what happened to his finger afterwards.

The Surrey staff of 1954.

P. B. H. MAY

M. C. COWDREY
2 9 ft.
KENT

Peter and Colin Cowdrey as the 'daring young men Down Under'; and the MCC party to Australia in 1954-55: (*back row, left to right*) G. Duckworth (baggage master), K. V. Andrew, P. J. Loader, T. W. Graveney, F. H. Tyson, H. W. Dalton (masseur); (*middle row*) J. H. Wardle, R. T. Simpson, J. V. Wilson, R. Appleyard, J. E. McConnon, J. B. Statham, M. C. Cowdrey, C. G. Howard (manager); (*front row*) T. E. Bailey, W. J. Edrich, P. B. H. May, L. Hutton (capt.), D. C. S. Compton, A. V. Bedser, T. G. Evans.

Leonard Hutton with Peter,
his vice-captain in Australia
and successor as captain.

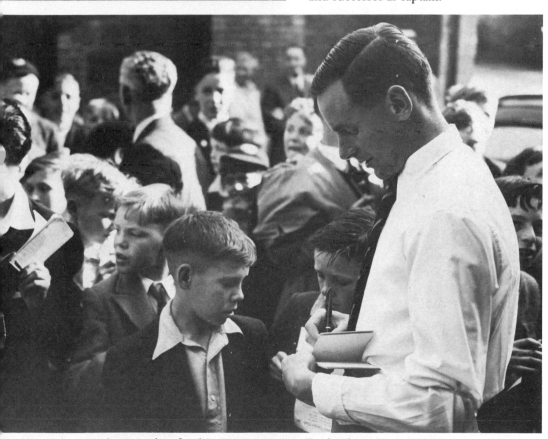

Autographs after his appointment as England captain in 1955.

Stuart Surridge, the epitome of enterprise as captain and fieldsman during
Surrey's great days in the 1950s.

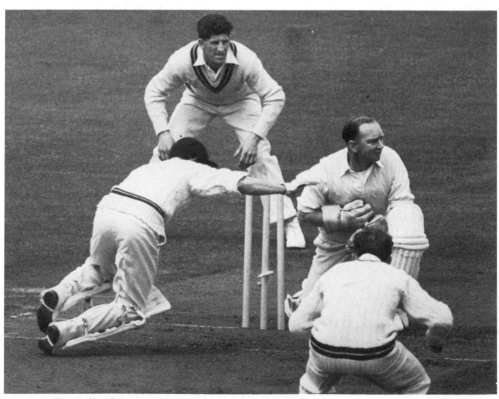

Typically alert Surrey fielding as McIntyre tries to stump Outschoorn of
Worcester, May 1957. Ken Barrington at slip.

The fightback against West Indies and Ramadhin in the first Test at Edgbaston in 1957. Peter batting (and Kanhai keeping wicket). (*Below*) May and Colin Cowdrey at end of play on 3 June, with May on 193 not out and Cowdrey 78 not out. The stand continued the following day until 411 runs had been added.

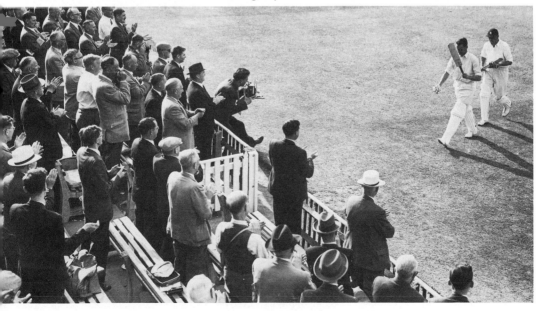

Qualities of a master batsman. Peter's intense concentration as he square-drives: (*below*) one of his magisterial strokes – the straight-drive.

Virginia and Peter May.
Doug Insole wrote that Peter
was an unlikely stable lad,
'but it had seemed possible
over the past few years that
he might turn up at Lord's
with the odd wisp of straw in
his hair'.

Selection Committee: Norman Gifford, Peter May, Alec Bedser, A. C. Smith.
(Photograph by Ken Kelly)

Reunion of Charterhouse school friends at a Butterflies C.C. dinner in 1994:
John Perry, Peter Nathan and Peter May. (*Below*) A family remembers:
the unveiling in the Long Room at The Oval of a painting of Peter May by
Penelope Reeve, June 1995. Virginia May (*centre*) with her daughters (*from left*)
Suzanne, Nicola, Tessa and Annabelle.

Laker responded: 'If there had been any logic in these arguments I would have done my damnedest to play. If I had thought I could do anything to help England win the match, no thought of the future would have stopped me. But I knew the truth; had I played I would have been letting down England who most likely would have been landed with a useless passenger.'

The morale of the team was also undermined by a succession of injuries. Willie Watson, one of three left-handers in the party, actually sustained his injury during the voyage. His knee collapsed when he rose from a deckchair. The subsequent x-ray revealed a loose particle inside the knee that had come adrift since a cartilage operation thirteen years before. Watson was out of action for nine weeks during which time the side was handicapped by the absence of a third opening batsman.

Subba Row was a later casualty; his thumb was broken by Frank Tyson in the nets just before the first Test at Brisbane. The injury situation was further compounded when Milton twice suffered a broken right finger, the same one in each instance, within three weeks, to end his active participation in the tour.

Confronting Peter May on his last and ill-fated tour of Australia were dubious challengers, unnerving and unpredictable in their powers. The cannonade of throwers was a demeaning assault, not offset by protestations that the livelihood of professionals was at stake. Throughout the 1950s a *laissez-faire* attitude persisted towards bowlers with suspect actions. The cries of outrage did not begin until serious injury – a maiming strike or worse – threatened with the arrival of throwers of unbridled speed.

The lingering revulsion is not lessened by the qualifying verdict of Alan Davidson, one of May's rivals in Australia. Davidson, not given to over-statement, maintains that he could list upwards of twenty bowlers, some respected names, around the world, who were guilty of transgression. Tony Lock, hailed as a master of vicious spin, was one who illegally rose to eminence during a regime of lenient stewardship.

Norman Preston, the editor of *Wisden*, considered that the authorities had only themselves to blame for the spread of the menace to the game. Too much responsibility had been left to umpires, who lacked support from the officials above them. Peter May recalled a diminished sensitivity in an unfair situation. Those brave umpires who did call offending bowlers, he said, were looked upon as publicity-seekers. 'The tendency was to sweep such unpleasantness under the carpet.'

England, it could be said, were hoist by their own petard in Australia;

but a breach in Anglo–Australian relations on the scale of the bodyline furore was only averted by careful diplomacy. May insisted that the tour, rather than being his greatest failure as England captain, was probably one of his greatest successes. 'At the end of it England and Australia were still speaking to each other.' His objective as an ambassador was to avoid friction so that controversial matters could be settled later, without recriminations, by administrators sitting amicably around a table. Asked for his views at the end of the series, he obliquely parried the question. 'I think your Norman O'Neill has a magnificent throw – from cover-point.'

The need for diplomacy was paramount in a country where throwing was a disfiguring feature in every state. There were 'draggers' as well, and they left behind them a wake of aggrieved batsmen. 'Having a ball thrown at you from eighteen yards blights the sunniest disposition,' said May. 'We saw boys' matches in parks in which bowlers were throwing without the slightest sign of discouragement from the presiding adults.'

Ian Meckiff, the chief target of criticism, was the Victoria left-arm bowler who had risen in the space of one year from South Melbourne first-grade cricket to represent his state and country. His swift progression had earned him a place in the victorious Australian team in South Africa the previous winter. This charming man, 'the honest chucker' in the words of Alf Gover, was to become castigated as a social oddity, a man people pointed to as a rebel.

Jack Pollard, the Australian writer, said Meckiff bowled with an arm that had a permanent bend in it and could not be fully straightened. 'He achieved his pace from double-jointed shoulders and from extremely thin wrists. Originally he made very little use of his front arm but when the chucking controversy raged he started to use the front arm more, lifting it up higher. The action of his bowling remained the same but the change in the use of the front arm made some critics believe he had altered his bowling action. Ironically, Meckiff had a poor throwing arm when fielding.' E.M. ('Lyn') Wellings, one of the English press corps, commented: 'Meckiff approaches the wicket in the deliberate manner of a bowler who delivers the ball at medium pace. He runs no faster than did Hedley Verity to bowl his slow spinners. And yet the ball leaves his hand at express pace.'

Peter Richardson, one of the English tourists, believes that the crucial error was made in not registering a complaint against Meckiff before the beginning of the series. Trevor Bailey had raised the issue at a team meeting. 'This man throws,' declared Bailey. 'I can assure you that if nothing is done, he will win at least one Test match for Australia. If we are going to complain, we must do it before he becomes lethal.' Richardson considers that Peter May must share some of the blame for not pursuing his players' fears.

Jack Fingleton, the former Test player and writer and an Australian spokesman, was supportive to a point in his view that the Australian bowlers would have been more at home 'knocking down coconuts on Hampstead Heath'. But he did believe that English critics were disposed to see illegal bowlers behind every gum tree. In addition, they were apt to regard every Australian umpire, including those involved in controversial decisions in the series, as embryonic Ned Kellys.

Fingleton considered that the worst bowling action belonged to Jimmy Burke of New South Wales. Burke was an obdurate batsman, forming a successful opening partnership with Colin McDonald, but a highly suspect off-spinner. On one occasion, as Fingleton recalled, a 'bleacher' advised Burke: 'Bowl him one for a change, Jimmy; you'll surprise him out.' Ian Peebles once likened Burke's bowling action to that of a policeman applying his truncheon to a particularly short miscreant's head.

Gordon Rorke, a giant of a man at 6ft 5in, was another member of the fearsome bowling battalion. Brian Chapman, writing in the *Daily Mirror*, described him as a 'honey of a chucker'. More of a problem to the English batsmen than Rorke's arm action was his 'drag', for he loomed extremely close to them before delivering the ball. Tom Graveney recalls: 'It was absolutely terrifying. We just stood there like rabbits against him. He had the longest drag of them all; his front foot pitched six feet beyond the popping crease.' Facing Rorke from a reduced distance of around seventeen yards was an unenviable experience. Graveney remembers the warning of his team-mate, Colin Cowdrey. 'Whatever you do,' said Cowdrey, 'don't play forward to him. He'll tread on your toes.'

Arthur Milton recalls his own baptism against the Australian throwers. 'The biggest problem with them was judging the line, length and pace.' He was opposed to Rorke in the state match at Sydney. 'I'd just picked my bat up and the ball glanced off it down to third man.' The eccentric nature of the bowling, fluctuating so wildly, could not be countered with any certainty. Rorke, at times, was so wayward that his wicket-keeper would have needed the assistance of stilts to prevent the ball soaring over his head. At Sydney, Rorke did eventually manage to direct a ball adjacent to the target. 'Around the third over I nicked one on to my off-stump,' says Milton. 'It snapped clean in half.'

147

The MCC side was required to follow-on but Rorke was no longer a threat in the second innings. Milton and Richardson put on 170 runs. 'Rorke had thrown out his arm while fielding,' says Milton. 'He was now just gentle medium-pace. After our big century stand, Peter and I walked off feeling rather pleased with ourselves.' Peter May also recalled their first meeting with Rorke. 'I never batted in a cap except under hot sun and I cannot believe that I would have taken readily to a helmet if they had been in vogue. But if I *had* worn one ever, it would have been against Rorke. I knew that if he pitched on the right spot, he would, as it were, hit double top, and there would not be much I could do about it.'

The first murmurings of the throwing furore stirred soon after the arrival of the MCC team in Perth in October. Keith Slater twice took May's wicket in the match against Western Australia. The dismissals occurred at less critical junctures than others (by Meckiff and Burke) during the forthcoming Test series. But they did carry alarming portents. Slater, in the MCC second innings, took four wickets. They included those of Milton and May – out to successive deliveries – and Graveney. In this spell of fourteen balls Slater did not concede a run.

'He was a tall fellow who electrified us by throwing slow off-breaks as obviously as Jim Burke threw his for New South Wales,' wrote Lyn Wellings. Graveney, with 177, and May had been happily unconcerned against Slater in the first innings. 'In the second innings,' continued Wellings, 'he was a fast-medium bowler and now his throw was far more important. It not only gave him zip off the sullen turf, but it enabled him to jerk the ball back from the off. The ball with which he bowled May was a vicious break-back.' It was, in the view of Tom Graveney, faster than any propelled by Ray Lindwall.

Across the continent in Melbourne the dangers of Meckiff were noted but disregarded. Jim Swanton said the fact that the Victorian bowler did not 'throw' particularly well deceived the MCC management. The lack of an official comment or complaint was to prove negligent and misguided. The qualms of the players did not, however, appear justified in the state match against Victoria. The measure of the MCC supremacy stifled any concern. Milton, with a century, Subba Row and Graveney all batted with refreshing assurance. Statham took seven wickets in Victoria's first innings and Lock six in the second innings, the last two in the final over of the match. The victory by 87 runs was a welcome sign as England moved undefeated towards the Test series.

Peter May did, however, remember his misgivings amid the joys of an exciting game. He had looked out from the pavilion on the home players engaged in fielding practice. 'One of them, a left-hander whom we knew to be Meckiff, was throwing the ball at a batsman. This seemed an odd way for a bowler to limber up. A few minutes later he was out in the middle bowling to Peter Richardson with exactly the same action.'

May later reflected that the wildness of a thrower contained in part the key to his effectiveness. 'A batsman has few hits at the ball, even in an eight-ball over. There is no rhythm about the action, the line and pace are unpredictable – just a sudden jerk and the ball arrives.'

A worried May was able to suspend his disbelief in a pleasurable batting interlude against an Australian XI at Sydney. The MCC won by 345 runs and in the match May scored two centuries, his second one in a single session of play. Graveney, with 70, assisted him in the first innings, combining in a stand of 149 after three wickets had fallen for 40 runs. Bill O'Reilly, in the *Sydney Morning Herald*, reported: 'May's innings dwarfed everything else. In partnership with Graveney, he played the dominant part in a batting display which collared the attack lock, stock and barrel.

'The most fascinating feature of May's brilliant on-side stroking,' continued O'Reilly, 'was his uncanny ability to take the ball actually on the rise and hit it powerfully while keeping it on the ground out of harm's way.' O'Reilly said the Australians could take comfort from the thought that May was always high-class entertainment value. 'His batting is beautiful to watch, even though it does cut painfully across the patriotic wishes that our bowlers will do well.'

One of those bowlers facing a batsman delightfully on song was a West Australian, Ray Strauss. The figures on the scoreboard moved around too rapidly for the Sydney crowd. A waggish barracker on the hill did find humour in the situation. As he watched Strauss dancing to May's tunes, he called out beseechingly: 'Push off to Vienna.' Raman Subba Row recalls: 'The game stopped. Everyone dissolved into laughter.'

The tempo of May's play was in marked contrast to that of a powerful Australian batting line-up. The Australian eleven was captained by Neil Harvey and included McDonald, O'Neill, Peter Burge and Bobby Simpson. In their second innings they were routed by Lock, bowling into the footmarks left by the fast bowlers. Richie Benaud recalls that Harvey played one of the great innings at Sydney. Harvey's 38 was scored out of a total of 103. His technique against the ball spinning wickedly out of the rough was inscribed with masterly defensive acumen.

May's decision not to enforce the follow-on yielded a century even more violent than in his first innings. This time he scored 106 of his 114 runs between lunch and tea. It earned him a prize of 500 dollars, equivalent to £400 sterling, offered by the *Sydney Telegraph*. 'The conditions were such that it did not seem to me that the newspaper was in much danger of spending much,' commented Lyn Wellings. 'Yet here was May collaring this big prize within days of the announcement of the inducement to bright cricket. He did so although there was a period midway through the afternoon when Subba Row (May's partner in a third-wicket stand of 180) had nearly all the bowling. His strokes were brilliant, whether orthodox or unorthodox. He drove balls of good length with tremendous power and he hit with equal power off the back foot anything even a fraction short.'

The target, with thirty-five minutes left before tea, was well within range. May had then scored 83, eight of which had been registered before lunch. Subba Row, during the next twenty-five minutes, so monopolised the bowling that May advanced his score by only one run. Signs from the dressing-room now communicated a need for urgent action. May, previously only vaguely aware of a prize on offer, now responded to the mounting excitement. He struck 13 runs off an over from Johnny Martin. A glorious off-drive for four off Strauss brought his century. At this point, Barry Jarman, the wicket-keeper, told him: 'You need 108.' Another boundary and a single to keep the strike took him into the last over bowled by Barry Fisher before tea.

'I had to refuse singles, which was against all my principles,' recalled May. 'But it would have put an intolerable burden on Raman. If anything had gone wrong, we would have neither of us have been able to face the rest of the team waiting in the dressing-room.' The uncertainty ended with two resounding boundaries. May pulled the third ball to the square-leg fence. He then rocked on to his back foot to square-cut the next ball for four. His mission completed, he relaxed to surrender his wicket to Fisher. 'It must have been the most generally popular innings I ever played,' said May. 'I gave a party with the proceeds of my prize and asked both teams and the press of both countries to it. It went very well.'

Colin Cowdrey says that May's innings at Sydney precisely described for him the blueprint of one-day batsmanship. 'Peter picked them up, all safe shots – and whack, the bowlers were helpless. Some of our modern players bowling against him would be given a severe shock. If he got to 40, they just wouldn't be able to hold him.' Two Australians also give voice to May's aptitude for the limited-overs game, which was not introduced until shortly after his retirement. Alan Davidson considers that his English rival would have decimated bowlers with his power. 'He would have disrupted the field with ones and twos and then found holes everywhere.'

Richie Benaud also extols a brilliance which can only be imagined. 'Peter was not only a great orthodox player, but also a wonderful improviser. I often followed the ball to the boundary with my eyes and then glanced at him to find just the hint of a smile at the corner of his lips. That was when he had picked me from the off stump through mid-wicket, or had hit a good-length ball through extra-cover off the back foot where other batsmen might have played it defensively off the front foot.'

Bill Bowes, writing in *The Cricketer*, said the worst piece of luck that could have happened at Brisbane was when Peter May won the toss in the first Test. England, against the odds and frozen by indecision, were beaten by eight wickets. The expectations were that the pitch would be lively until lunch. 'It was,' said Bowes, 'lively for three days, and at its most vicious in the mornings when the tarpaulin covers had been removed. The first ball of the series, bowled by Davidson to Richardson, lifted from a good length to strike the England opener in the chest.' England were dismissed for 134; but Bowes said that, if Meckiff had bowled anything like straight at his end, they would not have totalled 70. 'This bowler was almost a laughing stock. Never in my life had I seen such inaccuracy in a Test bowler. One forgot his jerky action. He aroused sympathy but, in the light of later events, this was a mistake.'

Benaud believes that England squandered their chance on a very green pitch at Brisbane, which should have suited them. As it was, Australia were restricted to a first innings lead of 52 runs. At this stage England held the initiative, with the prospect of bowling on a worn pitch in the fourth innings. The sense of adventure displayed by Australia's new batting star, Norman O'Neill, was in marked contrast to the painstaking vigil of Trevor Bailey. He was sent in by May at the fall of the first wicket in the second innings. It was, conceded the England captain, not one of his better moments.

Lyn Wellings said the decision committed England to a laborious defensive engagement. 'The Australian attack was never challenged and subdued as it should have been. It was allowed to retain its precarious balance to the end, while the England batsmen took their muted cue from Bailey.'

Bailey, either by design or under instructions, was content simply to occupy the crease. He was top scorer in both England's innings; his second innings of 68 was, though, a marathon spread over seven hours and thirty-eight minutes. He scored off only forty balls out of the 426 he received. Wellings ascribed the blame to May for framing a policy which took less account of runs than of time. 'It brought about the defeat it deserved,' he said. Benaud agrees that ultra-defensive batting cost England the match. 'It wasn't a very good game of cricket and Trevor's stint didn't do anything to help them; but it did immediately give us the idea that we might win.'

Benaud stole a march on his fellow captain in England's second innings. May, according to one Australian, had categorised Benaud as a merely competent leg-spinner. He then proceeded to show that he sincerely believed his own statement. Benaud bowled a couple of leg-breaks pitched outside the off stump. On each occasion May allowed them to pass through to the wicket-keeper. He then adopted the same measure in facing up to what seemed an identical ball. It turned back and hit his pads. May was out lbw without attempting a stroke. He had been foxed by Benaud's 'wrong'un', which he clearly thought did not exist.

England lost eight wickets in scoring 106 runs on a lamentable fourth day. Colin Cowdrey, sparkling alone amid the batting travesty, was controversially given out. His dismissal came at time when his form was such that it seemed likely that he could play England into a winning position. The stroke he played off Meckiff was fielded first bounce by Kline at backward square-leg. Cowdrey was so unconcerned at an apparently frivolous appeal that he did not even look at the umpire, Mel McInnes, who had swiftly given the decision against him. The version of a vexed incident, related by May, was that Cowdrey and even the adjacent fieldsmen seemed to think that the ball had fallen short of Kline. He was later asked for a statement and his response was that they did not question an umpire's decision.

'On the field the Australians gathered around Kline like conspirators,' reported Lyn Wellings. 'Neil Harvey, who was fielding on the other side of the wicket, advised Cowdrey not to go too quickly, the obvious inference being that he expected him to be recalled. Benaud had gone over to consult Kline, and afterwards we were informed that Kline had told him he had definitely made the catch. It did not look as if anyone on the field was very happy.'

May added: 'It was not McInnes's decision that bothered us but his indecision. He made what we thought were several other mistakes and misjudgements in the series. Having known him well and respected him in the past, we thought he was over the top.' McInnes was not, in fact, withdrawn until after another embarrassing error in the fourth Test. Jack Fingleton thought the Australian Cricket Board were grievously wrong and discourteous in not asking McInnes to stand down after the Brisbane Test as May had expressly requested.

In the second Test at Melbourne England were stunned by a devastating opening spell by Davidson. In the third over of the match Davidson took the wickets of Richardson, Watson and Graveney, the latter two with successive balls. The position was retrieved largely through May, who scored the first century by an England captain in Australia since Archie MacLaren in 1901–02. Australia, at one stage 255 for 2, collapsed against Statham and Loader to 308 all out. For this benefit they were indebted to another quality innings of 167 by Neil Harvey. 'A crowd of 71,000, on a working day, turned up to acclaim his hundred with the echoing roar that is peculiar to the vast Melbourne arena,' reported Jim Swanton.

This was the match in which Ian Meckiff confirmed the hostility which Trevor Bailey had forecast before the start of the series. He shared nine wickets with Davidson in the first innings and then wielded the thrust of a dagger to bowl out England for 87 in the second innings. It was their lowest score in Australia since 1903–04 when they were bowled out for 61 on the same ground. 'I never saw anything as blatant as Meckiff's action as, with the swell of the crowd in his ears, he came up that afternoon full pelt from the bottom end towards the pavilion,' said Swanton.

Meckiff recorded figures of six wickets for 38 runs in the rout. 'We were all thrown out,' is the scornful comment of Peter Richardson. The statement is endorsed by one Australian correspondent. He watched, from a square-leg vantage point, the dismissal of Peter May in the England first innings. 'I cannot believe that he even saw the ball with which Meckiff threw down his stumps. May was well set, the pitch was flat, the light was fine, and England needed runs. I would doubt that there was a lapse in his concentration. Meckiff chucked in his faster one and this was straight.'

Jim Swanton remembered a day of bright sunlight and looking on as May proceeded serenely beyond his century. His score had reached 113 and, as Peter himself related, 'I was thinking there were plenty more to come when Meckiff, with the new ball, produced an absolute thunderbolt. My bat was still in the air when it shattered my wicket.' Even at this stage, and despite his surprise, May and others in the England camp thought Meckiff was too uncontrolled to be considered a major threat. 'Suddenly, in our second innings on the Saturday afternoon, he got it right,' said May.

'His method was such that he had a devastating effect. He was very, very fast. Somehow one was mesmerised. It was an extraordinary feeling.'

In Australia there was anger at the insensitivity of some officials, umpires and players towards Meckiff. One observer said few of them knew him or understood what he was alleged to have done wrong or the law involved. Instead of trying to appreciate that Meckiff was a victim of what Sir Donald Bradman called the most complex problem cricket had known, they joined in the Fleet Street witch-hunt.

Meckiff, on his twenty-fourth birthday, was cheered from the Melbourne field after his Test triumph. 'But before long,' wrote Jack Pollard, 'he was sniped at by the people who had applauded him. His children were called "Chucker" by the neighbourhood kids and his relatives were repeatedly confronted by friends who asked: "Does Ian really throw?"' The severity of the pressures brought health problems and Meckiff had to receive medical care.

Meckiff made three tours – to South Africa, India and Pakistan – before he was officially branded as a thrower and expelled from the game. He was not called for throwing until his sixth series in 1963. Colin Egar was the umpire who no-balled him in the first Test against South Africa at Brisbane. At this time Meckiff had only been judged an offender twice in Sheffield Shield matches and never found guilty in seventeen previous Tests. His Victorian state side still supported him.

The disorder of illegal bowling tactics was, though, perceived by Meckiff's captain, Richie Benaud. He attended, along with other state representatives, a dinner hosted by Sir Donald Bradman at his home in Adelaide in January 1963. They were shown a selection of intriguing films, which Bradman had assembled over the years, spotlighting various bowlers who either had suspect actions or actions slightly out of the ordinary. Benaud was deeply affected by the parade of indiscretions. At the end of the evening he said that in future he would not continue to bowl anyone called for throwing by an umpire. Furthermore, he stated that he would not bowl anyone whom *he* considered to have a suspect action.

Gordon Rorke, one of the notorious bowlers against England, was the first to test Benaud's resolve in a match between New South Wales and South Australia. Rorke was underbowled for reasons not primarily connected with legitimacy. Benaud was firmly told that his duty was to captain the side; they, the selectors, would determine whether their nominated bowlers erred in fairness. Benaud was not to be bullied out of his convictions. He told the selectors that he would continue his crusade against illegal bowlers. To drive home his point, he would not only sideline them but open the batting with them as well.

The sequel, involving the sorely tried Meckiff, came at Brisbane in December 1963. Meckiff, reinstated in the Australian team against South Africa, was no-balled four times in his opening over. Benaud, in the light of his high-profile campaign, had no alternative but to remove him instantly from the attack. 'It was very sad because it had a detrimental effect on one of the nicest men ever to step on to a cricket field. Ian never played first-class cricket again. It left a hollow feeling with everyone who had taken part in the game.' The exit of Meckiff, strangely, ran parallel with the farewell of Benaud, who captained Australia for the last time at Brisbane. In a grade match following the Test he broke the third finger of his bowling hand, attempting a catch at slip. Before the end of the year he had handed over the reins of captaincy to Bobby Simpson.

Peter May, for different reasons, was malignly harassed as a scapegoat on his last tour of Australia. Even more sourly, on a personal note, was the treatment meted out to his then fiancée, Virginia. Allegations that he was neglecting his team to spend time with her were rejected by one sympathetic correspondent, Lyn Wellings. 'There was no evidence whatsoever that he was any less a leader than he had been before the arrival of Miss Gilligan. The attack was unjust and was resented no less among responsible members in the press box than in the dressing-room of May's side.'

The future Mrs May was the guest of her uncle and aunt, Arthur and Penny, in Australia. (Arthur Gilligan, the former Sussex and England captain, was working as a Test radio commentator.) As a broadcaster, Gilligan enjoyed a successful radio partnership with a former Australian adversary, Victor Richardson. Their buoyant conversation pieces enlivened the dark hours of English winter mornings and brought a healthy smack of fun to Australian homes. Gilligan did much to cement the bond between the two countries. The reunion of Virginia and Peter, following their engagement in the previous April, was a happy occasion. It coincided with Peter's batting feats against the Australian XI at Sydney. He was able to dip into his newspaper prize money to buy her a bracelet as a birthday present.

Virginia had selected a cherished holiday abroad to celebrate her twenty-third birthday. She had first travelled to New Zealand to visit relatives, including her uncle, Frank, the eldest of the Gilligan brothers, and headmaster at the Wanganui Collegiate School. In Australia she was to become embroiled in a sickening vendetta. Clouding her holiday was the newspaper fiction that she and Peter had been secretly married. Virginia recalls: 'The press rang my parents at our home at Shamley Green at two o'clock in the morning.' 'Do you know that your daughter and Peter May have married?' was the message given to her father.

The impertinent announcement was vigorously disputed by Harold Gilligan. 'My father let loose a stream of rude words down the line and put the phone down.' Virginia and Peter were horrified by the unjustified attack. It was followed by a series of frantic telephone calls to them to clarify the situation in Australia. 'Daddy,' insisted Virginia, 'you know me better than that. We've got wedding plans for when we return home. I'm not going to get married in some little Australian town.' The fabricated story fuelled May's resentment against the press. He never entirely forgave them for the intrusion into his private life.

Friends and contemporaries believe that a sensitive and vulnerable man did not subsequently have the same appetite for cricket. Colin Cowdrey believes that the scars of the tour never properly healed. 'Having been peerless as both batsman and captain, Peter was quite taken aback by the hostility of the criticism and badly hurt.'

The unsavoury episode involving Virginia was the crowning insult. England, despite their welcome resolution in an honourable draw in the third Test at Sydney, returned home in chastened mood. May and Cowdrey had hinted at a recovery at Sydney. Benaud was forced on to defence as the England pair sought quick runs before the declaration. The rekindling of aggression, hitherto lacking in the series, was demonstrated in their fourth-wicket stand of 182 runs. It now seems remarkable that they had batted as low as five and six in the earlier Test at Melbourne. Cowdrey hit an unbeaten century and, in the words of Lyn Wellings, 'swinging his bat freely and timing his strokes so exactly that there was no need to run as a precautionary measure when he struck his fours'.

The stand ended when May, eight runs short of his century, was bowled by Burke. It was a shortish off-break, delivered in Burke's 'dart-throwing' style, which overcame the English captain. Jim Swanton wrote: 'After lunch Benaud for the first time employed Burke whom I had too hurriedly supposed might not be used on the grounds of conscience'.

With Laker absent, Peter May had little choice but to gamble in the fourth Test at Adelaide. His bold decision to put Australia in to bat was an attempt to save the series. It misfired as McDonald hit 170 and Australia totalled 476. Peter Richardson recalls his captain's dismay at the turn of events. Motoring back to their hotel at Glenelg, May turned to his team, and said: 'I'm sorry Jim was so tired and couldn't play today.' Richardson says: 'We'd played our hearts out. Peter was angry – he'd been let down as we all had – but his remark was as nasty as he would ever get. It is not easy to be forgiving in such circumstances.' Benaud's leg-spin gave him nine wickets in the match; and Australia, victors by ten wickets, regained the Ashes. Ray Lindwall, 'the last of the straight-armers', was restored to the team at Adelaide in place of the injured Meckiff. It was singularly appropriate that a doughty campaigner should enjoy his own celebration in the final Test at Melbourne. He overtook Clarrie Grimmett's record of 216 wickets. Only three other bowlers – Lillee, Benaud and McKenzie – have taken more wickets for Australia.

England's unexpected downfall, despite protestations that Australia's peal of victory had a hollow ring, signalled the end of an era. The verdict was that Peter May carried the burden of a 'too elderly team'. The veterans of happier days had embarked on a tour when past their prime. Alan Davidson, of the triumphant Australians, presents a modest and tactful appraisal. 'We were on a learning curve and only going to get better. England's players had reached their peak.' For Richie Benaud, the rising star among Test captains, there was mingled pleasure and near bewilderment. 'I've played in three series against England over six years and I've never known what it's like to win one before.'

Peter May maintained that the apparent submissiveness amid the provocations of the tour did not affect the outcome of the series. 'We were always going to struggle. If you have lost your keen edge, Australia finds it out.' In a later conversation, he believed that one of the causes of England's decline was the outcry for results in the mid-1950s which had led to bad wickets at home. 'The policy rebounded on us in Australia because we had fewer batsmen who could put together a big score on any sort of wicket.'

The problem facing the selectors prior to the tour was separating good and ordinary players, May said. The consequence was that, although the right men, based on averages, went to Australia, very few possessed the technique to score 150 on a good pitch. 'They had all become accustomed to graft for seventies on slow turners.'

The onset of illness was to deprive the emerging young players, at the dawn of the 1960s, of the counsel and example of a champion who prospered in all conditions. Without Peter May, disabled by an internal problem which necessitated an operation, Surrey's tenure as champions ended in 1959. He captained them in only seven championship matches; and of these they won six, including two victories over Yorkshire, the eventual champions.

His well-wishers did not know then that a magnificent career was drawing to a close. His lamented retirement was premature but it was final because Peter May would never have accepted being second best. Nor was he a man to prolong the curtain calls.

Chapter 14

A Time to Declare

'Peter portrayed the traditional qualities of the game and these were within his thoughts right until the end.'

Micky Stewart

The 'unusually retiring man', in the words of Colin Cowdrey, describes a player who scattered his stardust on the field, but was rooted in detachment off it. Throughout his brilliant career Peter May kept his head firmly out of the clouds. He accomplished so much in a comparatively short time and yet he was the least inclined to linger in nostalgia. The paradox is that for a batsman of his high rank he did not consider that he was doing anything out of the ordinary.

Peter Richardson, his England contemporary and a close friend, often wondered whether May really enjoyed cricket. The instinctive talents, sublimely expressed from boyhood onwards, kept his admirers enthralled, but he was never seduced by the acclaim. He could be quietly pleased if one or other of his glittering strokes was complimented. Richardson, batting with him on one occasion, offered words of praise. May, after some moments of thought, said: 'You're right; it did go rather well.' Richardson says: 'Peter did like to be noticed, but without fuss.'

The contract May made with cricket was essentially the pleasure of a job well done; he was not held to ransom by fool's gold. As a captaincy record-holder, he would have been in accord with C. B. Fry. In a radio interview, dwelling on the qualities of winning teams, Fry was asked: 'They tell me, Sir, you were once a great captain?' His rejoinder bordered on the apoplectic. 'Young man, of course I was a great captain. I had *great* bowlers.'

Peter May was equally blessed during his halycon summers. His investment in those years was an immense pride as a player which he always tried to communicate to the men under his command.

159

All who knew him considered it a tragedy that he was so cruelly treated on his last tour of Australia. 'His enjoyment of cricket had been squeezed out of him,' observes one friend. Only a few years earlier May had recalled the jaded feeling which affects even the most dedicated on the daily cricket round. The sparkle was not long dimmed. His pulse would quicken at the prospect of new challenges. There was a buoyancy in his military stride as he walked to his city office on one pre-season morning. 'I broke my umbrella on the pavement. I was practising my off-drive and the ball must have kept low.'

In 1959, following the desolation of the downfall in Australia, May presided over a changing order. Trevor Bailey and Jim Laker had made their last Test appearances. Only six players – Cowdrey, Milton, Evans, Statham, Trueman and May himself – of the MCC party in the previous winter played in the first Test against India at Trent Bridge. Gubby Allen, the chairman of the selectors, had announced the manifesto of a three-year plan. His objective was to produce a team able to topple Australia on their next visit in 1961.

It was a propitious season for experiment against the Indian tourists, who were beaten in all five Tests, the first time this had been achieved in England. In a fine summer, and on now covered wickets, there was a feast of scoring throughout the land. The England selectors were able to spread their nets freely in this rehearsal for more taxing duels ahead. They auditioned or recalled as many as twenty-one players against India. M. J. K. Smith, a future England captain, and Ken Barrington, two of those reinstated, celebrated with compelling performances. There was also, impressively on view, one newcomer from Lancashire, Geoff Pullar, who registered a strong claim for the vacancy of opening batsman.

Peter May resumed his cricket in a heartening manner after his marriage in April. The sun shone with tropical warmth as he led the new-look England team to an innings victory at Nottingham. Spurring his recruits was a vintage century – his thirteenth in Tests – and the familiar relentless power, time and again, shuddered the field. One of his impotent rivals was Subhash 'Fergie' Gupte, who was often unplayable as a leg-spinner in Lancashire League cricket. He had been expected to pose a genuine threat to England's batsmen on this tour. Gupte's venom was expelled by May. His batting, almost unfair in its flawless execution, cast a spell as alluring as that of a snake-charmer.

In the third Test at Leeds, May made his fifty-second successive Test appearance to equal the record of Frank Woolley. Then, quite out of the blue, illness intervened. It clouded what should have been an exultant July occasion, with Surrey once again on the victory rampage against Yorkshire at Bradford. 'Towards the end of the match,' recalled May, 'I felt so awful that I handed over to Alec Bedser. I had never had to do anything like that before and I was very depressed as I drove over the Pennines to Lymm where the England team was staying for the fourth Test at Old Trafford.'

May's fitness did not improve and Colin Cowdrey, not selected for the match, was hurriedly called up from Kent to take over the captaincy. After two days as a disconsolate spectator at Manchester, May returned home to Surrey. His illness was diagnosed as an ischiorectal abscess. It was operated on at the Central Middlesex Hospital. Peter did not learn until later that recovery was protracted because the wound was deep inside and the tissues had to heal from inside out. He had not envisaged this development; but after his convalescence, lasting beyond the autumn, he pronounced himself fit to tour the West Indies.

It was to prove an unwise decision as the illness re-occurred in the Caribbean. Peter was joined by Virginia and her parents and they went on a cruise to Caracas immediately following the third Test in Jamaica. It was a welcome break from cricket, but Peter was becoming increasingly uncomfortable. At the end of the cruise a concerned Virginia cancelled the original plan to return home with her parents. 'Peter is not at all well and I'm staying with him,' she said. Peter had, to this point, optimistically thought the wound of the abscess would heal. He had not mentioned his discomfort to anyone outside the family. It had now reopened and was seeping blood. Brian Statham, as they showered one day, did notice it and was horrified.

Despite the pain, Peter actually played in the colony match at George-town, British Guiana. His problem increased when he lost the toss and fielded for nearly two days. 'It was this ordeal in the humidity of the Demerara River estuary that finished me,' he said. Medical counsel now prevailed and he was expressly forbidden to play any more cricket. Virginia rejoined Peter for the following Test match after which they flew home for him to undergo a second and satisfactory operation. A wiser man after the trauma of the persistent illness, Peter this time made sure that the healing process was complete. Another Australian tour was looming; and he withdrew from all cricket in 1960 to conserve his energies for the tussles in the following summer.

Colin Cowdrey, who had taken over as captain of the MCC team in

161

the West Indies, and now was again May's deputy in the first two Tests against Australia in 1961, maintains that this was a series England should have won. May returned as captain at Headingley on a ground where good fortune had always favoured him. One of his most loyal companions, Fred Trueman, routed Australia at Leeds. England won by eight wickets and Trueman, with Les Jackson as his staunch ally, took 11 wickets for 88 runs in the match. They were his best figures in Test cricket.

Australia, having reached 183 for two before tea on the first day, collapsed to 237 all out. In the course of six overs, Trueman took five wickets for 16 runs. Harvey and O'Neill, distinctly threatening before the interval, were overwhelmed by Trueman's speed. Australia were bustled into submission by the second new ball and lost their last seven wickets for 21 runs. It was to prove the turning-point of the match. England were, though, indebted to Cowdrey in establishing a lead of 62 runs. Harvey's presence and his mastery against the spin of Lock and Allen baulked England on the Saturday. He scored his second 50 of the match and such was his assurance that May once again looked to Trueman.

The Yorkshireman proudly remembers the exhortation of his captain. 'You're the only one I can rely on,' he was told. The fervour of his response was breathtaking. Off his third ball, Harvey was caught by Dexter in the covers. 'Fred then announced that he was going to shorten his run and bowl off-cutters,' remembered May. 'I had hesitated to ask him to try something unusual but I had underestimated his accuracy. From then on he kept getting batsmen out and a match which only a few minutes before had promised to be a hard struggle was racing to a finish.' Trueman took six wickets for five runs in 47 balls; and Australia from 99 for two were bowled out for 120. England required only 59 runs to win and the match was over with two days to spare. Trueman, heaving into furious action, had produced a winning counter and the series was now levelled. 'We were utterly bemused by the speed of it all,' declared a grateful captain.

The champagne tonic at Leeds ought to have bubbled over into another victory in the conclusive fourth Test at Old Trafford. The glasses were recharged as Ted Dexter thrillingly hoisted England on to the threshold of success. His assault brought another change in fortunes in a fluctuating game. Australia had earlier conceded a deficit of 177 runs on the first innings. May hit another of his nineties, so polished in certainty as to deserve the seal of a century. He shared a third-wicket stand of 111 runs with Pullar. A succession of dropped catches in Australia's second innings, one at slip reprieving the century-maker, Bill Lawry, was to prove costly in the final reckoning. May was later adamant that the absence of Colin Cowdrey, unable to play because of a throat infection, had an important bearing on the match. Cowdrey's fielding prowess alone, he contended, would have put an England victory beyond doubt.

Richie Benaud, the Australian captain, says that he had hoped to set a target of around 250 runs. This was eventually achieved but only because Davidson and McKenzie put on 98 in a last-wicket stand. Before this unexpected rally Australia were only 157 runs ahead. Defeat appeared a near formality. Allen had taken three wickets without cost in fifteen balls. Davidson transformed the game with a massively defiant assault; his unbeaten 77 included 20 in one over from Allen. England had been rebuffed in their thrust for victory. It could now only be countenanced by a fevered imagination. There were only three hours and 50 minutes left for play. Dexter's 76, cudgelled in 84 minutes, tilted the game in England's direction yet again. The impossible had become possible; at 150 for 1, the quest had to be pursued. The chance was there but May, soon to be implausibly snared, foresaw the dilemma and the risks involved in pressing for runs on a worn pitch.

Benaud recalls that the subsequent happenings had had their origins on the previous evening. In conversation with Ray Lindwall, who was visiting England in a press capacity, he suggested one possible measure if Australia ran into trouble. He asked Lindwall for his opinion on the then unusual tactic of bowling round the wicket into the footmarks to the right-handers. The answer was clearly in the affirmative, as is revealed by a remarkable spell of match-winning bowling. The series was decided in a dramatic twenty minutes before tea.

Benaud's tactic, while preying on the batsmen's nerves, was a gamble against Dexter in full flight. 'Ted played a magnificent innings; and it was only after I went round the wicket that I had him caught by Grout.' May was next man in; and by now he was compelled to follow Dexter's lead. 'I tried to bowl Peter behind his pads first ball but didn't get it far enough out into the footmarks,' relates Benaud. 'The second ball pitched OK though it could have gone anywhere on landing in the rough. It just happened to hit the stumps though I had again set out to bowl him behind his pads.' It was the crucial dismissal and the ball which won the match.

May, uncharacteristically sweeping, at first thought he had escaped. But a bail, dislodged by Benaud's looping delivery, had fallen silently to the ground. It lay there like a leaf disturbed by a capricious breeze. Neil Harvey, fielding at leg-slip, sported a huge grin. He turned to the perplexed batsman and said: 'Sorry, mate, you're out.' May was later, in a conversation with Alf Gover, to concede an untimely rush of blood. In his haste to force quick runs he had disobeyed the cardinal principle of playing straight. 'Yes, I was guilty,' he said. 'It was a big mistake.'

Benaud took four wickets in five overs in his astonishing coup at Old Trafford. His other victims were Brian Close, caught in the deep by O'Neill after one towering six, and Subba Row, bowled one short of a valiant half-century. Australia emerged, almost unbelievably, from the shadows of defeat to win by 54 runs and retain the Ashes.

Jim Swanton told Benaud that he had succeeded with a 'gigantic confidence trick'. Afterwards, in a happy Australian dressing-room, Benaud and Harvey could scarcely believe their luck. 'Neil and I just sat there having a few beers, and whenever we caught each other's eye we roared with laughter,' said Benaud. May, while acknowledging that he had been outsmarted by the impudent enterprise, understandably took a more sober view of the events. 'We should not have had to make so many runs. We lost because we did not hold our catches.'

As one writer has said, Peter May bowed out of Test cricket with music playing rather softly in the background. His farewell deserved the accompaniment of a composition in a major key. The fruitless series against Australia in 1961 was his last and, after one more season with Surrey, he declared his innings closed in first-class cricket.

The awesome command was, however, still in evidence in one of two county games he played in 1963. The match was against Sussex at Guildford. Ted Dexter remembers an 'old-fashioned county pitch, grassy but not firm, really a club wicket, with each ball taking out little divots. There were a few current England batsmen appearing, like Kenny Barrington, Jim Parks and myself, and we all struggled for runs. For Peter it was not a problem. He had no inhibitions about hitting it over the top and made it very difficult for the bowlers to find any sort of length. He was head and shoulders above the rest of us.'

Peter May was still only 32 when he left the first-class scene. Personal considerations of a growing family and a need to develop his business career were cited as the reasons for his early retirement. Over the following years there were pressing petitions to him to return to the game. The wistful overtures were in vain, but hopes still lingered throughout the 1960s. The formal tribute in *Wisden* was delayed until 1971.

May himself had few regrets about his departure. One was that he had failed by fifteen to reach one hundred centuries. He would have welcomed this seal on his career. It would have enabled him to emulate the achievement of W. G. Grace, the only amateur to reach this milestone. But it was an omission he was prepared to accept amid other preoccupations. 'I never saw the game as a personal thing, which was why I enjoyed it so much. I was always more interested in how we did as a team,' he said. Others, including John Warr, express a sadness at May's premature retirement. 'Had Peter played into his forties,' says Warr, 'he might well, on covered wickets and against modern bowling, have scored 200 centuries to overhaul Jack Hobbs's record.'

The conclusion, in the reflections of Peter's widow, Virginia, presents an intriguing postscript. 'Peter had done a big stint; he just didn't really enjoy cricket, and the pressures that went with it, any more.' In the years of his retirement, Peter would happily turn out to entertain the crowds in charity matches on the Surrey commons at Dunsfold and Cranleigh where the visiting celebrities included the entertainers, Harry Secombe and Eric Sykes. But these interludes began to pall when one family friend, an aspiring fast bowler, came to view his contests with Peter too earnestly. 'What's the big deal?' exclaimed Peter. 'I just want your wicket,' said the persevering opponent. This was now becoming too serious; it was an imposition to be confronted with trivial challenges in his leisure time. Virginia adds: 'Peter sold his boots and all his cricket gear, so that nobody could ask him to come along and play.'

Before he called a halt to cricket Peter was persuaded to play for the Charterhouse Friars against Harrow Wanderers in the first round of *The Cricketer* Cup in its inaugural summer of 1967. One Carthusian admirer described what was for him an unexpected, and unforgettable, epilogue. 'Peter May was still in his thirties and, in a properly ordered world, would still have been captain of England. On the dusty, turning wicket Harrow had struggled to 180, and had then made that total seem substantial by taking three wickets.

'From the start, May seemed to be playing a quite different game from everyone else, on a quite different pitch. In partnership with a young Oxford blue and future Hampshire captain, Richard Gilliat (a total contrast in everything except determination), he made an effortless, chanceless, peerless century, transforming a tense contest into a masterly exhibition. At the end, he provided me with my last indelible image of his greatness. Only a handful of runs were needed, and Harrow finally dispensed with their slip. The next two balls, from their quick bowler, were both on a good defensive length just outside the off stump; he late-cut both, off the full face of the bat, so delicately and so fine that each time the ball brushed the sightscreen on its way to the undergrowth behind the scoreboard.'

In the tumult of the apartheid controversy, the first murmurings of which were heard during the D'Oliveira affair in 1968, many good friends became estranged. It was to extend in its repercussions to the reign of Peter May as chairman of the Test selectors in the 1980s. Jim Swanton recalled a 'dire catalogue of high passions, bewilderment on one side and exasperation on the other'. The long and acrimonious chapter began in the summer of 1968 when the MCC called off their tour of South Africa after John Vorster (the South African prime minister) had said that D'Oliveira's presence in the MCC team to South Africa was unacceptable. The saga ended with the last-minute cancellation of the South Africa tour to England by the Cricket Council at the request of the government in May 1970.

In a complex issue, the breaches in some cricketing relations, including the one between Peter May and David Sheppard, were never fully healed. Sheppard took a high-profile stance as an anti-apartheid spokesman. May, while disagreeing with the political situation in the republic, was sympathetic towards those people, including cricketers, who went out to earn a living in South Africa. Virginia May recalls: 'Peter was very upset with David over the affair. They were in two camps. My father and Peter sincerely hoped that all cricketers would support cricket. They saw this as a genuine option and the way forward.'

Other long-standing friends, including John Perry and Peter Nathan, say that May was not easily dissuaded from relaxing his views once he had taken up a particular position. 'You would need to be a very good advocate to change his mind,' says Perry. David Sheppard also refers to the unswerving nature of a man with whom he vainly sought harmony after their friendship was disrupted. 'Peter could be very unyielding in certain circumstances,' he says.

May, writing in the mid-1980s, restated his view that England should play cricket with everybody possible in those relatively few countries that played the game. 'It seems to me that those who wish to isolate South African cricket . . . are harming the very people whom they profess to help. Moreover, by refusing to co-operate in the huge liberalisation in sport which is taking place there, we are strengthening the hands of those who oppose change in South Africa.' His good offices in South Africa during the long exclusion from international cricket are emphasised by his widow.

May was saddened by the knowledge that old friends in South Africa, who had, he said, served the non-whites better than their critics in England, should shroud our name in dishonour. 'I have not enjoyed seeing good men and good friends treated with contempt by critics often wilfully ignorant of the facts.'

Raman Subba Row, another opponent of apartheid, did not allow his friendship with May to be soured by recriminations. As chairman of the Test and County Cricket Board, he was later to observe at first hand the dilemma faced by May during his term as chairman of the selectors. The irony of the situation was that well-meaning English players going out to coach in South Africa, often in the townships, had become politically unacceptable. 'It did make Peter's position as chairman extremely difficult because inevitably even this worthy activity was coloured by political considerations.'

Subba Row was also mindful of the more mercenary rebel tours in the 1980s. Soon after taking over from Alec Bedser as chairman in 1982, May was disadvantaged in his selections. He was deprived of fifteen players outlawed by the TCCB after taking part in an unofficial tour in the previous winter. The future of English cricket, as Subba Row reveals, was severely imperilled. 'It was an unhappy situation. The knock-on effects of the apartheid furore were quite painful for us. It is not generally known, but we were as close as a whisker from having no one to play against.'

Peter May, having elected against all expectations to take on this high office at Lord's, was beset by so many insoluble problems. 'When times are hard you are constantly ducking and weaving,' says Subba Row. On a happier note, May had been, to his astonishment, nominated by Billy Griffith for the MCC presidency in 1980. At fifty, he was one of the youngest to be appointed to this office. 'Come on, let's do it,' said Virginia. 'You may not be asked again. Let's enjoy it while we can.' Sir Oliver Popplewell, one of May's successors in the post, says: 'Peter was the ideal person for this position. He was good with people and delightful without being over-effusive.'

May had resumed his links with first-class cricket as a selector in 1965. Doug Insole, then chairman, remembers their supportive relationship. 'Peter was utterly steadfast and reliable and we had a very happy alliance. In his new role he was much more imaginative and adventurous without the cares of playing.' Insole was among those who instigated May's

167

appointment as chairman in 1982. By this time the media involvement had intensified, as Peter was well aware, and he knew he was setting himself up as an easy target in a merciless shooting gallery. It is still a source of amazement to many people that he should expose himself to criticism and even, sadly, derision, however unwarranted. 'I was quite surprised that he agreed to our invitation and by the fact that he stayed on as long as he did,' says Insole.

May was swayed by the objective of restoring discipline, which had seriously declined in first-class cricket. Colin Cowdrey applauds the aim, but believes that the good intentions of his friend were dispersed by the gap in generations. It is a familiar story which has remained unresolved during the recent tenure of Raymond Illingworth. The irritations multiplied, as May found himself increasingly displeased by the lack of efficiency. David Gower, as the England captain, was a particular disappointment. Gower's casual approach was at variance with May's standards. 'He expected David and others to address themselves to the homework needed in big cricket,' says Cowdrey. 'In his playing days Peter would always prepare notes on the jobs he had to do.'

The verdict of Virginia May, a supportive and protective partner during an uneasy time, is that her husband's advice was spurned by the England players. 'You're behind the times,' they said. It is in the nature of young men to rebel against elders and want to chart their own courses. But it is incumbent upon them to listen, as others did before them, to gain increase in stature and wisdom. The values which Peter espoused can never be outdated. 'If they were not prepared to be guided by Peter,' adds Virginia, 'then they were not likely to listen to anybody.'

Christopher Martin-Jenkins, writing in *The Cricketer*, struck a note of understanding when May resigned in November 1989. He urged his readers to reflect upon an unlucky reign and said that many critics had invested May with powers which were not at his disposal. 'Like Alec Bedser before him, Peter May tried hard to persuade the TCCB that their first priority should be a strong England team. Yet during his period in office the number of overseas players in county teams fell only slightly; pitches in county cricket continued to provide, on the whole, an unsatisfactory preparation for Test cricket.'

Charges were made of a lack of continuity amid these crisis years. The roll-call of dethroned captains included Keith Fletcher, Bob Willis, Mike Gatting, David Gower, John Emburey and Chris Cowdrey. Some were justified but others open to question. May's cause was not helped by frequent injuries. Greater players than those available to him would have been hard put to resist the humiliations inflicted by the West Indies upon England in three successive series in the 1980s. The catalogue of reverses was later balanced by more satisfactory results, and May's pride was bolstered by triumphs against Australia, twice in successive series.

His departing recommendations included the need for a full programme of four-day championship cricket and the assertion of his strongly held views on restricted recruitment of overseas players. He always maintained that English cricket had suffered from the neglect of home-bred young-sters. Unproven candidates from overseas had blocked the progression of our own talents. He left cricket, unjustly pilloried by lesser men who refused to admit that the apprenticeship and craft of other days had been ousted by short-term options.

Jack Bailey also expressed the anger of many in cricket circles. 'It was a shame that the gifts of quiet charm, sensitive but firm handling of many issues, and a dedication – all of which he possessed in abundance but he was not always adept at showing the world outside – should have been scantily regarded at the end of his administrative career.'

Micky Stewart presents another salutary footnote on an honourable man. His friendship with Peter extended over forty years, so he is well able to judge the convictions of a master of cricket. 'When you have, as Peter had, cricket in your heart; when you see peripheral activities affecting the game, you feel it very deeply. He had a sense of responsibility to cricket and so much to offer.'

Epilogue
A Private Man in a Public World

'His gifts were sublime, even mysterious, and he bore them with honour, modesty and distinction.'

Wisden obituary

A November meeting at his Hampshire home in 1994, only a few weeks before his death, is my last memory of a brave champion. Peter May was clearly a sick man, but the sheaf of correspondence on his desk denoted his continuing industry. Unfailingly courteous as ever, he rose from his chair to welcome me. My visit was to discuss a collaboration on this biography, which sadly was not destined to be pursued.

There had been an uncharacteristic delay in his response to my earlier overture. I was much heartened by a cheerful note which seemed to indicate that the reported news of his illness was not as bad as feared. 'I have had a short spell in hospital which rather slowed me up,' he wrote. 'I am pleased to say that I feel much better.' Across the world in Melbourne, watching another Test match against Australia, I was saddened by the announcement of his death. It was a warm and sunny afternoon preceding the dawn of the New Year. The flags were at half-mast on a ground where, thirty-six years before, he had decorated the scene with a century mingling charm and resolution.

The misleading diffidence of Peter May led one observer to place him in the gallery of Harold Pinter portraits, buttoned up with a scarcely penetrable ambiguity. Peter would have thought it strange to be regarded in this enigmatic light. The excessive modesty was deceiving. Peter, in the delightful phrase of one of his daughters, was never a man to 'throw whoopees'. He was a kindly man who needlessly played himself down. In conversation a mischievous smile would be accompanied by a shy chuckle. For those who gained his trust he was attentive and supportive; as his

170

interviewer, I recall how he would offer supplementary questions for my investigation. They often provided me with new insights on given topics.

In the company of his family, or a close group of friends, Peter was a fountain of lively humour. He took an incorrigible delight in the foibles of people. As a public figure, he was ceremonially correct, but a chink in this demeanour was revealed on one overseas tour. Peter disliked the small talk which is commonplace at social events. After one interminable cocktail party conversation, he was clearly appalled by the chatter. He took a fellow cricketer and guest, Peter Richardson, to one side and said: 'How can anyone be *so boring?*' It was the simplest of sallies but Richardson says: 'Peter was being dismissive, but his dry response was also so very funny.'

Doug Insole presents another tour anecdote. The baritone voice, displayed to good effect in the Gilbert and Sullivan opera at school, was paraded again. 'Together with Peter Richardson, he and I made a recording of a version of Cole Porter's "Let's Do It". This had been written and performed for the team's Saturday Night Club in South Africa. Peter did his vocal stuff with great gusto and considerable enjoyment,' remembers Insole.

The polite shield was lowered in the bonhomie of relaxed gatherings. 'Peter was anything but a dry stick in those circumstances,' says another lifelong friend, John Warr. The laugh lines, exchanged with his adored daughters, reflected Peter's enjoyment of running gags. These comical sayings could reduce the family to laughter bordering on hysteria. Tears of joy would stream down their faces as they encored expressions which had aroused amusement weeks before. Onlookers would be bemused. 'We would all fall about laughing,' says Virginia. 'No one could understand why.' The incomprehension only served to heighten their laughter.

John Warr was affectionately known as 'Funny Uncle John' in the May household. J. J. describes Peter as a 'warm and emotional man', who was at his happiest and best within his family. Another long-running bout of repartee followed the presentation of a pair of silver pear trees to Virginia and Peter. The gifts marked their Silver Wedding anniversary. They also carried a reminder of Peter's only cricketing 'pair'. He was twice dismissed for a duck by Ron Hooker and Fred Titmus in the match against Middlesex at Lord's in 1961. The greetings of the Mays and the Warrs invariably touched upon the health of the trees, made animate by the names of the Middlesex bowlers. 'How are they?' was the jocular expression of concern. 'They're all right,' chimed Virginia and Peter in reply. 'Ron is a little better than Fred at the moment.'

The friendship of the families was sealed by the bestowal of god-parentages on their children. Anniversaries and birthdays were the times for convivial parties. On Peter's sixty-fourth birthday on New Year's Eve 1993, the decision was taken to surprise him with a celebration. J. J. and his wife, Valerie, were the only non-members of the family present at the party. Their invitation had been kept secret from Peter. The Warrs were staying with a neighbouring farmer and their arrival was unannounced. When Peter walked into the room, J. J. gestured in mock surprise. 'What are you doing here?' he said. Peter was bowled over by the sally. 'He thought it was absolutely hilarious that I should challenge him in this way at his own party.'

A sense of duty did carry Peter through his social obligations. 'He was so shy,' says Warr. 'We almost had to drag him to parties.' It was a symptom of his embarrassment as a guest at entertainments rather than taking the lead on an official basis, as he did as England captain and later as a meticulous host looking after company guests at Lord's. The ordeal of entering a crowded room coupled with the recognition of his celebrity left him nervous and ill-at-ease. It is a common malady which he shared with others, apparently more ebullient, and of similar status.

When he was on duty, prepared and in control, Peter cut a more confident figure. During his playing days, and while still a bachelor, he spent many winter evenings at cricket dinners. In 1957, he estimated an attendance at 75 events. He was required to speak at nearly all of them. They were not, as he said, dictated by a desire for oratory, but by an awareness of the need to keep himself informed of trends by meeting cricketers at all levels. He recalled one dinner which he attended during his reign as England captain. The first two speakers far overstepped the bounds of time. 'When my turn came, I got up and said that I wished our Test team were blessed with openers who would stay on their feet as long as the opening pair that evening.'

Peter was essentially a private man in a public world. He did, though, appear to have been unnecessarily discreet on one occasion. Two of his closest friends were excluded from his confidence. John Perry recalls that Peter was his best man at his wedding in Shrewsbury in April 1958. 'Peter quite literally stopped the traffic in the centre of the town. The crowds had all gathered to see the England captain.' Perry and his bride, Pat, went on to spend their honeymoon in St Mawes, Cornwall. Ten days into the holiday, Perry called into the local newsagents to buy a morning paper. One headline met his astonished gaze. It announced: 'England captain to marry.' The only possible explanation was that in the excitement of his own wedding Peter and Virginia had forgotten to advise him of their own imminent engagement. There were two interesting sequels in the weddings of Peter and of Colin Cowdrey. They both stayed, in their turn, at the same honeymoon hotel as the Perrys in St Mawes and occupied the same room, no. 12.

In the 1970s, following employment with the London insurance brokers, E. R. Wood, Peter was appointed as broker and Executive Director by Willis, Faber and Dumas Limited (now the Willis Corroon Group). Jerry Lodge, one business associate, recalls that Peter was the perfect company ambassador. 'Through his personality, he seemed to know somebody at the highest level in every major company in the land. This had a large bearing on Willis currently having the largest portfolio of UK corporate business of any insurance broker.' Lodge disputes the self-effacing statement by Peter that he knew very little about insurance and was primarily a 'contact man'. 'This was very far from being the truth as his knowledge of insurance was extensive and greatly appreciated by numerous clients.'

Peter retired from Willis Corroon in 1989 but was retained by the company as a consultant. He was instrumental in setting up the Willis Box at Lord's. 'Over the years,' says Lodge, 'he met and entertained virtually all of the company's major clients and, without exception, they had commented on his unflagging courtesy, attention to detail and phenomenal memory in recalling the names of people.' The May family remembers a brilliantly conceived operation and John Perry says that an invitation into the Willis Box was highly treasured. On all the major cricketing occasions at Lord's Peter was the gracious host, immaculate down to his beautifully polished shoes and invariably sporting an England or a Surrey tie. The man with the military gait supervised the hospitality with the precision of a military manoeuvre. Everything was ordered and mapped out with a smoothness which masked months of painstaking preparation.

The riding achievements of his four daughters – Suzanne, Nicola, Annabelle and Tessa – were Peter's special pride. Doug Insole said Peter was an unlikely stable lad, 'but it had seemed possible over the past few years that he might turn up at Lord's with the odd wisp of straw in his hair'. Peter did not ride himself. 'I am not exactly the right shape for a jockey,' he once said. But he was a marvellous supporter, sharing the triumphs and disappointments of his girls. As in his own sporting life, he wanted them to be the best if at all possible. He had always striven for pole position in cricket. The pursuit of this aim is just as earnestly the ideal of his family. Peter reflected on the advantages of a cricketer in comparison with the vicissitudes of riding. 'A batsman has another chance in the second innings, or perhaps next day in another match. A horse may not be fit to compete again for months. If a rider can raise a smile, forget the past and carry on again with the future in mind, he or she must be learning one of the more valuable lessons in life.'

Virginia May, an expert horsewoman in her heyday, today commands the equestrian operations of her family. The yield of her knowledge has aided the successes of her daughters. Suzanne, the eldest, was a junior international at dressage, representing Britain in the European Championships in Vienna in 1980. Nicola, at sixteen, followed her by winning a place in the British junior three-day event team, a position she held for two years. On the first occasion, she won the individual gold medal in the European Junior Championship held at Punchestown, Ireland. In the following year she came seventh but Britain won the team medals, so there was another gold to add to her collection. Annabelle, the third of the May sisters, is an accomplished sprinter and hurdler apart from following in the riding tradition. She narrowly failed to make it a hat-trick of international appearances and was first reserve for the European Championships in Poland in 1984.

Golf was an abiding interest for Peter in his retirement; the '19th hole', as he said, was within walking distance of his home. Alf Gover says Peter never had any tuition in the sport, but believes he had the potential to become a very good amateur golfer. Gover recalls one foursomes event which he organised at the Muirfield course in Scotland. The pairings included Peter with another Surrey cricketer, Eddie Watts. They were opposed by Ted Drake, the former Arsenal and England footballer, and Joe Davis, the billiards champion.

'Peter struck his first shot off the tee right out of sight,' says Gover. 'He then continued to hit long and drop all his putts.' Davis was prompted to make an inquiry after this unexpected display. 'I don't like to say anything, but is Peter an honest chap? He's supposed to be playing off 12, yet he's played to four.' He added: 'Next time we come to Scotland I'll play with him and not against him.'

Among the happiest of Peter's times were the tranquil holiday interludes, shared with Virginia, at the Torquay hotel of John and Pat Perry. He was often asked by John if other selected guests should be allowed to join the company. 'No,' he replied. 'I just want to be with Virginia and

Pat and yourself.' In this quiet sanctuary beside the sea, Peter was able to cast aside his weariness. There were cosy dinners, with steaks, or fish specially ordered from a local fishmonger – and lobster, as the frequent request of Virginia – followed by a measure or two of whisky and reminiscent talk. 'All Peter insisted upon was that matters should be arranged tidily and without fuss,' says Perry. 'He was a man of simple tastes.'

One of the great sadnesses of Peter's early death was that he missed the joys of assisting in the development of his grandsons, William, Oliver and Henry. Having brought up a family of horsewomen, there was the prospect of cricketing males to claim his attention. The most promising is Henry, a bouncy two-year-old, the son of Nicola and her husband, Harry, a former Junior Wimbledon tennis player. Henry has not yet graduated to holding a bat, but he catches and kicks a ball with zest and watchfulness. 'This little chap has so much talent,' says Virginia, the proud grandmother.

The first symptoms of the brain tumour which was to end Peter's life did not surface until late summer in 1994. Friends, including Alec Bedser, had noticed a certain vagueness in his manner on cricket occasions at Lord's and The Oval. It did not at the time arouse cause for alarm. There is now increased speculation that worries over a deteriorating personal financial situation and the Lloyds syndicate debacle was a stress factor in his illness. Peter Richardson voices the thoughts of many people that his friend was devoured by anxiety. 'It was completely frightening, a predicament made worse because it was beyond our control,' says Virginia. 'Peter had never owed a penny to anyone in his life. If there was a bill to be paid, it was met on the dot.'

Peter's condition, after a brief remission, worsened and he was re-admitted to hospital in November. He was brave and cheerful through the final days. There was the blessing of one last Christmas at home with all his family before his death on 27 December, four days before his sixty-fifth birthday.

John Perry presents a telling postscript on Peter's fortitude and generosity of spirit. Less than three months before his death he accepted an invitation to speak at a luncheon in the Livery Hall of the Worshipful Company of Butchers, close by Smithfield Market. The severity of his illness had been concealed from his friends. Perry, who was proposing the toast at the function, had no inkling of Peter's declining health. The newly installed Master, Henry Tattersall, had chosen cricket as his theme. He expressly asked if Peter would make the response. 'None of us knew how desperately ill he was, but Peter was determined to carry out the task.' Alerted by the news of Peter's appearance at Smithfield on 7 October, there was a packed assembly to greet him. The hall was not big enough to accommodate all those wanting to attend the lunch. 'Peter, with only the cues on a small postcard, held the company of nearly two hundred people spellbound with his cricket reminiscences,' says Perry.

The winning speech was delivered 'clear as a bell', betraying not a jot of the trauma affecting him. Peter once again rose to the occasion, conscientiously intent on upholding his standards in this last innings. The applause for a man, who was happy to be ordinary, should have told him that he would be remembered for his extraordinary qualities.

Bibliography

John Arlott: *Test Match Diary, 1953* (James Barrie, 1953); *Australian Test Journal* (Phoenix Books, 1955); *Days at the Cricket* (Longmans Green, 1950).

Alex Bannister: *Cricket Cauldron* (Stanley Paul, 1954).

Richie Benaud: *On Reflection* (Willow Books, Collins, 1984).

George Chesterton and Hubert Doggart: *Oxford and Cambridge Cricket* (Willow Books, Collins, 1989).

Colin Cowdrey: *MCC – The Autobiography of a Cricketer* (Hodder and Stoughton, 1976).

Norman Cutler: *Behind the South African Tests* (Putnam, 1955).

Michael Davie and Simon Davie, editors: *The Faber Book of Cricket* (Faber and Faber, 1987).

Ted Dexter, with Ralph Dellor: *Ted Dexter's Little Cricket Book* (Bloomsbury, 1996).

Louis Duffus: *Springbok Glory* (Longmans, Green & Co., 1955).

Jack Fingleton: *Four Chukkas to Australia* (Heinemann, 1960).

Charles Fortune: *The MCC Tour of South Africa – 1956–57* (Harrap, 1957).

Bill Frindall: *England Test Cricketers* (Willow Books, Collins, 1989).

Kenneth Gregory, editor: *From Grace to Botham* (Times Books, 1989).

Andrew Hignell: *The Skipper – Wilf Wooller* (Limlow Books).

Alan Hill: *The Family Fortune – A Saga of Sussex Cricket* (Scan Books, 1978); *Johnny Wardle – Cricket Conjuror* (David and Charles, 1988); *Bill Edrich* (André Deutsch, 1994).

Roy McLean: *Pitch and Toss* (Hodder & Stoughton, 1957).

Peter May: *Peter May's Book of Cricket* (Cassell, 1956); *A Game Enjoyed* (Stanley Paul, 1985).

Christopher Martin-Jenkins and Mike Seabrook, editors: *Quick Singles* (Lennard Books, 1986).

Don Mosey: *Laker – Portrait of a Legend* (Queen Anne Press, 1989).

A. G. Moyes: *Benaud & Co* (Angus & Robertson, 1959).

Ian Peebles: *The Ashes – 1954–55* (Hodder & Stoughton, 1955).

Pembroke College, Cambridge Society: *Annual Gazette, 1995.*

Jack Pollard: *Australian Cricket – The Game and the Players* (Angus & Robertson, 1988).

Anthony Quick: *Charterhouse – A History of the School* (James & James, London, 1990).

Simon Raven: *Shadows on the Grass* (Blond & Briggs, 1982).

Ray Robinson: *Between Wickets* (Collins, 1945); *On Top Down Under* (Cassell, 1981); *The Glad Season* (Collins, 1955).

Robert Rodrigo: *Peter May* (Phoenix House, 1960).

Alan Ross: *Australia '55 – A Journal of the MCC Tour* (Michael Joseph, 1955; *Cape Summer and the Australians in England* (Hamish Hamilton, 1957).

Gordon Ross: *The Surrey Story* (Stanley Paul, 1958); *Surrey* (Arthur Barker, 1971).

David Sheppard: *Parson's Pitch* (Hodder & Stoughton, 1964).

E. W. Swanton: *West Indian Adventure* (Museum Press, 1954); *Sort of a Cricket Person* (Collins, 1972); *Report from South Africa – With P. B. H. May's MCC Team, 1956/57* (Robert Hale, 1957); *Swanton in Australia – with MCC 1946–1975* (Collins, 1975).

E. M. Wellings: *The Ashes Thrown Away* (Bailey Bros & Swinfen, 1959).

Contemporary reports in *The Carthusian; The Daily Telegraph; The Times; Daily Express; Manchester Guardian; Cambridge Evening News; Yorkshire Post; Yorkshire Evening News; Sydney Morning Herald; Rand Daily Mail* (Johannesburg); *Natal Mercury* (Durban); *The Jamaica Gleaner; The Cricketer; Playfair Cricket Annual; Surrey CCC Yearbooks;* and various editions of *Wisden Cricketers' Almanack* have provided the nucleus of printed sources in this book.

STATISTICAL APPENDIX

P. B. H. May in first-class cricket

Compiled by Derek Lodge

P.B.H. MAY
IN FIRST-CLASS CRICKET

Born: Reading, Berkshire ..... Died: Liphook, Hampshire
31 December 1929 .... 27 December 1994.

Cambridge University: 1950–1952. Blues all three years.
First-class Debut: Combined Services v Hampshire, Aldershot.
16 June 1948.
Surrey Debut: vs Gloucestershire at Bristol.
19 July 1950.
Capped by Surrey: 29 August 1950.
England Debut: vs South Africa at Leeds.
26 July 1951.
Final Match for England: vs Australia at The Oval.
17 August 1961.
Final First-Class Match: vs Northamptonshire at The Oval.
17 July 1963.

Summary of teams represented

	Matches	Innings	N.O.	Runs	H.S.	Aver.
Combined Services	7	14	1	700	175	53.84
Cambridge University	37	58	12	2861	227*	62.19
Surrey	208	327	46	14168	211*	50.78
England	66	106	9	4537	285*	46.77
Others	70	113	9	5326	206	51.70
Total	388	618	77	27592	285*	51.00

* *signifies not out*

181

List of centuries: 85

175	Combined Services v. Worcestershire, Worcester	1949
227★	Cambridge University v. Hampshire, Fenner's	1950
118	Surrey v. Worcestershire, Worcester	1950
120	Cambridge University v. Sussex, Fenner's	1951
156★	Cambridge University v. Warwickshire, Fenner's	1951
120	Cambridge University v. Middlesex, Fenner's	1951
178★	Cambridge University v. Hampshire, Bournemouth	1951
119★	Gentlemen v. Players, Lord's	1951
121	Surrey v. Middlesex, Lord's	1951
138	England v. South Africa, Headingley	1951
167	Surrey v. Essex, Southend	1951
103★	Surrey v. Essex, Southend	1951
104★	Cambridge University v. Essex, Fenner's	1952
171	Cambridge University v. Yorkshire, Fenner's	1952
139★	Cambridge University v. Lancashire, Fenner's	1952
167	Cambridge University v. Sussex, Hove	1952
124	Surrey v. Kent, Oval	1952
143	Surrey v. Indians, Oval	1952
123★	Surrey v. Hampshire, Southampton	1952
197	Surrey v. Leicestershire, Leicester	1952
174	M.C.C. v. Yorkshire, Scarborough	1952
100★	M.C.C. v. Yorkshire, Scarborough	1952
137	Surrey v. Cambridge University, Fenner's	1953
136	Surrey v. Northamptonshire, Oval	1953
102★	Surrey v. Cambridge University, Guildford	1953
116	Surrey v. Kent, Blackheath	1953
135★	Surrey v. Nottinghamshire, Oval	1953
159	Surrey v. Middlesex, Lord's	1953
136★	Surrey v. Sussex, Hove	1953
157	Gentlemen v. Players, Scarborough	1953
124	M.C.C. v. Jamaica, Melbourne Park, Kingston	1953/54
135	England v. West Indies, Port-of-Spain	1953/54
169	Surrey v. Northamptonshire, Oval	1954
107★	Surrey v. Somerset, Oval	1954
211★	Surrey v. Nottinghamshire, Trent Bridge	1954
207	Surrey v. Cambridge University, Oval	1954
117★	Surrey v. Hampshire, Guildford	1954
112★	Gentlemen v. Players, Scarborough	1954
129	M.C.C. v. Combined XI, Perth	1954/55
105★	M.C.C. v. Victoria, Melbourne	1954/55
114	M.C.C. v. South Australia, Adelaide	1954/55
104	England v. Australia, Sydney	1954/55
122★	Surrey v. Lancashire, Oval	1955
112	England v. South Africa, Lord's	1955
102	Surrey v. Kent, Blackheath	1955

List of centuries: 85 (*cont.*)

117	England v. South Africa, Old Trafford	1955
125	Surrey v. The Rest, Oval	1955
107	Surrey v. Kent, Oval	1956
128★	Surrey v. Kent, Blackheath	1956
101	England v. Australia, Headingley	1956
162	M.C.C. v. Western Province, Cape Town	1956/57
118	M.C.C. v. Eastern Province, Port Elizabeth	1956/57
124★	M.C.C. v. Rhodesia, Bulawayo	1956/57
206	M.C.C. v. Rhodesia, Salisbury	1956/57
107	M.C.C. v. Natal, Durban	1956/57
116	M.C.C. v. Western Province, Cape Town	1956/57
151	Surrey v. M.C.C., Lord's	1957
117	Surrey v. Sussex, Oval	1957
285★	England v. West Indians, Edgbaston	1957
100	Surrey v. Lancashire, Old Trafford	1957
125	Surrey v. Yorkshire, Oval	1957
104	England v. West Indies, Trent Bridge	1957
119	T. N. Pearce's XI v. West Indies, Scarborough	1957
165	Surrey v. New Zealanders, Oval	1958
163	Surrey v. Nottinghamshire, Trent Bridge	1958
174	Surrey v. Lancashire, Old Trafford	1958
113★	England v. New Zealanders, Headingley	1958
155	Surrey v. Yorkshire, Oval	1958
101	England v. New Zealanders, Old Trafford	1958
112★	Surrey v. New Zealanders, Oval	1958
131	T. N. Pearce's XI v. New Zealand, Scarborough	1958
113	M.C.C. v. Combined XI, Perth	1958/59
140	M.C.C. v. Australian XI, Sydney	1958/59
114	M.C.C. v. Australian XI, Sydney	1958/59
113	England v. Australia, Melbourne	1958/59
136	M.C.C. v. New South Wales, Sydney	1958/59
124★	England v. New Zealand, Auckland	1958/59
106	England v. India, Trent Bridge	1959
143	Surrey v. Kent, Blackheath	1959
124	M.C.C. v. Jamaica, Melbourne Park, Kingston	1959/60
153★	Surrey v. Somerset, Taunton	1961
100	T. N. Pearce's XI v. Australians, Scarborough	1961
119	Surrey v. Pakistanis, Oval	1962
123★	Surrey v. Middlesex, Oval	1962
135	Surrey v. Warwickshire, Edgbaston	1962

Double-century partnerships: 17

P'ship	Wkt	May	Partner	Score	For	Opponents	Venue	Season
411	4	285*	M. C. Cowdrey	154	England	West Indies	Edgbaston	1957
301	4	206	T. E. Bailey	110	M.C.C.	Rhodesia	Salisbury	1956/57
261	3	163	B. Constable	96	Surrey	Nottinghamshire	Trent Bridge	1958
241	2	167	M. R. Barton	117	Surrey	Essex	Southend	1951
234	6	114	D. C. S. Compton	182	M.C.C.	South Australia	Adelaide	1954/55
233	3	227*	M. H. Stevenson	109	Cambridge University	Hampshire	Fenner's	1950
224	3	207	B. Constable	104*	Surrey	Cambridge University	Oval	1954
218*	4	122*	K. F. Barrington	135*	Surrey	Lancashire	Oval	1955
218	4	118	D. J. Insole	118	M.C.C.	Eastern Province	Port Elizabeth	1956/57
215	2	120	D. S. Sheppard	143	Cambridge University	Middlesex	Fenner's	1951
213	3	116	D. G. W. Fletcher	115	Surrey	Kent	Blackheath	1953
210	3	137	B. Constable	119	Surrey	Cambridge University	Fenner's	1953
209	2	227*	J. G. Dewes	101	Cambridge University	Hampshire	Fenner's	1950
208	4	139*	M. H. Stevenson	96	Cambridge University	Lancashire	Fenner's	1952
207	3	104	T. W. Graveney	258	England	West Indies	Trent Bridge	1957
205*	3	123*	K. F. Barrington	91*	Surrey	Middlesex	Oval	1962
205	4	157	M. C. Cowdrey	100	Gentlemen	Players	Scarborough	1953

Two Hundreds in a Match

Innings		For	Against	Ground	Year
167	103★	Surrey	Essex	Southend	1951
174	100★	M.C.C.	Yorkshire	Scarborough	1952
140	114	M.C.C.	Australian XI	Sydney	1958/59

Fifty and a Hundred in one Match

Innings		For	Against	Ground	Year
97	175	Combined Services	Worcestershire	Worcester	1949
171	50	Cambridge University	Yorkshire	Fenner's	1952
88	102★	Surrey	Cambridge University	Guildford	1953
135★	73★	Surrey	Nottinghamshire	The Oval	1953
159	58	Surrey	Middlesex	Lord's	1953
116	79	M.C.C.	Western Province	Cape Town	1956/57
117	64	Surrey	Sussex	The Oval	1957

Two Fifties in one Match

Innings		For	Against	Ground	Year
80	90★	Combined Services	Gloucestershire	Bristol	1949
73	86★	Cambridge University	Worcestershire	Worcester	1951
64	53	England	Australia	Lord's	1956
90	63★	Surrey	Kent	The Oval	1959

Centuries for Surrey: 39

v. Kent (6) 143, 128★, 124, 116, 107, 102
v. Cambridge University (3) 207, 137, 102★
v. Lancashire (3) 159, 122★, 121
v. Nottinghamshire (3) 211★, 163, 135★
v. Essex (2) 167, 103★
v. Hampshire (2) 123★, 117★
v. Northamptonshire (2) 169, 136
v. Somerset (2) 153★, 107★
v. Sussex (2) 136★, 117
v. Yorkshire (2) 155, 125
v. New Zealanders (2) 165, 112★
v. Leicestershire (1) 197
v. Warwickshire (1) 135
v. Worcestershire (1) 118

Centuries for Surrey: 39 (*cont.*)

v. M.C.C. (1) 151
v. The Rest (1) 125
v. Indians (1) 143
v. Pakistanis (1) 119

For Cambridge University (9)

v. Hampshire (2) 227★, 178★
v. Sussex (2) 167, 120
v. Essex (1) 104★
v. Lancashire (1) 139★
v. Middlesex (1) 120
v. Warwickshire (1) 156★
v. Yorkshire (1) 171

Where the Centuries were made

England

The Oval	17	Blackheath	4	Worcester	2
Fenner's	8	Headingley	3	Bournemouth	1
Scarborough	7	Edgbaston	2	Leicester	1
Lord's	5	Guildford	2	Southampton	1
Trent Bridge	4	Hove	2	Taunton	1
Old Trafford	4	Southend	2		

Abroad

Australia: Sydney 4, Melbourne 2, Perth 2, Adelaide 1
South Africa: Cape Town 2, Bulawayo 1, Durban 1, Port Elizabeth 1, Salisbury 1
West Indies: Melbourne Park, Kingston 2, Port-of-Spain 1
New Zealand: Auckland 1

Season-by-Season record

In England

Season	Matches	Inns	NO	Runs	H.S.	100's	50's	Average	Catches
1948	1	2	0	5	3	0	0	2.50	0
1949	6	12	1	695	175	1	5	63.18	2
1950	26	38	3	1187	227★	2	4	33.91	10
1951	26	43	9	2339	178★	9	9	68.79	17
1952	27	47	7	2498	197	10	7	62.45	15
1953	34	59	9	2554	159	8	11	51.08	21
1954	29	41	7	1702	211★	6	6	50.05	26

Season-by-Season record (*cont.*)

1955	25	42	5	1902	125	5	12	51.40	33
1956	30	50	7	1631	128★	3	8	37.93	31
1957	29	41	3	2347	285★	7	15	61.76	29
1958	29	41	6	2231	174	8	9	63.74	27
1959	11	16	2	663	143	2	4	47.35	12
1961	22	42	5	1499	153★	2	10	40.51	16
1962	20	31	5	1352	135	3	8	52.00	16
1963	3	4	0	90	85	0	1	22.50	1

Overseas

In Australia

Season	Matches	Inns	NO	Runs	H.S.	100's	50's	Average	Catches
1954–55	14	23	3	931	129	4	3	46.55	13
1958–59	13	22	1	1197	140	5	5	57.00	4

In New Zealand

1954–55	4	6	0	165	48	0	0	27.50	3
1958–59	4	4	1	315	124★	1	2	105.00	1

In West Indies

1953–54	10	18	2	630	135	2	3	39.37	0
1959–60	9	12	0	389	124	1	1	32.41	1

In South Africa

1956–57	16	24	1	1270	206	6	4	55.21	4
Total	388	618	77	27592	285★	85	127	51.00	282

Test Matches

	Matches	Inns	NO	Runs	H.S.	100's	50's	Average	Catches
Australia	21	37	3	1566	113	3	10	46.05	10
South Africa	12	22	1	906	138	3	4	43.14	10
West Indies	13	21	2	986	285★	3	3	51.89	5
New Zealand	9	11	2	603	124★	3	2	67.00	6
India	7	10	1	356	106	1	2	39.55	8
Pakistan	4	5	0	120	53	0	1	24.00	3
Totals	66	106	9	4537	285★	13	22	46.77	42

County Championship Matches

Season	Matches	Inns	NO	Runs	H.S.	100's	50's	Average	Catches
1950	11	17	1	529	118	1	3	33.06	2
1951	7	10	2	614	167	3	2	76.75	2
1952	8	14	2	804	197	3	3	67.00	5
1953	20	34	8	1488	159	5	6	57.23	12
1954	18	24	5	947	211★	4	2	49.84	17
1955	16	26	4	921	122★	2	6	41.86	23
1956	20	36	5	1007	128★	2	2	32.48	22
1957	19	27	2	1391	125	3	12	55.64	20
1958	18	27	4	1274	174	3	6	55.39	18
1959	7	10	1	481	143	1	4	53.44	7
1961	12	23	3	718	153★	1	4	35.90	13
1962	17	27	5	1180	135	2	8	53.63	12
1963	2	3	0	86	85	0	1	28.66	0
Totals	175	278	42	11440	211★	30	59	48.47	153

Record on each UK Ground

Ground	Matches	Inns	NO	Runs	H.S.	100's	50's	Average	Catches
Aldershot	1	2	0	5	3	0	0	2.50	0
Blackheath	8	12	1	809	143	4	3	73.54	11
Bournemouth	2	4	2	250	178★	1	0	125.00	1
Bradford	3	5	0	141	63	0	2	28.20	3
Bristol	5	9	1	296	90	0	3	37.00	1
Cardiff	3	5	0	87	60	0	1	17.40	2
Chelmsford	1	1	0	91	91	0	1	91.00	0
Chesterfield	1	2	0	14	10	0	0	7.00	0
Clacton-on-Sea	1	2	0	20	13	0	0	10.00	3
Derby	2	3	0	35	30	0	0	11.66	1
Edgbaston	7	13	1	776	285★	2	2	64.66	2
Fenner's	26	36	9	2219	227	8	9	82.18	23
Gillingham	2	4	0	99	52	0	1	24.75	1
Gloucester	1	2	0	42	34	0	0	21.00	0
Guildford	11	15	3	685	117	2	4	57.08	11
Hastings	1	2	0	69	37	0	0	34.50	0
Headingley	10	15	2	762	138	3	3	58.61	7
Hove	6	11	2	560	167	2	1	62.22	4
Ilford	1	2	0	84	59	0	1	42.00	2
Kettering	1	2	0	9	7	0	0	4.50	1
Leyton	1	2	0	45	33	0	0	22.50	0
Leicester	5	8	0	451	197	1	3	56.37	5
Lord's	39	69	6	2467	159	5	15	39.15	32

Record on each UK Ground (*cont.*)

Loughborough	1	1	0	8	8	0	0	8.00	0
Northampton	3	4	0	199	96	0	1	49.75	2
Pontypridd	1	1	0	4	4	0	0	4.00	0
Old Trafford	11	17	2	963	174	4	3	64.20	5
Portsmouth	2	3	0	112	97	0	1	37.33	0
Scarborough	16	30	2	1539	174	7	4	54.96	8
Sheffield	3	6	0	166	68	0	1	27.66	3
Southampton	1	2	1	143	123*	1	0	143.00	0
Southend	1	2	1	270	167	2	0	270.00	0
Swansea	1	2	0	20	20	0	0	10.00	0
Taunton	3	4	1	252	153	1	1	84.00	0
The Oval	114	178	31	7023	207	17	40	47.77	108
Trent Bridge	12	15	3	1009	211	4	4	84.08	11
Weston-super-Mare	2	3	0	193	62	0	1	64.33	3
Worthing	1	2	0	13	9	0	0	6.50	1
Worcester	8	13	1	765	175	2	4	63.75	5
Totals	318	509	69	22695	285*	66	109	51.57	256

Record at The Oval

May's record at the Oval is just a little inferior, statistically, to his record on English grounds generally, which may give just a little colour to the theory that the Oval pitches favoured the bowler – but it is still impressively consistent.

Season	M	Inns	NO	Runs	H.S.	Average
1950	8	13	1	243	92	20.25
1951	4	6	0	211	87	35.16
1952	7	12	1	615	143	55.90
1953	13	21	4	869	136	51.11
1954	12	17	3	779	207	55.64
1955	11	18	3	683	125	45.53
1956	14	24	6	686	107	38.11
1957	10	14	2	651	125	54.25
1958	12	15	3	846	165	70.50
1959	3	5	1	183	90	45.75
1961	8	16	3	517	99	39.76
1962	11	15	4	739	123*	67.18
1963	1	2	0	1	1	0.50
Total	114	178	31	7023	207	47.77

Australian Grounds

Ground	Matches	Inns	NO	Runs	H.S.	100's	50's	Average	Catches
Adelaide	3	5	0	237	114	1	1	47.40	5
Brisbane	4	8	1	176	77	0	1	25.14	1
Hobart	1	1	0	80	80	0	1	80.00	0
Launceston	1	1	0	80	80	0	1	80.00	0
Melbourne	6	10	2	423	113	2	1	52.87	1
Perth	4	6	1	313	129	2	1	62.60	5
Sydney	8	14	0	819	140	4	2	58.50	5
Totals	27	45	4	2128	140	9	8	51.90	17

South African Grounds

Ground	Matches	Inns	NO	Runs	H.S.	100's	50's	Average	Catches
Bulawayo	1	1	1	124	124★	1	0	–	0
Cape Town	4	6	0	405	162	2	1	67.50	3
Durban	2	4	0	112	107	1	0	28.00	0
East London	1	1	0	79	79	0	1	79.00	0
Johannesburg	4	7	0	166	73	0	2	23.71	0
Kimberley	1	1	0	15	15	0	0	15.00	1
Port Elizabeth	2	3	0	163	118	1	0	54.33	0
Salisbury	1	1	0	206	206	1	0	206.00	0
Totals	16	24	1	1270	206	6	4	55.21	4

West Indian Grounds

Ground	Matches	Inns	NO	Runs	H.S.	100's	50's	Average	Catches
Bridgetown	4	7	0	198	69	0	3	28.28	0
Georgetown	3	3	0	33	12	0	0	11.00	0
Grenada	1	1	0	38	38	0	0	38.00	0
Kingston									
(Melbourne Park)	2	3	1	261	124	2	0	130.50	0
(Sabina Park)	4	7	1	233	69	0	1	38.83	0
Point-a-Pierre	1	1	0	25	25	0	0	25.00	1
Port-of-Spain	4	8	0	231	135	1	0	28.87	0
Totals	19	30	2	1019	135	3	4	36.39	1

New Zealand Grounds

Ground	Matches	Inns	NO	Runs	H.S.	100's	50's	Average	Catches
Auckland	2	2	1	172	124★	1	0	172.00	1
Christchurch	2	2	0	102	71	0	1	51.00	3
Dunedin	2	3	0	120	97	0	1	40.00	0
Hamilton	1	1	0	23	23	0	0	23.00	0
Wellington	1	2	0	63	41	0	0	31.50	0
Totals	8	10	1	480	124★	1	2	53.33	4

Aggregates

	Matches	Inns	NO	Runs	H.S.	100's	50's	Average	Catches
In England	318	509	69	22695	285★	66	109	51.57	256
In Australia	27	45	4	2128	140	9	8	51.90	17
In South Africa	16	24	1	1270	206	6	4	55.21	4
In West Indies	19	30	2	1019	135	3	4	36.39	1
In New Zealand	8	10	1	480	124★	1	2	53.33	4
Totals	388	618	77	27592	285★	85	127	51.00	282

Runs against various opponents

In England

Versus	Inn	NO	Runs	H.S.	Average
Derbyshire	12	1	356	88	32.36
Essex	16	2	740	167	52.85
Glamorgan	14	1	309	82	23.76
Gloucestershire	15	2	372	90★	28.61
Hampshire	21	6	1038	227★	69.20
Kent	24	3	1438	143	68.47
Lancashire	24	8	1055	174	65.93
Leicestershire	19	2	799	197	47.00
Middlesex	38	7	1370	159	44.19
Northamptonshire	15	0	717	169	47.80
Nottinghamshire	25	8	1284	211★	74.52
Somerset	15	3	694	153	57.83
Surrey	4	1	109	61	36.33
Sussex	29	3	1307	167	50.26
Warwickshire	14	1	693	156★	53.30
Worcestershire	21	4	1015	175	59.70
Yorkshire	34	1	1495	174	45.30
Oxford University	8	0	256	91	32.00

Runs against various opponents (*cont.*)

	Versus	Inn	NO	Runs	H.S.	Average
	Cambridge Univ.	11	1	836	207	83.60
	M.C.C.	13	1	620	151	51.66
	Australians	15	1	483	100	34.50
	South Africans	3	0	138	62	46.00
	New Zealanders	6	1	487	165	97.40
	West Indians	7	1	269	119	44.83
	Indians	6	1	288	143	57.60
	Pakistanis	5	0	301	119	60.20
	Free Foresters	3	1	122	83★	61.00
	Rest of England	5	0	272	125	54.40
	England	2	0	2	2	1.00
	Players	26	2	943	157	39.29
Tests in England						
	Australia	18	3	810	101	54.00
	South Africa	12	1	753	138	68.45
	West Indies	6	1	489	285★	97.80
	New Zealand	6	1	337	113★	67.40
	India	10	1	356	106	39.55
	Pakistan	5	0	120	53	24.00
	Total	57	7	2865	285★	57.30
In Australia						
	Australian XI	3	0	299	140	99.66
	Combined XI	3	0	322	129	107.33
	N.S.W.	7	0	243	136	34.71
	Queensland	4	1	101	77	33.66
	South Australia	1	0	114	114	114.00
	Tasmania	1	0	80	80	80.00
	Victoria	3	2	142	105★	142.00
	West Australia	4	1	71	60	23.66
	Australia	19	0	756	113	39.78
	Total	45	4	2128	140	51.90
In South Africa						
	Border	1	0	79	79	79.00
	Combined Univ.	1	0	25	25	25.00
	Eastern Province	1	0	118	118	118.00
	Griqualand W.	1	0	15	15	15.00
	Natal	2	0	108	107	54.00
	Rhodesia	2	1	330	206	330.00
	Transvaal	3	0	85	73	28.33
	Western Province	3	0	357	162	119.00
	South Africa	10	0	153	61	15.30
	Total	24	1	1270	206	55.21

Runs against various opponents (*cont.*)

In New Zealand

Versus	Inn	NO	Runs	H.S.	Average
Canterbury	1	0	31	31	31.00
Northern and Central Districts	1	0	23	23	23.00
Otago	1	0	97	97	97.00
Wellington	2	0	63	41	31.50
New Zealand	5	1	266	124★	66.50
Total	10	1	480	124★	53.33

In the West Indies

Versus	Inn	NO	Runs	H.S.	Average
Barbados	4	0	128	69	32.00
British Guiana	1	0	9	9	9.00
Jamaica	4	0	270	124	67.50
Trinidad	5	0	77	25	15.40
Windward Island	1	0	38	38	38.00
West Indies	15	1	497	135	35.50
Total	30	1	1019	135	36.39

Test Match record

Series by series

Season	Opponents	Test	Ground	Runs	How Out
1951	S. Africa	4	Headingley	138	b A.M.B. Rowan
	S. Africa	5	Oval	33	b Chubb
				0	c E.A.B. Rowan b A.M.B. Rowan
1952	India	1	Headingley	16	b Shinde
				4	c Phadkar b Ghulam Ahmed
	India	2	Lord's	74	c Mantri b Mankad
				26	c Roy b Ghulam Ahmed
	India	3	Old Trafford	69	c Sen b Mankad
	India	4	Oval	17	c Manjrekar b Mankad
1953	Australia	1	Trent Bridge	9	c Tallon b Hill
	Australia	5	Oval	39	c Archer b Johnston
				37	c Davidson b Miller
1953/54	W. Indies	1	Kingston	31	c Headley b Ramadhin
				69	c McWatt b Kentish
	W. Indies	2	Bridgetown	7	c King b Ramadhin
				62	c Walcott b Gomez

Test Match record (*cont.*)

Season	Opponents	Test	Ground	Runs	How Out
	W. Indies	3	Georgetown	12	lbw b Atkinson
				12	b Atkinson
	W. Indies	4	Port-of-Spain	135	c Pairaudeau b King
				16	c Worrell b McWatt
	W. Indies	5	Kingston	30	c sub b Ramadhin
				40	not out
1954	Pakistan	1	Lord's	27	b Khan Mohammad
	Pakistan	2	Trent Bridge	0	b Khan Mohammad
	Pakistan	3	Old Trafford	14	c Imtiaz Ahmed b Shujauddin
	Pakistan	4	Oval	26	c Kardar b Fazal Mahmood
				53	c Kardar b Fazal Mahmood
1954/55	Australia	1	Brisbane	1	b Lindwall
				44	lbw b Lindwall
	Australia	2	Sydney	5	c Johnston b Archer
				104	b Lindwall
	Australia	3	Melbourne	0	c Benaud b Lindwall
				91	b Johnston
	Australia	4	Adelaide	1	c Archer b Benaud
				26	c Miller b Johnston
	Australia	5	Sydney	79	c Davidson b Benaud
	N. Zealand	1	Dunedin	10	b MacGibbon
				13	b MacGibbon
	N. Zealand	2	Auckland	48	b Hayes
1955	S. Africa	1	Trent Bridge	83	c McGlew b Smith
	S. Africa	2	Lord's	0	c Tayfield b Heine
				112	hit wkt b Heine
	S. Africa	3	Old Trafford	34	c Mansell b Goddard
				117	b Mansell
	S. Africa	4	Headingley	47	b Tayfield
				97	lbw b Tayfield
	S. Africa	5	Oval	3	c Goddard b Fuller
				89	not out
1956	Australia	1	Trent Bridge	73	c Langley b Miller
	Australia	2	Lord's	63	b Benaud
				53	c Langley b Miller
	Australia	3	Headingley	101	c Lindwall b Johnston
	Australia	4	Old Trafford	43	c Archer b Benaud
	Australia	5	Oval	83	not out
				37	not out
1956/57	S. Africa	1	Johannesburg	6	c Goddard b Adcock
				14	c Endean b Heine
	S. Africa	2	Cape Town	8	c Waite b Tayfield
				15	c Waite b Heine

Test Match record (*cont.*)

Season	Opponents	Test	Ground	Runs	How Out
	S. Africa	3	Durban	2	c Goddard b Tayfield
				2	lbw b Tayfield
	S. Africa	4	Johannesburg	61	b Adcock
				0	c Endean b Tayfield
	S. Africa	5	Port Elizabeth	24	c Duckworth b Goddard
				21	lbw b Goddard
1957	W. Indies	1	Edgbaston	30	c Weekes b Ramadhin
				285	not out
	W. Indies	2	Lord's	0	c Kanhai b Gilchrist
	W. Indies	3	Trent Bridge	104	lbw b Smith
	W. Indies	4	Headingley	69	c Alexander b Sobers
	W. Indies	5	Oval	1	c Worrell b Smith
1958	N. Zealand	1	Edgbaston	84	c Petrie b MacGibbon
				11	c Petrie b MacGibbon
	N. Zealand	2	Lord's	19	c Alabaster b MacGibbon
	N. Zealand	3	Headingley	113	not out
	N. Zealand	4	Old Trafford	101	c Playle MacGibbon
	N. Zealand	5	Oval	9	c Petrie b Blair
1958/59	Australia	1	Brisbane	26	c Grout b Meckiff
				4	lbw b Benaud
	Australia	2	Melbourne	113	b Meckiff
				17	c Davidson b Meckiff
	Australia	3	Sydney	42	c Mackay b Slater
				92	b Burke
	Australia	4	Adelaide	37	b Benaud
				59	lbw b Rorke
	Australia	5	Melbourne	11	c Benaud b Meckiff
				4	c Harvey b Lindwall
	N. Zealand	1	Christchurch	71	c Hough b Moir
	N. Zealand	2	Auckland	124	not out
1959	India	1	Trent Bridge	106	c Joshi b Gupte
	India	2	Lord's	9	b Surendranath
				33	not out
	India	3	Headingley	2	b Desai
1959/60	W. Indies	1	Bridgetown	1	c Alexander b Hall
	W. Indies	2	Port-of-Spain	0	c Kanhai b Watson
				28	c and b Singh
	W. Indies	3	Kingston	9	c Hunte b Hall
				45	b Hall
1961	Australia	2	Lord's	17	c Grout b Davidson
				22	c Grout b McKenzie

Test Match record (*cont.*)

Season	Opponents	Test	Ground	Runs	How Out
	Australia	3	Headingley	26	c and b Davidson
				8	not out
	Australia	4	Old Trafford	95	c Simpson b Davidson
				0	b Benaud
	Australia	5	Oval	71	c Lawry b Benaud
				33	c O'Neill b Mackay

May as Captain

May was sensationally successful as the captain of England when playing at home, rather less so abroad, though this judgement is somewhat distorted by the disastrous series of 1958/59. Wherever the matches were played, he led from the front as the table showing the number of times he made the top score in an innings, or the top aggregate in the match, will indicate.

	W	D	L	Top score	Top aggregate
Home	16	6	4	16 out of 38	11 out of 26
Away	4	5	6	5 out of 27	4 out of 15
Total	20	11	10	21 out of 65	15 out of 41

Captaining Surrey, he was even more successful. He only led them for the two full seasons, missing much of the seasons of 1959, 1961 and 1962, but his record in 1957/58 was formidable. (The figures relate to all matches, and not only to the championship.)

Season	W	D	L	Surrey's final position
1952	0	0	1	1st
1953	1	1	1	1st
1954	4	0	0	1st
1955	1	0	1	1st
1956	1	0	1	1st
1956	1	0	1	1st
1957	17	4	1	1st
1958	14	5	3	1st
1959	6	1	0	3rd
1961	3	6	6	15th
1962	8	9	2	5th
Total	55	26	16	

During Surrey's seven winning years, they defeated each of the other sixteen counties more often than they lost to them, their best 'score' being 11–0 against Middlesex, their worst 5–4 against Northamptonshire and Warwickshire. It was occasionally alleged that one reason for their unprecedented run of success was that the Oval pitches were prepared to suit Laker and Lock, but this is comprehensively disproved by a comparison of the records of those two great bowlers at home and away.

	Laker		Lock	
	Home	Away	Home	Away
1952	42 wkts/11 matches	44/7	64/13	52/11
1953	67/12	26/7	47/8	20/3
1954	60/12	52/11	53/11	48/13
1955	50/14	52/10	68/12	81/10
1956	34/8	23/5	49/10	68/7
1957	29/8	56/10	83/9	70/11
1958	45/9	48/11	67/12	47/8
Total	327/74	301/61	431/75	386/63

Overall, then, Laker took 4.42 wickets in each home game, 4.93 in each away fixture; Lock's corresponding figures were 5.75 and 6.13.

Miscellany

In 1956/57 May scored four successive centuries, as follows:

162   v. Western Province at Cape Town.
118   v. Eastern Province at Port Elizabeth
124* v. Rhodesia at Bulawayo.
206   v. Rhodesia at Salisbury.

Twice he scored three successive centuries;

In 1952   197   for Surrey v. Leicestershire at Leicester
          174   and 100* for M.C.C. v. Yorkshire at Scarborough
In 1958   155   for Surrey v. Yorkshire at The Oval
          101   for England v. New Zealanders at Old Trafford
        112* for Surrey v. New Zealanders at The Oval

He bowled only 17 overs in first-class cricket, all for Cambridge University. He took no wickets, and conceded 49 runs; there is no record of his bowling method.

He was out 541 times in his career, and in the following ways:

Mode	Number	Percentage of Total
Bowled	136	25.1
Caught	338	62.4
LBW	38	7.0
Stumped	13	2.4
Run out	9	1.6
Hit wicket	7	1.2

He was out LBW rather less often than most of his contemporaries (Hutton, for example, was LBW in 13% of his dismissals, and Compton in 9%) and caught slightly more often – most batsmen of consequence are out caught in between 50% and 60% of their dismissals, the general average, for batsmen and non-batsmen alike, being round about the 50% mark.

Thirteen bowlers defeated him six or more times.

F. S. Trueman	12
R. Benaud	9
H. J. Tayfield	9
J. H. Wardle	9
J. A. Young	9
R. R. Lindwall	8
F. J. Titmus	7
R. Appleyard	6
P. S. Heine	6
W. A. Johnston	6
A. R. MacGibbon	6
J. B. Statham	6
R. Tattersall	6

In Test cricket, there are several points of interest:

In the 1955 series against South Africa, his second innings scores were 112, 117, 97 and 89 not out, a record which has not been surpassed except, arguably, by C. L. Walcott in 1955, against Australia, when he made 39, 110, 73, 83 and 110 again.

In seven innings in the 1956 series against Australia, May was only once out for under 50. His scores in a relatively low-scoring series were 73, 63, 53, 101, 43, 83* and 37*.

His greatest innings, statistically and in every other way, was his 285* at Edgbaston in 1957. This was then the highest innings in a Test by an England captain. It has since been surpassed by Graham Gooch with 333 against India at Lord's in 1990.

May's 285* was the highest Test innings at Edgbaston, surpassing the 138 made by J. T. Tyldesley in 1902, and again by W. R. Hammond in 1929. The nearest approach since has been 274 by Zaheer Abbas, in 1971, and the nearest by an Englishman, 215 by D. I. Gower in 1985.

May and Cowdrey added 411 for the fourth wicket, the highest partnership for any wicket for England, and the highest for the fourth wicket by players from any country.

Index